Unruly Audience

Unruly Audience

Folk Interventions in Popular Media

Greg Kelley

UTAH STATE UNIVERSITY PRESS
Logan

Published by Utah State University Press
An imprint of University Press of Colorado
245 Century Circle, Suite 202
Louisville, Colorado 80027

ASSOCIATION of UNIVERSITY PRESSES   The University Press of Colorado is a proud member of
the Association of University Presses.

The University Press of Colorado is a cooperative publishing enterprise supported, in part, by Adams State University, Colorado State University, Fort Lewis College, Metropolitan State University of Denver, Regis University, University of Colorado, University of Northern Colorado, University of Wyoming, Utah State University, and Western Colorado University.

∞ This paper meets the requirements of the ANSI/NISO Z39.48–1992 (Permanence of Paper)

ISBN: 978-1-60732-989-3 (paperback)
ISBN: 978-1-60732-990-9 (ebook)
https://doi.org/10.7330/9781607329909

Library of Congress Cataloging-in-Publication Data

Names: Kelley, Greg, 1960– author.
Title: Unruly audience : folk interventions in popular media / Greg Kelley.
Description: Logan : Utah State University Press, [2020] | Includes bibliographical references and index.
Identifiers: LCCN 2020008853 (print) | LCCN 2020008854 (ebook) | ISBN 9781607329893 (paperback) | ISBN 9781607329909 (ebook)
Subjects: LCSH: Folklore.
Classification: LCC GR67 .K45 2020 (print) | LCC GR67 (ebook) | DDC 398.2—dc23
LC record available at https://lccn.loc.gov/2020008853
LC ebook record available at https://lccn.loc.gov/2020008854

Cover art: "I Don't Believe in Fairy Tales" by street artist TRUST. iCON, first appearing in Bethnal Green, East London, 2015. Permission of use and original photo courtesy of the artist.

Contents

Acknowledgments

THIS PROJECT UNFOLDED AS A SERIES OF DISCOVERIES about the wonderfully creative world of disruption, about the myriad ways that active audiences assert themselves to undermine, refashion, expand, or otherwise fracture the messages of popular media. Along that path, a number of good-hearted people provided me with resources, inspiration, and encouragement.

Vital portions of the research were made possible by the Faculty Research Fund at the University of Guelph-Humber. I wish to thank George Bragues specifically for supervising that fund and John Walsh for the administration's ongoing support of faculty research and professional development. Thanks go to the Rollins family and Angele Nunez, manager of operations at Jamaica's Rose Hall Great House, who facilitated my research by granting liberal access to tours and plantation grounds. I am particularly grateful to Doug Prout, artistic director of the interactive nighttime tour at Rose Hall, for graciously agreeing to an interview and for kind allowances as I recorded and studied his theatrical production. I extend my thanks also to Jonny Davies at the special collections of the British Film Institute and the staff of the BFI Reuben Library for access to materials housed there. The cover art "I Don't Believe in Fairy Tales" appears by generous consent of UK street artist TRUST. iCON, to whom I am deeply obliged.

Through the full span of the project, Sue Hunter and Roland Vila of Library Services at Guelph-Humber graciously lent their reference-sleuthing skills in helping me track down esoteric sources. And the kind collaboration of my colleague and friend Marc Tavares, media technologies specialist at Guelph-Humber, has been boundlessly helpful. Further, I am lucky to have worked with two very capable research assistants: Curtis Nelson, who deftly handled all the digital details of our fieldwork at Rose Hall, and Cal Campos, whose careful transcription and editing skills served us well at the BFI archive, making the most of our limited research time there.

Iterations of this work were presented at meetings of the American Folklore Society and the Folklore Studies Association of Canada. I am grateful to participants and panelists at those meetings for their comments and suggestions as I worked through the ideas that shaped the arc of the book. Earlier versions of chapters 1 and 6 have appeared previously in print (Kelley 2012, 2015, respectively). I also thank the editors at Utah State University Press—Michael Spooner, Rachael Levay, and Laura Furney—for their direction and kind encouragement throughout. And Robin DuBlanc's exceptional copyediting in the final stages was a godsend.

I benefited immeasurably from the insights and support of friends who have inspired my work: Ray Cashman, Charlie Doyle, Michael Evans, Michael Dylan Foster, Henry Glassie, Bill Hansen, Wolfgang Mieder, Tom Mould, Elliot Oring, and Pravina Shukla. Many fruitful conversations with other friends and colleagues have proved instrumental in the ferment of this book, memorably with Kristie Andrews, Ron Baker, Simon Bronner, Jan Brunvand, Eric Eliason, Bill Ellis, Natalie Evans, Diane Goldstein, Brian Huss, Mikel Koven, Janet Langlois, John Laudun, Jim Leary, Carl Lindahl, Moira Marsh, Jay Mechling, Adam Miller, Danny O'Quinn, Jill Terry Rudy, Jeannie Banks Thomas, Tok Thompson, Libby Tucker, Tad Tuleja, Rory Turner, Kathy Ullyott, and Theresa Vaughan. All the while, David and Maxine Schacker have been kindly supportive.

In the time that I have written this book, both of my parents passed away. In the face of that heavy loss, the bond with my brothers (Harry, Bryant, and Eric) and their partners (Judy, Jennifer, and Dawn) remains close as ever. They are individuals of complexity and character, and my shared history with them is an inspiriting presence in my life and work.

Foremost, I am thankful for the abiding support of my partner and best friend Jennifer Schacker, whose helpful advice and loving encouragement sustained me through the long process of research and writing, from beginning to end, even as we worked together to establish—with Jax Mill, Chloe Mill, and Frida Kelley—a compassionate and cheerfully offbeat household.

Unruly Audience

Introduction

Reception and Resistance

W̲ʜᴇɴ I ᴡᴀs ᴀ ʟɪᴛᴛʟᴇ ʙᴏʏ, a blocky Zenith brand TV the size and weight of a bank safe graced our family living room. There, after school and on weekends, my three brothers and I would sit—or lounge with pillows on the crimson shag carpet—watching programs like *The Addams Family*, *The Brady Bunch*, and *Get Smart*. This was long before the convenient affordances of remote controls, home recording, and on-demand viewing: we were captive—though not always captivated—media consumers who had no choice but to endure the frequent commercial interruptions to our favorite programs, which at the time we reckoned as an endless nuisance. So together we devised a game to mitigate the boredom. When a commercial flickered onto the screen, one of us would extract himself from his comfortable nest and turn down the TV volume (a task that usually fell to me, as the youngest), and then we would all collaborate to create spontaneously our own sardonic content to the advertisements. Often we slipped quickly into irreverent, distasteful, or subversive themes. I recall that contamination was a common leitmotif: a handsome fellow shaving at the bathroom mirror was, by the alchemy of our invention, inexplicably slathering mayonnaise onto his face; a married couple at the breakfast table gleefully sipped murky motor oil, not coffee; aerosol room fresheners were reimagined as fire extinguishers, mouthwash as kerosene, liquid floor wax as accidental urination on the kitchen floor, and so on. We replaced the existing narration

DOI: 10.7330/9781607329909.c000

and dialogue of the commercials with our own voice-overs and we adapted the visuals to scenarios that veered inevitably toward the ridiculous. I recall an instance when one brother chimed in with an extemporaneous voice-over for a sugarless gum commercial. He exaggerated the deep-toned inflection of a professional announcer, trumpeting: "People who chew Trident gum have 20 percent fewer cavities . . . because they have 40 percent fewer teeth." The game became a regular part of our family folklore and something of a contest as we all jockeyed for the honor of getting off the next best gag or one-liner, each of us trying to match wits with the other—and laughing all the while. Sometimes we were disappointed when the regularly scheduled program resumed, bringing our improvised fun to a sudden halt. In fact, on occasion, when we were particularly engaged with it, the game continued right into the program itself. And so our afternoon TV time was not just passive viewing; rather, it was spontaneously creative and immersive as we interacted purposely with the network programming and its interspersed ads. At the time I did not comprehend the notion of brandwashing (Lindstrom 2011) or corporate control, nor did I recognize the ludic routines with my brothers as interventions against the onslaught. But those early games disrupting commercials may have set me in the direction of musing on the relationship between dominant media and disorderly audience reception—what has been a long pathway leading to this volume and its central focus on folk intervention in popular media.

Try as they might, media texts can never finally control or contain the meanings that they generate. They form only one station of a polysemous discourse, and embedded within them are resources out of which active audiences augment or undermine the aims of production. "The hegemony of the text is never total," John Fiske observes, "but always has to struggle to impose itself into that diversity of meanings that the diversity of readers will produce" (2011, 93). Folklore is one mechanism in that process, an intervention whereby creative individuals inject alternate meanings into the media that they consume—and in doing so disrupt dominant ideologies.

ROOTS

In the 1970s, about the same time that my brothers and I were giggling in the living room, cultural theorists like Stuart Hall offered a new theoretical model for studying mediated communication. Repudiating the conventional view that communicative acts were essentially static processes with a sender, a message, and a receiver, Hall and cohorts at the Centre for Contemporary Cultural Studies in Birmingham posited that meaning was neither transparent nor predetermined by a hegemonic sender.[1] Gone were the old assumptions that media messages were fixed, unidirectional communications delivered to a passive audience. Instead, Hall opened up an understanding of the complexities of audience reception—negotiated meanings, subjective interpretations, and the agency of media consumers in creating their own cultural texts. Hall's groundbreaking essay "Encoding/Decoding" (2000) outlined different cultural positions or codes by which media texts might be interpreted: (1) the dominant-hegemonic position, which embraces wholesale the political and ideological messages of dominant culture—that is, the "preferred readings" institutionally encoded into the texts; (2) the negotiated position, operating similarly within a general understanding of the hegemonic viewpoint, but texts are decoded according to more particular or locally situated logics, the so-called near view; this position is inherently contradictive, Hall concedes, as it both adapts to and, at the same time, resists dominant ideology. And then there is (3) the oppositional stance, which is unequivocally counter-hegemonic. Readers reject the media codes that are "structured in dominance" (57), instead injecting an alternative frame of reference in order to "retotalize" (61) the message.

Hall's conceptualization is one of the taproots of reception studies, which in some ways is an inapt label given that so much hangs on audience agency in the act of decoding. Rather, the moment of media consumption on the part of readers, listeners, or viewers is more precisely a form of audience *construction* rather than the passivity connoted by the term *reception* (Corner 1983, 267). In any case, reception theory, sometimes called active audience studies, addresses the entanglement of social structure and agency—specifically, here, the relation between media production and the interpretive consumption of that media.

Not that production and consumption are discrete or easily separable categories. Consider, for example, a standard practice among ratings-hungry producers of reality television. They shoot vast quantities of video from which to edit selectively.[2] And then they closely monitor audience feedback on blogs, chatrooms, fan sites, and all manner of social networking to determine preferred plot points that are then fed back into a master narrative. Add to that programmed audience participation like voting (as in *Big Brother* and *American Idol*), and the assumed antithetical binary of production and consumption gets muddled (Jones 2003, 404; Tincknell and Raghuram 2002, 211). In effect, consumption becomes a part of the production—blurring the distinction between encoder and decoder.

But this complication is not entirely postmodern or solely a function of contemporary electronic media. Theorists talk about new media, communication after the rise of the internet; and new new media, essentially social media in which the users interact with the content. To demonstrate the longevity of the production/consumption quandary, let's consider a case from old old media, before the printing press.

INTERVENTION IN OLD OLD MEDIA

The art of illuminating manuscripts—adding decorative marginalia to scripted texts—dates back to antiquity, but during the Gothic period especially, up until the advent of the printing press, it became an extensive media enterprise. Between the twelfth and fourteenth centuries, the trade of copying and illuminating manuscripts underwent significant changes: monks who had labored freely in cloistered cubicles (for remission of sins) were replaced by wage-labor lay copyists who worked together, on commission, in urban commercial scriptoria to meet the increased demand for books (Eisenstein 1983, 10–11). In that social environment, as the sacred monastic tradition gave way to nascent capitalism, a secular vocational subculture emerged amid the increasingly collaborative production of manuscripts. Even as most of the illuminated texts during that time remained religious in nature—Bibles, Psalters, books of hours (Christian devotional books), decretals (compilations of papal letters on church doctrine)—the sensibilities of scribes drifted toward the profane. The copyists were often unruly consumers of the very ecclesiastical texts they produced, and their disruptive point of view found (often humorous) expression in the illuminations themselves.

The illuminations include a zoological menagerie of horses, cats, hares, foxes, apes, and birds of all sorts as well as eclectic hybrid beasts, grotesque human figures, and depictions of royalty and clergy. One of the most commonly recurring figures is the curious image of a snail battling a knight. The motif is generally construed as a mockery of human cowardice, though scholars have asserted other possible meanings. For example, the nineteenth-century bibliophile Alexander Comte de Bastard, who published the first facsimiles of illuminated manuscripts, interpreted the motif of the snail emerging from its shell as a symbol of resurrection (based on a pair of images he noticed in the margins of a French book of hours—an archer shooting a snail adjacent to a miniature of the raising of Lazarus [1850, 172]). Lilian Randall (1962) argued that snails battling knights were associated with the Lombards, an ethnic group in the early Middle Ages denigrated for their legendary cowardice. Still others have read the pervasive motif as a portrayal of the poor in their struggle against ruthless aristocracy, as a critique of social climbers, or as a symbol of male and female sexuality. The image has been explained also in practical terms: snails, which love to eat damp paper and could devour manuscripts stored in dank cellars, presented something of an occupational nuisance to bookish scribes, who then illustrated in the margins their contempt for the pests (see comments in Biggs 2013). In this view, the scribes perhaps identified with the knights, seeing themselves as heroic defenders of the text, although that would not explain why, in more instances than not, the snails seem to be winning the fight. In any case, whatever its emergent meanings at the moment of inscription, the ubiquitous snail was for the scribes an iconographic emblem of their occupational lore—and, if nothing else, suggestive of the sluggish tedium of their work.

Other motifs more radically destabilized the host texts they decorated. Clergy figure prominently in the such illuminations— sometime comically partaking in secular pleasures, like the bare-footed nun in the Maastricht Hours (c. 1300–1325) who hitches up her habit to perform a rude country dance to music scratched out by a friar playing a bellows like a fiddle with a distaff as the bow. These images are sometimes more carnal, as the lustful friar grop-ing a woman on the December calendar page in a fifteenth-century book of hours.

Sometimes the religious figures are scatological: for instance, a nude bishop appears in the margins of the famous Gorleston Psalter (c. 1320) chastising a defecating cleric. In the same volume we find the partially erased images of a nun and cowled figure, whose rude sexual gambols we are left to imagine as the offending illustration of their lower halves was long ago expunged (by some individual who, inexplicably, left alone the defecating cleric and any number of other unflinchingly offensive illuminations elsewhere in the codex). Clerics are not the only ones to engage in erotic shenanigans: in the Feischi Psalter (c. 1290) one male peasant is shown spanking a woman with a paddle, apparently to their mutual delight. A book of hours from Paris (c. 1460) includes this devo-tional passage from Psalms 32: "I have acknowledged my sin to thee, and my injustice I have not concealed. I said I will confess against myself my injustice to the Lord: and thou hast forgiven the wickedness of my sin." Meanwhile, in the margin are two charac-ters (a man and a woman) holding distaffs with threads that twine down to the corner of the page where two naked male figures are intimately occupied, curiously joined together anus to anus with a spindle. Cavorting characters in the illuminations are not always human, or even from the same species; for example, one fifteenth-century French book of hours depicts a fox copulating with a cock.

Apes became favorite figures of the illuminators. Their imi-tative nature made them ideal devices by which human behavior might be satirized. Their depiction is routinely scatological, and often they represent and ridicule the holy order. One series of images from a thirteenth-century English Psalter has the appear-ance of a simian bacchanal: one ape is vomiting as another presents its posterior for an ape cleric who, with fingers extended, positions himself for what looks like a pontific proctologic exam; one ape aggressively sodomizes another, while still another on a separate page is graphically penetrated by a stork with a prodigious phallic beak. Elsewhere, an ape pays homage to the bishop while being penetrated similarly by a blue jay, and the whole affair is witnessed voyeuristically by another cleric, who leers from above in a historiated letter D. Birds buggering monkeys with their beaks is a recurring image in medieval illuminations. The simians are also commonly penetrated by arrows shot from across the page, sometimes forcefully from a distant crossbow, as in the Pontifical of Guillaume Durand from Avignon (pre-1390).

The Rutland Psalter (c. 1260), a prized holding of the British Library, flourishes the text of Psalm 86:14: "O God, the proud are risen against me, and the assemblies of violent men have sought after my soul; and have not set thee before them." Underneath is a demon wielding a bow, having sent the arrow up the backside of an albino hybrid figure. The text itself (the tail of the letter P) has been commandeered by the demon in the pointed pederastic attack. This connotes the melding together of visual and lexical forms that is the signature of illuminated manuscripts; these are not just extraneous marginal doodles—as many medieval scholars dismissed them for years. Rather, on the pages of these codices, the illuminations interact in meaningful ways—semiotically and sometimes literally—with the scripted text. There is another ape in the Rutland, a mock knight brandishing a spear and riding an ostrich. His unarmed target waits on the facing page. It's a bearded man—possibly Christ—bent over in a passively willing posture.

Musical instruments appear regularly, sometimes played in unconventional ways, as with a number of naked figures playing trumpets with their buttocks. Fans of Monty Python's *Holy Grail* will no doubt remember this motif featured in one of Terry Gilliam's animated sequences. There's an equine variation in the Maastricht Hours: a horse plays a trumpet from its anus while prancing about just underneath the text "Gloria Patri" ("Glory to the Father"). A fourteenth-century Flemish book of hours depicts a naked musician who theoretically could play a duet with himself;

he holds two long trumpets, one to his mouth and the other to his buttocks. The mimetic apes that populate the illuminations also on occasion play trumpets from their nether regions.

Though these enigmatic drawn and painted figures are literally pushed to the side of the manuscript, in no way are they just trivial doodles—or only marginal, in the contemporary sense of the word. They add an extra dimension, argues Michael Camille, whose monograph *Image on the Edge* is one of the most important studies of the subject. The illuminations form a pictorial "supplement, that is able to gloss, parody, modernize and problematize the text's authority while never totally undermining it" (1992, 10). Illuminated medieval manuscripts provide us with an antique case study of what Hall (2000) may have considered a negotiated position, as the scribes essentially vandalized the very texts they had a hand in producing. Their marginal images were "conscious usurpations, perhaps even political statements about diffusing the power of the text" (Camille 1992, 42)—pointing up the fraught codependent relationship between production and reception. This is the arena where my interest lies, especially in the role that folklore plays as consumers of culture—whether medieval or modern—actively construct their own meanings. Overworked and impish medieval scribes amending, reimagining, and editorializing on venerated ecclesiastical texts with their own impious pictographs on manuscript edges is an early model for the sort of performative disruption in folk culture that animates this study of unruly audiences.

Individuals devising profane expressive forms to undermine established institutions is a well-practiced tradition; the implementation of these forms need not be public or face-to-face, although it is implicitly social. We might point to one particular variety of latrinalia that first appeared in the late 1970s (about the same time that Hall was formulating his theories on audience reception). It involves altering the (pretentiously obvious) stenciled instructions on electric hand dryers in public washrooms, which read as follows:

PUSH BUTTON.
RUB HANDS GENTLY UNDER WARM AIR.
MACHINE STOPS AUTOMATICALLY.

With a sharp device, individuals would scratch away specific letters, revealing another set of instructions with an entirely different message:

PUSH BUTT.
RUB GENTLY UNDER ARM.
STOP(S) AUTO.

In 1980, Charles Doyle conducted an informal regional study of this traditional practice, which at the time had been in circulation for no more than just a few years. Observing scores of examples in situ, he discovered that the alterations of the first two lines remained uniform. However, notable variations occurred in the treatment of the final line, which was sometimes left intact, sometimes excised altogether. Those instances in which it was modified to read "Stop auto," Doyle argues, "[imply] that the carrying out of instructions 1 and 2, 'Push butt' and 'Rub gently under arm,' will leave someone in such a state of excitement or enervation as to make driving unsafe or impossible" (1981, 50). More generally, this latrinalic custom is an act of defiance against institutional authority; invitingly anti-bureaucratic, it defaces an official directive outright and inscribes another message of erotic nonsense in its place.

Some years after Doyle's survey, additional textual manipulations began to appear in the stenciled instructions: a few medial characters were excised, rendering the final line as "STOP AUTO AT ALLY." The underlying logic remains the same: carrying out the previous steps of the instructions would impede one's ability to operate a motor vehicle properly. But this version goes further yet, as the reader is directed to park the car in an alleyway, a location more privately conducive to illicit butt pushing and arm rubbing. That the word *alley* was misspelled in this iteration apparently did not discourage practitioners who were determined to amend the original form. One model of hand dryer carried these verbose instructions:

SHAKE EXCESS WATER FROM HANDS.
PUSH KNOB. STOPS AUTOMATICALLY.
RUB HANDS LIGHTLY AND RAPIDLY.
TURN LOUVER UPWARD TO DRY FACE.

Which, through excision, were transfigured into an X-rated directive:

SHAKE KNOB. RUB LIGHTLY AND RAPIDLY.
TURN UPWARD TO FACE.

In its various constructions, this one tradition of epigraphy by subtraction, as Doyle calls it, would not last long. When the World Dryer Corporation, the leading global manufacturer of hand dryers, and other similar companies systematically replaced the stenciled instructions on the machines with procedural pictographs, there was no text left to deface. The first image shows a disembodied hand depressing a circular button; the second image (illustrating the essential step of rubbing hands gently under warm air) shows a pair of hands side by side under parallel, wavy red stripes. The industry had effectively co-opted the folk process, and eradicated the subversion, by removing *all* of the letters—a maneuver that, whatever may have been intended, echoed a well-rehearsed hegemonic strategy: regulating, muzzling, and sometimes eliminating altogether the media of disturbance.

Interestingly, the World Dryer website promotes its most popular hand dryer, the World Model A, as "suitable for high traffic facilities needing vandal-resistant features." It is not clear whether the vandal resistance is a function of the machine's rugged cast-iron construction, its porcelain enamel finish, or its relative paucity of instructional text that might be subversively refashioned with a sharp object. Agitators with a mind to flout authority and a will to scratch away letters found themselves without a medium, so their ingenuity turned elsewhere.

A new folk practice emerged in the form of captions to the institutional pictographs, invented instructions written to the side or above the images, depending on their horizontal or vertical arrangement: "Press [or push] button" and "Receive bacon." Once the wavy red lines had been decoded as a stylized depiction of bacon, this graffito proliferated. Models of the Nova brand of blowers included a third image, a human facial profile in front of the red lines, inviting individuals to air-dry their washed faces, a much less common ablution in public restrooms. Not surprisingly, the folk mind was ready to extend the emendations to a tripartite grafitto: "Press button," "Receive bacon," "Enjoy [or eat] bacon." Though these examples do not have the sexual energy of their precursors, as playful subversions of a conventional institutionalized message they are no less iconoclastic. In fact, the implied act of dispensing and eating food in a restroom violates a culturally mandated sense of order/separation; as such, it is, in the parlance of Mary Douglas, pollution and therefore memorably *dangerous* (2002, 36–37). My own informal observation during a recent road trip across the Midwest and Upper South shows that this latrinalic practice is still very much alive. When the wavy red lines became further abstracted as simple straight black lines emanating from the air nozzle, the pictograph no longer resembled bacon, and as a result the folk captions mutated once again, to the nonsensically surreal "Applaud the jellyfish." Sometimes, the verbal or illustrated instructions were followed by a single sardonically practical tip: "After five minutes, wipe hands on pants," lampooning altogether the general inefficiency of institutional procedures and equipment.

CULTURE JAMMING AS INTERVENTION

Iconoclastic though they are, the sabotaged directives on hand dryers in public restrooms reach only small audiences. When the same principle of message disruption finds expression in mass media, the defiance is bolder and broader—and the stakes are higher. We are constantly assaulted by commercial messages, and it appears that no print or digital medium is exempt from the strategies of publicists. Ads appear before films, and through product placement the films themselves become vehicles of branding; advertising crawlers stream across every available electronic screen; postboxes overflow with direct mail and glossy flyers; corporate images overrun cityscapes—on busses and taxis, billboards, transit shelters, marquees, sports arenas, ad infinitum. Corporate advertising occupies every bit of negotiable public space, and as a result, it persuasively infiltrates cognitive terrain as well as our thought processes.

As advertising tactics have grown increasingly sophisticated and insidious, it is no wonder that recent years have given rise to subcultures of activists who passionately challenge the corporate rhetoric that dominates our space and minds. Some are artists, some are hackers, some grassroots protestors, but they are allied in their shared effort to disrupt corporate media messages; they employ a common tactic of adbusting, or culture jamming: using ad parodies, media hoaxes, trademark infringement, and sabotage to undermine and reconfigure the commercial saturation of public life.

Naomi Klein notes that the most sophisticated culture jams are not isolated parodies but rather "[ad] interceptions—counter-messages that hack into a corporation's own method of communication to send a message starkly at odds with the one that was intended" (2000, 281). So, in practices that are enacted as part of a discourse of civic responsibility, jammers, also called "subvertisers" or "hacktivists," use corporations' own well-funded resources against them. This anti-consumerist pranksterism is a kind of rhetorical jujitsu that "resists less through negating and opposing dominant rhetorics than by playfully and provocatively folding existing cultural forms in on themselves." But the end goal is always the same: to "impede the machinery of marketing" (Harold 2004, 190–91). Furthermore, Kembrew McLeod argues, such pranking and culture jamming operate as "twisted versions of participatory democracy" (2017, 401), an observation particularly resonant with the notion of folk intervention.

The Gap's popular 1993 print ad campaign "Who Wore Khakis?" featuring images of iconic celebrities such as James Dean, Steve McQueen, Andy Warhol, and Marilyn Monroe, backfired when Australian jammers propagated parody ads closely mimicking the look of the originals, down to the grayscale photography and placement of the Gap logo, showing Adolf Hitler sporting khakis as well. That idea was pressed further when freelance writer Christopher Corbett penned a humor piece for the *Los Angeles Times* titled "So, Just Who Is a Khaki Kind of Guy?" (1993) associating the pants with other famous twentieth-century personalities like Goebbels, Himmler, Mussolini, Baby Doc Duvalier, Idi Amin, and cult leader Jim Jones. Once the Gap executives openly denounced Corbett, the modest spoof escalated into a full-blown media controversy, receiving coverage in the *New York Times, Wall*

Street Journal, Baltimore Sun, and Associated Press. "Everybody but The Gap got the joke," Corbett observed (Olesker 1993); and with its advertising campaign effectively jammed, the company came across as humorless, defensive, and—the worst thing possible from a marketing standpoint—*uncool* (see Klein 2000, 68–73).

More recently British Petroleum became the target of numerous culture jams after the disastrous explosion of the Deepwater Horizon offshore drilling rig in April 2010. Eleven people lost their lives in the initial explosion, and the rig, after burning for thirty-six hours, eventually sank, leading to the largest marine oil spill ever. Almost two months passed before the streaming oil plumes on the seafloor could be permanently sealed, and in that time an estimated 5 million barrels of oil had leaked into the Gulf of Mexico. The catastrophic environmental impact of the accident, coupled with the public's growing awareness that BP had enjoyed enormous profits while cutting corners on safety regulations (Lyall 2010), made the company a prime target for anti-corporate culture jammers. While the oil was still leaking, Greenpeace UK initiated a rebranding contest inviting participants to redesign BP's "Helios Sunflower" corporate logo—a logo that, when it was unveiled in 2000, had cost more in development than BP had spent on renewable energy in the entire preceding year (Macalister and Cross 2000). Within a few weeks the contest received more than 2,000 entries, many adapting the logo's signature geometric form and color scheme but with splashes, drips, and pools of added black to signify the oil spill. A number of entries also replaced the attendant corporate slogan "Beyond Petroleum" with mordant phrases like "Black Planet," "Business Profits," "Banking Pollution," "Bitter Poison," and "Bad Plumbing."

Some anonymous activists opened Twitter account under the name BP Public Relations (@BPGlobalPR), ostensibly representing the commercial interests of the oil conglomerate. But tweeted comments soon revealed otherwise:

> Negative people view the ocean as half empty of oil. We are dedicated to making it half full. Stay positive America!

> We are starting a movement to fix the oil leak. Just mail your
> garbage to New Orleans and we'll take it from there. The bigger
> the better! (Torben 2015)

Beyond just using the BP's method or style of communication, this
media prank is an instance of outright impersonation, a strategy
defined by the culture-jamming network the Yes Men as *identity
correction*, "impersonating big-time criminals in order to publicly
humiliate them, and otherwise giving journalists excuses to cover
important issues" (http://theyesmen.org/). It makes sense that
tactics like these came to be nominally associated with the jamming
of radio waves, which similarly involves deliberate disruption of
dominant frequencies.

FAN PARTICIPATION

Not all media disturbances come from ardent protesters, however.
Contradictory though it seems, some interventions emanate from
fan culture. Henry Jenkins has written extensively about the relationship between the producers and consumers of cultural texts,
exploring the ways in which fans, particularly, play a participatory
role in re-forming popular media. "[Fans'] pleasures often exist on
the margins of the original text," Jenkins writes, "and in the face of
the producer's own efforts to regulate its meanings" (2013, 24). In
that sense, contemporary fandoms might be likened to the medieval copyists who long ago inscribed their own editorials literally
into the margins of commissioned ecclesiastical texts. Jenkins used
the term *poaching* to describe the manner in which fans construct
unauthorized expansions of the media franchises to which they are
devoted. The sheer amount of fan labor in that process is astounding: there is fan art in every medium—videos, music, costumes,
theatrical reenactments, and fan fiction, to name a few examples.
Fandom energizes a participatory subculture that augments and
refashions familiar commercial materials; but, according to Jenkins,
those media manipulations are not necessarily subversive: "To
say that fans promote their own meanings over those of producers is not to suggest that the meanings fans produce are always

oppositional ones . . . Readers are not always resistant; all resistant readings are not necessarily progressive readings; the 'people' do not always recognize their conditions of alienation and subordination" (34). That said, the case studies in Jenkins's seminal work *Textual Poachers: Television Fans and Participatory Culture* continually point up what appears to be built-in conflicts of interest between producers and consumers of media.

One example, a subgenre of fan fiction, is slash literature, fan-generated writing that amends and recasts the narratives of primary media texts to develop explicitly homoerotic pairings of central characters that may have been nonexistent or only hinted at in the original. The slash (/) itself comes to represent all of the unspoken sexual tension between same-sex characters that is then made transparent in fan fiction. The first slash literature appeared in fanzines in the early 1970s with the illicit coupling of James Kirk and Spock from *Star Trek*, designated as K/S. Since then, many fandoms across different media have developed their own couplings: Wilson and House from *House*, Draco and Harry from the *Harry Potter* series, Frodo and Sam from *Lord of the Rings*, Captain America and Iron Man from *The Avengers*, Holmes and Watson from the BBC's *Sherlock*, and so on. This queering of mainstream media is a literary response to patriarchal constructions of sexuality, and it may strike outsiders as curious that, although the couples are overwhelmingly male/male, slash fiction is written and consumed almost exclusively by women (see Jenkins 2013, 191–93; Hellekson and Busse 2006, 17). The genre asserts emotional warmth, sensuality, intimacy, and affection over the sexual objectification and self-serving physical pleasure typical of most male-oriented pornography. Slash fiction allows a fluidity of sexual expression in an erotic universe where gender, in essence, becomes irrelevant. Just as it overtly resists heteronormative masculinity, slash fiction also confronts patriarchal constructions of femininity, argues Joanna Russ, imagining "a love that is free from the culture's whole discourse of gender and sex roles" (1985, 89). Such fan appropriations of "authorized" popular media create new, alterative expressive forms through which disenfranchised consumers undercut the hegemonic powers of production.

❊ ❊ ❊

These preliminary illustrations—medieval scribes, anonymous latrinalists, jammers, and dedicated fandoms—form an eclectic assembly of folk groups, to be sure; diverse as they are, they demonstrate a shared principle: consumers of media are not passive, and they produce their own meaningful expressive culture in the *reception* of that media. Economic and ideological dominant culture manipulates the means of communication to reify the status quo—that much should not surprise us. But nested within that media are resources of resistance. Hegemonic messages proliferate, but those messages are differently activated by the disenfranchised, who formulate alternate meanings to—and thereby contravene—the prevailing discourse of a social system that disempowers them. These are the "contradictory lines of force" that foment popular culture. As John Fiske argues, "If the cultural commodities or texts do not contain resources out of which the people can make their own meanings of their social relations and identities, they will be rejected and fail in the marketplace. They will not be made popular" (1989, 2). This presses to the central focus of this book—the fluid interplay between production and audience reception, between forces of cultural domination and cultural resistance. Most important, this is an exploration of the ways in which folklore operates as a mechanism in that interplay. I will discuss these processes in terms of remediation, "the formal logic by which new media refashion prior media forms" (Bolter and Grusin 1999, 173), and intervention—a conceptual framework for the creation of new expressive forms as social action, and a means of disrupting dominant modes of media discourse. It is within this larger theoretical universe that I situate *Unruly Audience*. The case studies explored here demonstrate that folklore is instrumental in the agentic, often disruptive, audience reception of popular music, film, tourism, television, advertising, and multi-mediated jokes.

Popular music lends itself to parody. In a sense, its popularity facilitates its undoing by encouraging manipulation of the original form. No authored popular melody demonstrates this more clearly than "The Colonel Bogey March," the famous military march composed in 1914 by Lieutenant F. J. Ricketts, British bandmaster and director of music for the Royal Marines at Plymouth. The melody, sometimes identified (anachronistically) simply as the whistling tune from *Bridge on the River Kwai*, is a staple in Western military and popular culture—and a perfect case study of the cross-pollination between popular media production and folk reception. Although the march was written as a melody alone, without words, it quickly became the conduit for numerous comical folk lyrics, partly because the tune was so infectious. None of the adaptations has been more tenacious—or memorable—than "Hitler Has Only Got One Ball," which emerged initially among British troops in 1939 and remains in oral tradition even today. The song sits comfortably with a wide range of other satirical treatments of Nazism in folklore and popular culture, like the 1943 propagandistic song "In Der Fuerher's Face" recorded by Spike Jones; Disney's animated cartoon by the same title; Mel Brooks's musical number "Springtime for Hitler" from his film (and later Broadway play) *The Producers*; recent parodic internet videos of a single clip from the German film *Downfall* (2004) that have propagated across YouTube in more than 100 versions; and Godwin's Law, a playfully conceived media theory regarding the proliferation of Hitler/Nazi comparisons in the blogosphere (related to the logic fallacy reductio ad Hitlerum). In chapter 1, I trace the provenance of "The Colonel Bogey March" from its martial, patriotic beginnings to its amplification as a satirical wartime folk song in World War I, World War II, and beyond ("Hitler Has Only Got One Ball" and other military and civilian adaptations). I look at its diffusion among British Tommies and American GIs, and its continued circulation in children's folklore on both sides of the Atlantic.

A number of scholars have examined the far-reaching influences of Disney, Inc., interrogating the company's politics (Dorfman and Mattelart 1984; Shortsleeve 2004), its labor practices (Grover 1991; Kuenz 1995; Klugman 1995), its consumerist and capitalistic inclinations (Schickel 1997), and its role as an arbiter of American values (Watts 1997). Moreover, several have critiqued the "Disneyfication" of traditional fairy tales—notably Jack Zipes (1995; 1997, 89–110), Waller Hastings (1993), Naomi Wood (1996), and Kay Stone (1975). In chapter 2, I build on that line of criticism to consider the dialogic relationship between the Grimms' version of "Snow White," Disney's film adaptation, and contemporary jokes that target the film and its characters. Disney is among the world's most recognizable corporations, and everything we associate with the brand—the far reaches of its media and entertainment empire—is built upon the initial achievements of *Snow White* (1937), the first full-length animated feature in the motion picture industry. It was Walt Disney's pet project and he personally supervised every facet of the production. As we know, the film was enormously successful: the plot, characters, and songs became indelibly etched into American popular consciousness. Along with that, however, a corpus of salacious Snow White jokes surfaced in folk culture, far afield from the tightly managed picture of wholesomeness presented in the film. The jokes invite us to look at Disney's emblematic film through a different lens altogether. Of the case studies in the present volume, this one demonstrates perhaps the greatest divergence between the prescribed dominant message of a media producer and the disorderly reception of that media.

Humor is not the only tool that audiences employ to undermine media texts, however. The charged social negotiations of tourism comprise another sort of mediated performance that can be appropriated, refashioned, or sabotaged in audience reception. North Americans alone spend well over $100 billion a year as international tourists, much of that money flowing into the local economies of the places they visit. Many sites are crucially dependent on tourism for their economic vitality, but the exchange is not unidirectional; it is, rather, transactional, as all parties (tourists, foreign investors, local entrepreneurs, and workers) receive something in the process. As a result, the invention and management of exotic interest in local custom has become commercial strategy. The transaction is especially fraught when viewed through a postcolonial theoretical lens, as the various participants bring divergent national, economic, and ethnic sensibilities to the touristic stage. In chapter 3, I examine the tourist site of Rose Hall, a nineteenth-century sugar plantation in Jamaica that is supposedly haunted by its onetime proprietress, Annie Palmer. Hailing from

England, Annie is said to have been a diminutive white landowner who exploited and terrorized her slaves at every turn, eventually earning the moniker "the White Witch of Jamaica." The legends of Rose Hall have been soundly, publicly debunked on several fronts, but there remains staunch local attachment to narrated details of an alleged slave uprising there, coinciding temporally with the well-documented Jamaican Slave Revolt of 1831. The regional touristic narrative about Rose Hall, touted as "the most haunted house in the Western hemisphere," has been symbolically transformed into a metaphor for Jamaica's historical struggle for emancipation—and as such, it holds tremendous symbolic power. Literary versions of the legend of Rose Hall in the nineteenth and early twentieth centuries are themselves influenced by an enduring local oral tradition, and manifestations of the legend in popular media (music, television, film, and tourism) have become poignantly and problematically entangled with Jamaica's troubled history of slavery. This particular nexus of oral tradition, literature, popular culture, tourism, and national identity creates a distinctively rich subject for a study of cultural production and folk reception.

The popular NBC series *The Office*, which concluded in 2013 after nine seasons, featured the inept and bombastic office manager Michael Scott, played by Steve Carrell. One marker of Scott's obnoxious character was the frequent injection of inappropriate humor into the workplace, the most notable of which was the recurrent suggestively lewd wisecrack "That's what she said" as a riposte to some innocent comment uttered by a coworker. Although this rhetorical device was launched into wide popularity from repeated use on the television show, it was in play in folklore long before *The Office* first aired. In fact, it has roots in an earlier humorous trope from Edwardian England, "As the actress said to the bishop," which itself is linked to an even older proverbial expressive form, the Wellerism. By way of these related expressions, chapter 4 examines the form and social use of "That's what she said" jokes in folk culture and their recent leap as a meme into popular media. This case exemplifies the fluidity between folk and popular culture, and that gray intermediate zone where media production and audience reception commingle in what Jenkins calls "convergence culture," the cultural space where "old and new media collide" (2006). It demonstrates the bilateral pathways of cultural production, appropriation, and reintegration that characterize the "folkloresque," that is, "popular culture's own (emic) perception and performance of folklore . . . [derived] directly from existing folkloric traditions," which, in some instances, "inspires a feedback loop in which the folkloresque version of the item is (re)incorporated into the folk cultural milieu that it references" (Foster and Tolbert 2016, 5).

Children are exposed to thousands of brands every day (Lindstrom and Seybold 2004, 6). In the face of that assault, it is not surprising that their folklore demonstrates significant brand awareness, and that they have developed elaborate strategies to deflect the endless barrage of commercial advertising. While a few folklorists have commented on the numerous name brands that appear in children's lore (e.g., Tucker 2008, Bronner 1988, Sherman and Weisskopf 1995), their observations tend to be primarily tabulations; there has been little substantive analysis of the dynamic process by which children's folklore disarms and undermines dominant corporate messages. Chapter 5 addresses that gap in the discourse. Children's folklore draws a wealth of material from commercial culture, and because children are not just spectators or passive consumers, on the playground they frequently adapt and satirize popular advertisements. I examine salient examples, including childhood parodies of ads for Pepsi, KFC, and McDonald's. A few remarkable parodies linger in children's verbal play *long after* the original targeted advertising blitz has faded from popular/commercial consciousness. With these and other relevant examples, this chapter draws a theoretical framework regarding the ways in which children perform subversion in their lore and attempt to deflate the power of corporate branding.

Several of these chapters demonstrate that humor is a commonly employed instrument by which audiences disrupt and repurpose the media messages of dominant culture: soldiers invent incongruous, bawdy lyrics for a majestic martial tune and snicker as it circulates irreverently through the ranks; the moviegoing public reimagines cloyingly adorable Disney characters as a rowdy cast of lewd degenerates; children parody ads from the endless wave of commercial material aimed at them; and fans respond to a familiar TV joke with countless comical remediations in other digital forms. Even the sort of acerbic social critiques and guerrilla tactics of culture jamming mentioned above are realized in terms of dark humor called "laughtivism" (Delaure 2017, 419). Humor is the apparatus of all these folk interventions, whose raison d'être is upending established social order. But curiously, in a postmodern turn, certain self-referential forms of humor effectively upend themselves. That is, metajokes, the subject of chapter 6, operate both as vehicle and object of their own intervention. Variations on the practice of self-referential and self-aware joking include parodies of joke templates (formulaic joke patterns manipulated and reconditioned in new jokes), meta-humor (jokes about jokes), joke metonyms (abbreviated allusions to familiar jokes), and anti-jokes (non-jokes performed as jokes). Metajokes create generic ambiguity. Like the ancient Ouroboros, the curled serpent eating its own tail, these self-referential jokes effectively incorporate themselves as they playfully recalibrate our expectations about what jokes do.

* * *

Corporations and institutions that own and manipulate the means of communication expend untold resources to maintain power and shape cultural meaning, generally in the interest of increasing profits. That is not to say, however, that the relationship between producers of media and consumers is a one-way street—or that the marketplace holds total control of meaning. Active audiences have developed strategies of participation (engaging, sharing, promoting, adding content, retooling [see Gjoni 2017, 64]) and resistance (critiquing, parodying, culture jamming, subverting) to assert themselves in the face of hegemonic mediated discourse. They mobilize corporate-driven popular media for their own purposes and engage with it in varying degrees—from unorthodox participation to unruly disruption—as a form of social activism. And folklore, as we'll see, is one important appliance in that linkage between controlled media production and divergent audience reception, which can be subversive, participatory, or a measure of both.

1

Colonel Bogey's Parade of Parody

CATCHY MELODIC PHRASES AND LYRICAL TWISTS from popular music lodge themselves in our brains; because they are so familiar and instantly retrievable, these little tuneful figures are ripe for manipulation. Professional song parodists like Spike Jones, Allan Sherman, and Weird Al Yankovic built profitable careers burlesquing popular music, and more recently hordes of amateurs on YouTube are dabbling in the creation of their own song parodies. But these tend to be transient and pitched narrowly to specialized audiences, few lasting in popular consciousness for more than a year or two. The more democratized song parodies emanating from folk culture, however, have greater longevity and resonance with broader public appeal. "The Colonel Bogey March" presents us with an extraordinary and enduring case study, as a legacy of folk parodies, some of which still circulate, has followed this famous military tune for more than a century since its composition.

THE COMPOSER

Frederick Joseph Ricketts, venerated as the "British March King," stands as one of Britain's finest composers of military music. He is touted as England's answer to Sousa. Born in East London to a Shadwell coal merchant in 1881, Ricketts was orphaned by the age of fourteen and lied about his age in order to join the

24

DOI: 10.7330/9781607329909.c001

army as a bandboy. In 1904, after seven years' service in India, he returned to England to study at the Royal Military School of Music where, surprisingly, he was ranked bottom of the class for his original march composition. In 1908 he took charge of his first band, but with the onset of World War I his bandsmen were called back to service and Ricketts found himself directing a band composed primarily of overaged musicians and bandboys. In that capacity, he spent the war leading concerts for service charities and other wartime causes (Richards 2001, 428–29). After the war, Ricketts directed several military bands, finally transferring in 1930 to the divisional band at Plymouth, where he served as director of music for the Royal Marines until his retirement as a major in 1944. He was composing all the while, using a pseudonym (Kenneth J. Alford) because service personnel during this time were discouraged from developing professional careers outside the military. Of the eighteen marches he composed in the span of his active career, the best known by far is "The Colonel Bogey March," familiar to most Americans as the theme melody from the film *Bridge on the River Kwai*.

Alford composed "Colonel Bogey" in 1914, a portentous year for marches, to be sure. Legend has it that the original inspiration for the march came from an eccentric colonel whom Alford met while stationed at Fort George near Inverness in Scotland just before the war began. The composer played golf, and on the local course he occasionally encountered the colonel, whose nickname among fellow golfers was "Bogey." Instead of shouting "Fore!" to warn of an impending drive, the colonel had the peculiar habit of whistling a two-note phrase, descending in the minor third. This little musical figure took root in Alford's receptive mind—spawning the signature motif of his memorable march.

When Alford penned "Colonel Bogey," he could not have foreseen its destined fame. One authority on the bawdy folk culture of World War I, Brophy and Partridge's *The Long Trail*, claims that "Colonel Bogey" was "the most frequently heard marching tune in the Army . . . whistled and hummed everywhere" (1965, 16). It was to be Alford's masterwork and a significant commercial success. By the early 1930s, the sheet music of the march had sold more than a million copies, and the tune had been recorded countless times (Graves 1999). Beyond licensing and recording, however, "Colonel Bogey" enjoyed a vibrant other life in parody.

EARLY PARODIES

Ultimately, what permanently stamped the melody into the popular consciousness was not its commercial achievement but rather its function as a vehicle for numerous comical folk lyrics. As Jeffrey Richards observed, the march's "rhythmic structure was so appropriate for words that marching soldiers rapidly attached to it obscene lyrics, which were cheerfully sung by squaddies [British infantry soldiers] in both world wars" (2001, 431). The catchy two-note introductory figure lends itself to bawdy disyllabic lyrics, and within a few years of its composition, the march had inspired several ditties like this one:

> Bullshit! That's all the band could play,
> Bullshit! They played it ev'ry day
> Bullshit! Ta-ra-ra bullshit!
> Ta-ra-ra bullshit! bullshit! bullshit!

Given that Alford's marches were composed as "affirmations of his patriotism," "tributes to the fighting forces," and "morale boosters" (Richards 2001, 431), this stanza appears lyrically hostile to those intentions. The band is roundly berated, and then, suggestively, patriotism is impugned as well. "Ta-ra-ra bullshit" unmistakably invokes "Ta-ra-ra-boom-de-ay," the song made famous by Lottie Collins, the British music hall singer who first performed it in London in the 1890s. With an accompanying dance routine, she performed the song all over London and then toured America and Australia. The song was memorialized around the world and by the time of World War I had become shorthand for British patriotism (*Era* 1895; Busby 1976, 39). So with their lyrics, British soldiers were simultaneously undermining the understood jingoism of both "Ta-ra-ra-boom-de-ay" and "Colonel Bogey." Military hard-liners may have reacted like World War I British commander in chief Douglas Haig upon overhearing one battalion singing a bawdy rendition of "Turkey in the Straw": "I like the tune . . . but you must know that in any circumstances the words are inexcusable" (Macdonald 1993, 208).

Poetically, however, the "Ta-ra-ra bullshit" lyric to "Colonel Bogey" is not especially imaginative, nor does the last line scan easily with the original rhythm of the march. We might compare another rendition from the same period, whose irreverence, stated in terms of the disintegrated body and cannibalism, is considerably more graphic:

> Bollocks, and the same to you,
> Bollocks, they make a damned good stew,
> Bollocks, mixed up with scallops,
> And a nice tasty arsehole or two.
> (Sometimes an alternate third line is inserted: "Knackers,
>   go well with crackers.")

Considering the parodies that would imminently emerge during World War II, it is notable that by the mid-1930s the word *bollocks* figured prominently in many British renditions of the march: in the folk mind the melody was already being associated with the realm of the testicular. Although Alford was dismayed at the lyrics that had become attached to his composition (Trendell 1991, 33), on occasion he affably recounted an incident that had occurred in 1919, while he was listening to the Royal Marine Artillery Band playing at Ryde, Isle of Wight. "As the band struck up 'Colonel Bogey,' an unknown officer turned to [Alford], who was dressed in civilian clothes, and said 'There's that bollocks tune again! How I'd like to strangle the bloke that wrote it'" (quoted in Trendell 1991, 67).

WORLD WAR II AND THE THIRD REICH

From there it was a logical progression that led to the most persistent—and memorable—adaptation of the march, "Hitler Has Only Got One Ball," which appeared initially among British troops sometime in 1939 and remains in oral tradition even today. One typical variant goes this way:

Hitler has only got one ball,
Göring has two but very small,
Himmler is rather sim'lar,
But poor old Goebbels [Go-balls] has no balls at all.

A means of ridiculing the Nazis, "Hitler Has Only Got One Ball" became immensely popular among both British and American troops (Cleveland 1994a, 85), who in transmitting this song were exercising something of a wartime convention by demeaning the sexual faculties of enemy leaders. But the mockery extended further. Since the 1920s, the words *balls* or *ballsy* had come to denote notions of courage, nerve, or fortitude. In that sense, defective testicles rendered the Nazis defective soldiers. This song's itemized taxonomy of malformed German genitalia—the monorchid, the micro-orchid, the anorchid—was particularly forceful, and satisfying, to Allied soldiers in that it scattered satiric buckshot across the whole Nazi high command (Hitler; Hermann Göring, commander in chief of the Luftwaffe; Heinrich Himmler, Reichsführer of the SS; and Goebbels, Reich minister of propaganda).

The song's genesis in this form is unclear. In his autobiography *Fringe Benefits* (2000), Anglo-Irish writer Donough O'Brien claims that the original was written by his father, Toby O'Brien, in August 1939 when the latter was working as a publicist for the British Council. His version started with the words "Göring has only got one ball," and went on to describe Hitler's two diminutive ones—contradicting virtually all later versions, in which the positions are transposed. But the composer and broadcaster Hubert Gregg also professed to have authored the lyrics. Allegedly, he penned the bawdy verse and proffered it anonymously to the British War Office, which welcomed the contribution enthusiastically as an implement of wartime propaganda. The award-winning BBC radio play by Neville Smith titled *Dear Dr. Goebbels* (2001) posits yet another origin of the song. Purportedly nonfiction, the play recounts the story of a World War II prosthetic seller named Philip Morgenstern who goes undercover with MI6 to Germany. There, he meets Goebbels and is commissioned to fit the doctor with new prosthetic surgical boots. In the process, he learns scandalous details of Goebbels's private life, which he then versifies to the tune of the "Colonel Bogey March." Churchill later offers Morgenstern an honor, officially for bravery in service but unofficially for the propagandistic musical jewel. The play closes with Churchill, on his last day of office, singing the song with Morgenstern. These claims all remain unsubstantiated, and authorship of "Hitler Has Only Got One Ball" has never been definitively established. There is no known attempt by anyone to acquire or enforce a copyright on the lyrics—listed in the Roud Folk Song Index as number 10,493. In 1939, Ray Sonin set wholesome patriotic lyrics to Alford's march with "Good Luck and the Same to You," but the sanitized song failed to obscure the bawdy folk versions already in circulation.

It is impossible for us to know just from the texts what the verses may have meant to specific informants at the time, but it is probable that this song would have elicited from Allied soldiers some amusement at disparaging the enemy with the added social benefit of morale boosting. It would be misleading, though, to suggest that the song served an express institutional strategy of propaganda. As Christie Davies has argued, political and military institutions are generally unsuccessful in using humor as a strategy in war, strictly speaking. "Jokes belong to the black market" rather than to authorities, and "popular humour operates independently of any strategy that the official controllers of war-time propaganda would like to impose on it" (2001, 402; see also Oring 2016, 122). The strategic prospects for authorities are doubly limited when the humor is conveyed through melody, because a song's success, like a joke, depends upon audience reception rather than political imperative. According to Les Cleveland, a noted scholar of military occupational lore, the US music industry's efforts to establish a "correct" formula for World War II songs were ineffectual. The US Office of War Information considered the potential of popular songs as military propaganda, only to determine that there "was no payoff in high purpose or patriotic intent. A song had to be accepted by the mass audience on its own merits" (1994b, 167). So it was with "Hitler Has Only Got One Ball," which obviously found fertile soil into the 1940s but has flourished in folk and popular culture ever since—beyond the military, beyond the war—notwithstanding (dubious) assertions, like O'Brien's, that it was launched as a propagandistic initiative through government channels.

Some propose that the song, no matter the circumstances of its origins, developed from a simple linguistic glitch—namely, the difficulty of English speakers to pronounce Goebbels's name properly—and that the rest of the song unfolded organically from there. It is worth noting that some later variants among children, who probably had no idea who Goebbels was (and who probably could not pronounce his name), replaced "Go Balls" with a fictional character called "Joe Balls." But regardless of the subject's name, all collected versions of the opening stanza reach the same poetic denouement at line 4: "no balls at all." That is to say, in this musical catalogue of testicular disorders, the definitive last entry is always anorchism—the physical signifier of a lack of courage or character.

A second, less familiar, verse adds more details about other Third Reich personalities and introduces the notion of deformity in terms of overabundance rather than deficiency:

> Rommel has four or five, I guess,
> No one's quite sure bout Rudolf Hess,
> Schmeling is always yelling,
> But poor old Goebbels [Go-balls] has no balls at all.

Unlike his counterparts, Erwin Rommel's affliction is one of excess. If in these rhymes testicles are equated with fortitude, then Rommel, Germany's highly decorated field marshal, comes across as hypermasculine, which diverges from the general tenor of the rest of the song. He does not fit easily into the song's central message because he was the least hated of the Nazi high command: a respected adversary who was one of the few senior officers not involved in war crimes, the "Desert Fox" was even implicated in the plot to overthrow the Führer near the end of the war. These ambiguities may account for the relative obscurity of this verse compared to the well-worn first verse. It is telling that Goebbels, who was among the most reviled Nazis, appears in virtually every variant and suffers most severely in the song's inventory of testicular defects. As for Rudolph Hess, Hitler's devoted deputy

Führer, no one is sure about him, perhaps because of the mysterious circumstances surrounding his capture and incarceration. He remains one of the most enigmatic personalities of the Third Reich: he secretly flew solo to Scotland in 1941 to negotiate peace with England but was arrested and detained for the remainder of the war and then imprisoned for life after a conviction at the Nuremberg trials.

The appearance of the boxer Max Schmeling in line 3 may strike us as more puzzling yet. As the only nonsoldier and the only one without an expressed testicular abnormality, he seems at first to be incongruously yoked with the others. But any American GI old enough to fight in World War II would well remember Schmeling's backstory. His matches against Joe Louis were monumental events of the 1930s. Schmeling delivered the best performance of his career in 1936, knocking out the then undefeated Louis in the twelfth round. Back in Germany, Schmeling was swept up in the Nazi propaganda machine and his victory was trumpeted as evidence of Aryan superiority. The subsequent rematch between Schmeling and Louis for the World Championship in 1938 at Yankee Stadium was at that time the most anticipated and politicized sporting event ever held on American soil. Billed as the "Battle of the Century," it had deep racial implications and became an epic morality play between the forces of Nazism and American democracy. Louis beat Schmeling soundly with a technical knockout in the first round. A decisive punch of the match was a blow to the left kidney, at which point Schmeling "grimaced and let out a high pitched cry that echoed throughout the stadium" (Margolick 2005, 298). Symbolically, this was a yell heard around the world; countless spectators and sportswriters commented on the scream and it was remembered vividly as part of the national narrative about the fight. And within five years of the match, we find American versions of "Hitler Has Only Got One Ball" with the Schmeling line inserted. Like "Himmler is rather sim'lar," "Schmeling is always yelling" is an irresistible rhyme, but it clearly is there for more than just poetic reasons. It is an iconic moment of American victory over Nazism frozen in time. In the artistic frame of the verse, Schmeling is always yelling; that is, he is doomed to relive the moment of defeat perpetually. That image of the enemy would serve American soldiers well, and it fits precisely with the song's theme of derision.

Other subsequent British verses amended Hitler's bizarre testicular history, as it were, and narrowed the audience appeal through regional vocabulary and reference to local landmarks:

> Hitler has only got one ball,
> The other is in the Albert Hall,
> His mother, the dirty bugger,
> Chopped it off when Hitler was small.
> She threw it, into the apple tree
> The wind blew it into the deep blue sea
> Where the fishes got out their dishes
> And ate scallops and bollocks for tea.

It's not entirely implausible that Hitler may have been monorchid (as we shall see), or that his mother may have been abusive to the point of mutilation (an explanation for his pathology, perhaps). But it is unfathomable how, in the "plot" of the song, his severed testicle could find its way to such a place as the Royal Albert Hall after (nonsensically) having been a side dish for anthropomorphized fish at high tea. Founded in 1871, the Albert Hall is a famous performance and exhibition venue in Westminster and appears most often in these additional stanzas. It is significant that the ultimate resting place of the Führer's testicle is an arena of public display. Exhibition in that kind of space is a public assertion of ownership and subjection. The Albert Hall, then, becomes the municipal custodian of a wartime trophy, a symbolic means by which the British state is taking proprietary rights of Hitler's diminished power. Variants from other regions of the UK provide a casebook of oikotypes, as the second line of the stanza is frequently altered to reference local buildings. In Manchester the other ball is in the "Free Trade Hall"; further north it is the "Leeds Town Hall"; in Glasgow the "Kelvin Hall"; and in Northern Ireland the "Ulster Hall." As a narrative device, this localization emphasizes the singer's implied "civic" participation in immortalizing and exhibiting domination over Hitler.

Despite the poetic function of celebrating Nazi testicular deformity, some individuals have sought empirical explanations for these lyrics. An alleged Soviet autopsy on Hitler's remains made shortly after the war, released in 1968, is clear in its assertion of monorchism (see Bezymenski 1968; Waite 1977, 150). But the medical report has been dismissed by historians as its own bit of propaganda (see, e.g., Ainsztein 1969; Rosenbaum 1998). The authenticity of the autopsy is questionable, given that Hitler's death by suicide and the subsequent almost complete burning of his body left little for doctors to examine. Records do show, however, that as a soldier in the German Army during World War I Hitler was wounded in 1916 during the battle of the Somme, and although sources disagree as to the exact location of the wound, a few maintain that it was in the thigh or the groin. Some historians postulate that Hitler may have been monorchic from birth or that one of his testicles may have failed to descend at puberty. In any case, Hitler's World War I company commander claimed that a venereal disease exam revealed that Hitler had only one testicle (letter to *Die Zeit*, December 21, 1971, cited in Waite 1977, 152, 450n65). "Psycho-historians" with a Freudian bent have made much of these findings, viewing Hitler's "putatively half-empty scrotal sack as the root cause of his murderous character, his sexuality, and his anti-Semitism. The rumor offers one-stop shopping for Hitler explainers" (Rosenbaum 2008). For example, Robert G. L. Waite, whose book *The Psychopathic God: Adolf Hitler* (1977) is often touted as the definitive psychological portrait of Hitler, argues that Hitler's alleged childhood monorchism formed in him a lifelong complex of deficiency, which contributed significantly to his pathological personality. "The problem of the Fuehrer's testicles" is a foundational premise of Waite's biography, and he declares outright that "the British Tommies were right all along in the first line of their version of the Colonel Bogey March" (although, he adds, "they were manifestly mistaken in the last [regarding the supposed anorchism of Goebbels, who fathered six children]") (150).

In November 2008, the discovery of an eyewitness account by World War I army medic Johan Jambor electrified the press. Jambor was said to have discovered an injured Hitler at the battle of the Somme in 1916 and saved his life. Hitler was screaming for help as a result of injuries. Apparently, in the 1960s Jambor had revealed all this to a priest, who then dutifully wrote down the revelation in a document that surfaced in 2008, twenty-three years after Jambor's death (Roberts 2008). Appearing originally in the *Sun* (London), the story was quickly picked up by Commonwealth and American tabloid newspapers, which had a field day with the headlines: "One Ball, After All," "Half the Man He Used to Be," "Ballsy Ditties," and this jocular gem from the online newspaper the *Register:* "Hitler Had One Ball: Official—Other Not in Albert Hall, However." These headlines demonstrate that the lyrics were still well known in 2008. A separate, less publicized account says that his genitals were mangled by a goat when, as a child, Hitler tried to urinate into its mouth (Redlich 1999, 18).

In any case, the proximate cause of Hitler's presumed disorder (be it birth defect, bombshell, or goat) and whether it sprung from deliberately publicized misinformation or verifiable historical fact are not the central concerns. What irresistibly attracted the popular consciousness of the 1940s was the very idea that Hitler and his eugenic minions would have defective physiognomies. That notion, coupled with the medium of an already famous song, had all the makings of what we might call a "folk hit." And "Hitler Has Only Got One Ball" has remained on the charts ever since.

THIRD-WAVE POPULARITY: POST–WORLD WAR II

Assorted postwar variants of the first line delineate Hitler's peculiar testicular "arrangement": "only one big ball"; "only one left ball" (a curious description, given that having one left testicle is considered the norm); "only one meat ball" (certainly suggestive of the testicular, but specific to the mid-1940s as it emerged just after the Tin Pan Alley song "One Meat Ball"—a novelty tune about the high cost of eating out—had been made famous by the Andrews Sisters).

Any chance of the melody slipping from popular awareness evaporated when the tune appeared memorably in David Lean's Oscar-winning *Bridge on the River Kwai* in 1957. In fact, the march is often referred to simply as the *River Kwai* theme, with the common assumption that it was composed specifically for the film. But the march's rich prior folk history unquestionably figured into Lean's decision to place it in the film. He remembered the parodies from his youth, and he originally wanted the British soldiers in the film to be singing the lyrics of "Bollocks, and the Same to You" or "Hitler Has Only Got One Ball" as they entered the camp (Phillips 2006, 236). Producer Sam Spiegel, however, found the lyrics too offensive and Alford's surviving widow granted permission to use the melody only under the express condition that the bawdy lyrics not be included. It is reported that she cautioned the producers unequivocally, "A lot of rude words have been made up around that song and I don't want my husband made a mockery of " (Brownlow 1996, 354). Thus, the now-famous whistling version was substituted. Malcolm Arnold, the film's music director, recalled the method of his musical arrangement: "The whistlers . . . were a piccolo and seventeen members of the Irish Guards. They weren't handpicked; anybody can whistle. I said, 'Look, gentlemen, we all know both world war versions of "Colonel Bogey." But here, because of censorship, you've got to whistle it'" (381). In the end, Lean was pleased with the whistling rendition, conceding that even without the bawdy lyrics, "the English audience will know what we're after" (351). By that, he presumably meant the yoking together of martial protocol with implied irreverence. To the degree that Lean was correct about the audience's perception is a testament to the general awareness of "Colonel Bogey" parodies in Britain. Since then, the number of pop culture allusions, citations, oblique references, and send-ups of the song has been remarkable.

On the *Benny Hill Show*, for instance, the melody of the "Colonel Bogey March" was used in a sketch (original air date, April 16, 1980) mimicking the game show *Name That Tune*. Asked to identify the song, one female contestant guesses "After the Ball," which the host (played by Hill) tells her is half right. Then the gentleman contestant guesses "The Cobbler's Song," to uproarious laughter from the audience (*cobblers* being British slang for *testicles*). His second guess is the 1944 novelty song "I've Got a Lovely Bunch of

Coconuts." Much is left unsaid here, but the allusion is transparent. Associating the melody of the "Colonel Bogey March" with anything ball-istic instantly conjures up the song about Hitler.

The lyrics are alluded to in a 2003 advertisement for an English ale called Spitfire. A banner caption reading "Spot the ball" accompanies a photograph of Hitler in full Wehrmacht uniform. The advertisement refers to print media "Spot the ball" promotions that used soccer match photographs from which the ball had been electronically edited out. Readers would then compete by guessing the position of the missing ball. The phrase "Spot the ball" is innocuous by itself, but when paired with the photograph of Hitler the two together become unmistakable imagistic shorthand of the theme that has been propagated by the folk song for more than seventy-five years. Similarly, a brief bit by transgender comic Lara Rae at the Winnipeg Comedy Festival in 2016 obliquely references Hitler's legendary monorchism:

> I am changing my hormones to match my true gender . . . At 52, I am completely changing my endocrine system—not by myself, with the help of a doctor. This is not something you want to leave to the YouTube video [laughter]. I learned this the hard way when I tried to neuter the cats [laughter]. Spend the 80 bucks is all I'm saying! It might start out okay, but you really have to finish the job. A cat with no balls is mellow; a cat with one ball is Hitler [laughter].

The idea of a do-it-yourself cat neutering is funny in itself, but the clincher for the joke, and what prompts the biggest laugh from the audience, is the punctuating inference of the Hitler comment. This a reminiscent of a truncated form that Bill Ellis (1989) has termed "legend metonym," which reduces narrative to the level of simple allusion. These metonymic forms emerge when texts are so familiar that audiences "no longer need to re-experience them through performance"; that is, the well-known texts are distilled down to abbreviated verbal tags (40). In the same way, Rae's joke, Benny Hill's sketch, and the Spitfire ad work comically only if the fuller source text of "Hitler Has Only Got One Ball" is well known (which it most certainly is).

In his 2007 comedy tour *Fame*, Ricky Gervais builds a full minute of material around the song, emphasizing the endurance of the "Albert Hall" stanza and the logical problematics of it:

> No, it's a great gig, and it is at the Albert Hall, home to Hitler's other testicle. [*laughter*] "Hitler has only got one ball / The other is in the Albert Hall."
>
> I didn't see it, and I looked around for it, which is suspicious. If I had that, I'd have it in the foyer, on a plinth in a glass cabinet . . . in an eggcup. [*laughter*] I'd love to look at that, not in a gay way. I wouldn't be going, "Oh, there's a lovely bit of old bollock." I'd be going, "That's the physical and symbolic embodiment of pure evil. That's Hitler's seed."
>
> "Hitler has only got one ball / The other is in the Albert Hall / His mother has got the other." What? Did he have three? It doesn't make any sense at all. [*laughter*] Why would she have that? Why would your mother keep that, really? Unless she's going "Look, he's my son, and I love him. He's a wrong 'un. I know it. I don't want him breeding. I'm keeping back Hitler's testicle." Well, she would say "my Adolf's," wouldn't she? That name's died out, hasn't it? [*laughter*]

That same year, an episode of the British sketch comedy television program *The Armstrong and Miller Show* included a short bit playing off apocryphal reports about the origins of "Hitler Has Only Got One Ball." In the hallway of a government building, an officious-looking intelligence agent carrying a top-secret file folder approaches an operations officer.

OPERATIONS OFFICER [O.O.]: What's this?

INTELLIGENCE AGENT WALDUCK [W]: Possibly the single biggest intelligence coup of the war. It seems there's a dark secret lurking at the heart of the Nazi state. A secret which in the right hands just might turn the tide of the war.

O.O. [*perusing the contents of the file*]: Who else has seen this?

W: No one, sir. Enderby rang it through from Austria about twenty minutes ago.

O.O.: Rang it through?

W: I fear he shan't be coming back.

O.O.: But this is dynamite [*reading, as from a Morse code communiqué*].

Hitler. One ball. [*audience laughter throughout*]

Göring. Two but small.

Himmler. Similar.

Goebbels. No balls at all.

[*Returning file to Walduck*] I think you know what to do with this, Walduck.

ANOTHER SCENE—*in a dimly lit tavern*

HAROLD, THE SONGWRITER [H]: What do you want?

W: A song.

H: You lot, you think this stuff grows on trees. You wanted bawdy barrack-room ditties to raise morale. I poured out my soul. "Göring's prick is full of diseases / that's why he has to piss with tweezers." [*laughter*]

W: I remember the songs, Harold. But they had a crucial flaw. They were always based on speculation. This time it's different [*passes folder to Harold, who examines it slowly*].

H: Get me my old piano!

ANOTHER SCENE—*in a sparsely furnished apartment, Harold at piano*

H [*mumbling and humming*]: Ah! One ball! If Hannibal had many balls up in the air, there'd da da da da. Can't have Hannibal! Hannibal, that's not going to work! . . . Testes, testes—the Führer has only one [*laughter*] . . . It's no use! It's no use! [*outside window, a passing vehicle sounds horn, unmistakable as the disyllabic introductory figure from "Colonel Bogey." Composing on the spot, Harold tentatively fingers remaining six notes on piano keyboard (laughter)*]

ANOTHER SCENE—*Harold playing before panel of military officials*

Hitler has only got one ball, [*laughter throughout*]

Göring has two, but very small

Himmler has something sim'lar

And poor old Goebbels has no balls at all.

O.O. [*stands up slowly*]: Gentlemen, I think we've just won ourselves a war. [*laughter*]

The individual who posted the clip on YouTube describes it as "the single most important piece of intelligence from WW2."

These tenacious folk and popular adaptations of "Hitler Has Only Got One Ball" have engendered what Hitler biographer Alan Bullock labeled disdainfully as the "one ball business" (see Rosenbaum 1998, 78). But it should not surprise us, given its immense popularity, that the melody of "Colonel Bogey" inspired a number of other folk songs as well.

CHILDREN'S APPROPRIATIONS

The march has become a classic in children's folklore, existing in multiple versions that mark it as a vibrant artifact of post–World War II oral culture. Most Americans who were children during the 1960s and 1970s will likely remember the playground songs about Comet cleanser, which took "Colonel Bogey" into the world of consumer goods.

Comet, it tastes like gasoline,
Comet, it makes your teeth turn green,
Comet, it makes you vomit,
So get some Comet and vomit today.

Children's folklore draws a wealth of material from commercial culture, and popular advertisements are frequently adapted and satirized on the playground (see full discussion in chapter 5). Some folk parodies of commercials outlast by decades the advertising campaigns that initially inspired them. For example, children still sing spoofs of "McDonald's Is Your Kind of Place" commercials, which originally aired in 1967 and ran for only a few years after that. Similarly, variants of "Comet" linger in oral tradition years since it first appeared in the late 1960s. The song is not a parody, technically, because there was no existing jingle from Comet commercials that children then adapted and mocked. Rather, like the singing soldiers before them, they crafted new comical lyrics for music that was already floating in the popular ether. "Colonel Bo-gey," by then undergoing a revival following *Bridge on the River Kwai,* rhythmically accommodated the disyllabic word "Comet" perfectly (as it had done earlier with the names of Hitler and his gener-als). And because the product's name formed such a conspicuous rhyme with the word "vomit," most variants predictably became fixated on that bodily function. Indeed, like the standard Goebbels line in wartime versions, in the many incarnations of this folk song the "conclusion" of line 4 remains stable: the listener is invited to ingest the cleanser and enjoy its emetic properties. There is wide variance in the first two lines, however, where the rhyming possi-bilities seem endless—as in these few examples:

> Comet tastes like Listerine,
> Comet will make your eyes turn green.

> Comet, it makes your teeth turn red,
> Comet, it makes you wet your bed.

> Comet will get your bathroom clean,
> Comet will make your hair turn green.

> Comet, it makes your mouth turn square,
> Comet, it makes your butt grow hair.

Sherman and Weisskopf posit that rhymes about cleaning products appear in children's lore as a subversive response to famil-iar parental warnings about handling and ingesting such substances (1995, 162). But advertising itself is also targeted here. Constantly assailed by commercial images and jingles, children grow to resent the bombardment and use folklore as a means to "defend themselves against becoming mere bundles of reflexes that are dominated by the ads" (Knapp and Knapp 1976, 165). With songs like "Comet," they scoff at the relentless advice that advertisements have foisted upon them. Moreover, the song suggestively mocks commercially projected claims about domestic perfection. Uncleanness is seen in terms of damage or harm to the body: eyes, teeth, and hair change to unnatural colors; unwanted body hair sprouts in private areas; and sheets are soiled with regressive bed wetting.

It is commonly observed that children sometimes explore delicate or taboo subjects symbolically "behind the smokescreen of playful rhyming" (Bronner 1988, 52). Although that is certainly true, on occasion their rhymes are remarkably blunt, as with this adaptation of "Colonel Bogey" that addresses its touchy theme with candor:

> Herman, look what you've done to me,
> Herman, I think it's pregnancy,
> Herman, you put your sperm in,
> And now it's Herman, and Sherman, and me. (Mahoney
> 1994)

The self-referential monologue of a girl confronting the boy who has impregnated her, this rhyme depicts an unusual narrative stance. Lines 1–3 are directed at Herman alone, but we are drawn in as voyeuristic spectators to what would normally be a very private conversation. The speaker accuses her partner, speculates as to the consequences of their behavior, and reviews explicitly the activity that led them to that point (some versions offer a more decorous third line: "Herman, you were determined"). Taken together, the verses demonstrate considerable agency on the part of the speaker: she has confronted her partner, held him accountable for his actions, and proceeded on the expectation that they would naturally form a family unit with the newborn. That this version was an observed exchange between two ten-year-old girls is instructive, bearing out theoretical claims that children's play is an arena of rehearsal and preparation for adulthood (e.g., Burn 2016, 14–17; Knapp and Knapp 1976; Bronner 1988, 32–34). These girls are contemplating in song the connection between sex, pregnancy, and birth at a moment just before those things will have monumental importance in their lives. Alford could scarcely have imagined his patriotic march functioning as the underpinning for such lyrics a century after its composition.

MILITARY REDUX

While the march has been widely adopted by civilians, including children, its martial applications were not exhausted by 1945.

Some early baby boomers who had been exposed to World War II versions found themselves fighting in Vietnam. There, the song was reinvigorated with new themes and rhetoric suited to the context—like the following lyric that had more to do with the waning morale of American GIs than with demoralizing the enemy:

> Re-up, and buy a brand new car,
> Re-up, show what a fool you are,
> Re-up, I'd sooner throw up,
> I'd sooner throw up than re-up today.

When discharged, a soldier in the final stages of out-processing would see a recruitment counselor, whose unenviable job it was to encourage reenlistment. Personnel who extended for six or more months were entitled to thirty days' special leave to any place in the world, and as further enticement they were offered a reenlistment bonus, several thousand dollars exempt from taxation. According to the 25th Infantry Division reenlistment office, and reported in *Tropic Lightning News,* the division's weekly newsletter in Vietnam, the highest reenlistment bonus offered as of August 1968 was $9,540 (*Tropic Lightning News* 1968). As a point of comparison, the US Census Bureau reported that $8,600 was the median income of American families in 1968. It certainly would have been possible then to purchase a brand-new car with the reenlistment bonus. Nevertheless, it was an extremely difficult sale for recruiters to make. One blogger recalled the aphoristic reply that "short timers" would typically give when asked if they had thought about reenlistment: "Yes. Thought about it. Laughed about it. Forgot about it." The song's purpose, of course, was to steer GIs away from the redoubtable decision of reenlistment; in that sense, "Re-up" functioned as a sort of public-service announcement among fellow recruits. It is a tortuous path that brought "Colonel Bogey," an imperial military march with patriotic flair, to Vietnam—into the singing repertoire of American GIs who were counting the days until their discharge. This single melody became a sounding board for antithetical ideologies. Soldiers singing "Re-up" in the late 1960s may easily have had fathers who in World War II sang "Hitler Has Only Got One Ball" which, lewd though it was, elevated the morale and determination of Allied troops by ridiculing the common enemy. Conversely, "Re-up" is a picture of ambivalence: a jaunty military march conveys a message of antimilitaristic cynicism. Each version reflects the ethos of its time.

The utility of "Colonel Bogey" as a soldier's plaything is still in evidence. A video posted on YouTube in 2010 (with the heading "Explosions, Predator missiles, etc. in Iraq"), for example, shows footage of real-life explosions from the Iraq War. In what seems surely intended as ironic, the two-and-a-half-minute clip takes as its soundtrack the familiar *River Kwai* whistling arrangement of "Colonel Bogey." The bouncy and triumphant tune provides the backdrop for images of violent destruction, and soldiers' voices can be heard celebrating the blasts; war is depicted as glorious, victimless fun. The poster invokes the film clearly by tagging the video as the "River Kwai March." To be sure, explosives also figure prominently in *River Kwai,* with its unforgettable climactic scene of demolition. But there is playful manipulation at work in the video: seemingly incompatible sensibilities are merged when cheerful whistling accompanies conflagration. Here, as before, we see the multivalent social uses of the "Colonel Bogey March"—which in performance can be simultaneously both majestic and irreverent, patriotic and subversive.

❊ ❊ ❊

The evocative melody has endured, but perhaps not exactly in the manner that Alford would have preferred. "Colonel Bogey" is arguably the most famous march ever composed—and that is due in no small part to the persistent folk-lyrical ruminations on the alleged testicular oddities of the Nazi high command. "To this day," argues John Trendell, "a mere reference to the opening notes of the first four bars [of 'Colonel Bogey'] is sufficient to 'cock a snook' [a gesture of disdain] at any ill-favored or potential enemy" (1991, 98). The comically derisive lyrics may indeed have played some role in boosting the morale of Allied troops, but the popular appeal of "Hitler Has Only Got One Ball" has long outlasted that utilitarian function. The catchy little melodic motifs that made "Colonel Bogey" a great military march also created the perfect conduit for terse humorous lyrics, and so a host of disyllabic names and nouns—bollocks, bullshit, Hitler, Göring, Himmler, Goebbels, and later Comet, vomit, Herman, and Sherman—all found a natural poetic home. The lasting legacy of the "Colonel Bogey March" in many ways is indebted to these lyrics and their pop culture manifestations.

2

"There's Dirty Work Afoot"

On the Reception of Disney's Snow White

IN THE HISTORY OF FEATURE-LENGTH ANIMATED FILMS, WALT Disney's *Snow White and the Seven Dwarfs* (1937) is the first and, by many accounts, the fairest of them all. It is universally recognized as a monumental cinematic achievement and has garnered numerous institutional accolades. The National Film Registry officially designates *Snow White* as "culturally, historically, or aesthetically significant"; the American Film Institute places *Snow White* among the 100 greatest American films and ranks it as the top animated feature of all time; and in 1939, Walt Disney accepted an honorary Academy Award for the film (one regular-sized Oscar statuette and seven miniature ones) in recognition of "a significant screen innovation which has charmed millions and pioneered a great new entertainment field" (Bedi and Tatarewicz 2016). Within a month of its release, *New York Times* film critic Frank S. Nugent effused: "[*Snow White*] is so delightful, so engaging, so very merry a fantasy that I suspect Santa Claus himself must have had a hand in its making. For there is magic in the film, and hearts' ease, and tonic for disillusion . . . More than 250,000 New Yorkers already have seen this picture, have smiled contentedly together, have been united for a time—and for a time thereafter—in a common bond of enchanted delight" (1938, 157). *Snow White* far exceeded expectations at the box office, earning $8 million in initial release, more

DOI: 10.7330/9781607329909.c002

than any other film up to that point—an astounding figure considering that movie tickets in 1938 cost only 25 cents. Adjusting its gross earnings for inflation, the film still registers among the most profitable pictures of all time.

FAIRY-TALE FERMENT

Fairy tales had been a longtime favorite subject of Disney well before *Snow White*. His first attempt at animated storytelling, in fact, was a seven-minute silent cartoon version of "Little Red Riding Hood" that he worked on for six months in 1922 when he was a struggling commercial artist in Kansas City (Solomon 1998). Many of his cartoons with the short-lived Laugh-O-Gram studio in the 1920s were inspired by traditional fairy tales, as were a number of "Silly Symphonies" under the Walt Disney Productions banner in the early 1930s. But the spectacular success of *Snow White* in 1937 took things to a different level, establishing the Disney Studio as a major force in the film industry and setting the stage for several other full-length animated pictures based on fairy tales, which would become the studio's stock in trade but also pique considerable criticism from scholars of media and culture over the years.[1] This chapter is positioned within that critical universe to consider the dialogic relationship between the Grimms' version of "Snow White," Disney's film adaptation, and contemporary jokes that target the film and its characters. These literary, cinematic, and jocular folk iterations of the "Snow White" tale—and their linkages—provide us with an illuminating case study of the dynamic tensions between mediated texts and audience reception.

In production from 1934 to 1937, *Snow White* ran over its allotted budget, ultimately costing $1.5 million, an unprecedented figure at that time. In the industry (and even in house), the project became known as "Disney's Folly," for many believed that American moviegoers would be reluctant to pay regular ticket prices to see an animated feature, albeit a full-length one. After an advance screening of the partially completed film in 1937, Disney solicited written feedback from his staff; among the 359 responses was buried one bit of pointed anonymous advice, "Walt, stick to shorts!" Over the years it became something of an occupational joke at the studio, one that reflected on Disney's managerial style, that any time an employee challenged one of his ideas, Disney would counter, "I bet you're the guy who wrote 'stick to shorts!'" It was later rumored that the fiery response had originated with none other than Roy Disney, Walt's older brother and business partner (Watts 1997, 426; Holliss and Sibley 1987, 34–35). The Disneys had put all of their eggs in the *Snow White* basket, depleting the family fortune and borrowing several hundreds of thousands of dollars from the Bank of America to complete the project. John Grant observes that "the huge effort and expenditure were an investment not just in a single movie but in the whole of the studio's future" (2001, 69). As we all know, the gamble, and dedication, paid off—financially at least—and everything that we associate with the Mickey Mouse monopoly—animated and live-action feature films, theme parks, merchandising, media control—owes something to the initial success of *Snow White and the Seven Dwarfs*. To that point, the film is so often referred to as "the one that started it all" that Walt Disney legally registered the phrase.[2] The vast material assets of the Disney Corporation, one of the world's most recognizable brands, amassed from humbler beginnings at "the Studio the Dwarfs Built" (Croxton 2014).

In fact, Disney had been thinking about Snow White long before production began in 1934. On more than one occasion, he publicly reminisced about his grandmother reading him tales from the Grimms and Andersen when he was a child, recalling that "Snow White" was his favorite: "It was the best time of day for me. . . . The stories and characters in them seemed quite as real as my schoolmates and our games. Of all the characters in the Fairy Tales, I loved *Snow White and the Seven Dwarfs* the best" (Behlmer 1982, 49). Nostalgic as these remembrances may have been, Disney's *Snow White* is just as indebted to a series of popular theatrical and cinematic re-mediations of the fairy tale. In 1912, Broadway producer Winthrop Ames, under the pseudonym Jessie Braham White, wrote a children's play based on "Snow White," inspired by a long-standing tradition of Christmas pantomime and children's musical theater that commonly adapted fairy-tale sources.

As an adolescent, Walt Disney saw the 1916 silent film version of Ames's play, starring Marguerite Clark (reprising her stage role), with what was the largest single audience for a movie to date. In a free showing for newsboys at the Kansas City Convention Center on January 17, 1917, the film was projected onto four screens simultaneously to 16,000 children, many of them squeezed two to a seat in the 12,000-seat auditorium. The event was a formative experience for Disney, as remembered by the director of the film, J. Searle Dawley: "Seated in one of the top galleries was . . . Walt Disney. Years afterwards at a Special Dinner given to Marguerite Clark at the Disney Studios in Hollywood he told Miss Clark that [the] Snow White picture he saw in Kansas City—from the loft gallery seat—was the inspiration that caused him to create the first long cartoon picture" (Merritt 1998, 119n22). A few scenes in Disney's *Snow White* appear to have cognates in the silent film, one notable example being the framing shot of the evil queen appearing suddenly in the window of the dwarfs' cottage. If these were conscious imitations on Disney's part, then they emanated from his childhood memories, for there were no extant prints of the silent film in the 1930s that he might have accessed during production of *Snow White*. It is known, however, that Disney did consult the text of Ames's play (Merritt 1998, 111).

In light of these broader popular influences on Disney, it may seem unfair that he is so often maligned for being unfaithful to the presumed solitary blueprint of the Grimms' tale. Perhaps Disney brought those criticisms on himself with the introductory sequence of the film: the title frame dissolves into the beginning credits, which prominently herald the film as an adaptation of the Grimms' tale, with no other source attributions. And then there is the much-imitated cinematic trope of the opening tome and turning pages—which fetishizes the book (that is, the Grimms' collection) as source: antique, embossed in gold, and ensconced delicately in satin, the book is enshrined as the textual authority of the Snow White tale.[3] In a story conference on December 22, 1936, Disney summarized for his staff the full plot of the Grimms' Snow White, digested from books he had purchased during a European trip the previous year. We're not sure which translation or version Disney read, but his detailed summary attests that he was well acquainted with the Grimms' original. After the synopsis, Disney added,

> In our version of [Snow White] we followed the story very closely. We have put in certain twists to make it more logical, more convincing and easy to swallow. We have taken the characters and haven't added any. We have the Queen, the Mirror, the Prince, the Huntsman, Snow White and the Seven Dwarfs. The only thing we have built onto the story are the animals who are friends of Snow White's. This wasn't in the original fairy tale. We have developed a personality in the mirror and comic personalities of the seven dwarfs. (Inge 2004, 135)[4]

Disney manipulated the story of Snow White more than those comments let on, but it is not my intent to castigate him (as some have done) for every minor deviation from his sources, whether they be the Grimms, Ames, Dawley, or others. For well over a half century before Disney began production on *Snow White*, a number of adaptations and intermediary variants of the tale—literary, theatrical, and cinematic—were floating about in popular culture (McGowan 2016, 3). Disney was free to handle the fairy tale as he wished—and the Grimms' tales of whatever version, after all, are not untouchable Holy Scriptures. My interest lies in the fact that expurgated themes or plot elements (that Disney may have deemed inappropriate or offensive) still found unconscious expression in the film, and, suggestively, in circulating jokes *about* the film in folk and popular culture. And while it is well documented that Walt Disney himself tightly managed the creative vision and production of the film, the *reception* of the film—the purview of an unruly audience—was beyond his control. What I am proposing is an intertextual exercise, exploring Snow White in these cross-pollinated expressive forms.

"SNOW WHITE" AND SEXUALITY

To start, we might point to the oft-cited Bruno Bettelheim (1989). It is easy to critique his generally essentialist readings of fairy tales, but there are shining moments within them and I think he makes a few useful observations about "Snow White"—namely, as he traces the arc of Snow White's symbolic journey to sexual maturation and particularly in her relationship with the dwarfs. His perspectives on the Grimms' tale offer us a footing as we consider Disney and Snow White jokes. For Bettelheim, the central problem of the tale lies in the tension between sexual innocence and sexual desire. The tale essentially tracks Snow White through primary stages of her psychosexual development. She enters her Oedipal stage once the queen is defined as her rival. When Snow White's budding sexuality is confirmed by the magic mirror, the queen forces her stepdaughter from home at the age of seven; then, living with the dwarfs, Snow White passes into a stage of latency. We are never told how long she remains with the dwarfs, but hints of her sexual self do emerge at a few key moments: when the queen entices her with the poisoned comb—an object of beautification—and when the queen laces her tightly into the corset, a tempting prospect to Snow White as its purpose is to shape her girlish body into the figure of a fully developed woman. And finally, Snow White's awakening carries her into the genital or mature sexual stage, when she will experience love, marriage, and presumably parenthood.

The recurring colors of white and red become emblems of this process. White signifies innocence and purity, while red, associated with menstrual blood and childbirth, suggests sexual maturity and desire. The queen's poison apple is bifurcated in these colors, and when Snow White takes her bite from the red part (the poison part), Bettelheim argues, she passes the point of no return in her sexual maturation. No longer will she be able to retreat into latency, for her presumed death marks the end of her childhood. She revives (the Grimms' tale specifies years later) into sexual maturity and adulthood (see Sale 1978, 42–43). Mae West's famous quip, "I used to be Snow White, but I drifted," was perhaps more pointed than she realized. If we consider the implications—what Snow White drifted from (innocence and purity) and what she drifted toward (sexual awakening and experience)—then West's pun actually speaks to the very essence of the Grimms' tale.

The dwarfs can be viewed as primarily phallic: they are short and stubby and vocationally dedicated to penetrating dark tunnels.[5] At the same time, paradoxically, they are stuck in the stage of latency that Snow White must transcend. "[The dwarfs] certainly are not men in any sexual sense," Bettelheim argues. "Their way of life, their interest in material goods to the exclusion of love, suggest a pre-oedipal existence . . . They are satisfied with an identical round of activities; their life is a never-changing circle of work in the womb of the earth" (1989, 210). In the Grimms' tale, the dwarfs do not comprehend or sympathize with Snow White's inner conflicts. She is overwhelmed by temptations toward sexual life, and the dwarfs rescue her by recalling her into their own stage of latency. Importantly, the sexual tension is within Snow White herself.

DISNEY'S SNOW WHITE VISION

Snow White the film is framed quite differently, certainly more dramatically than Disney's conference comments suggest. The prince is introduced briefly near the very beginning, just long enough to set the stage for romantic possibility. The effect is to give Snow White an amorous longing throughout the film, and to provide occasion for songs like "I'm Wishing" and "Someday My Price Will Come."[6] When the prince does return at the end, sentimental expectations have been fulfilled and satisfied. This is not a young girl's journey into sexual awareness and adulthood, but rather a formulaic romance.

Disney had determined early on that Snow White and the other realistic characters in the film (the queen, the huntsman, and the prince) would not be cartoonish or caricatured, but creating lifelike movements for them proved considerably difficult for even the most seasoned animators. Some of the problems were solved with rotoscoping, the process by which live-action film is projected through glass and then traced over frame by frame to create drawn animation. Somewhat ambivalent with the method as a shortcut, Disney insisted that the rotoscoped scenes be heavily animated in order to camouflage the source. The live-action

model for Snow White was the sixteen-year-old dancer Majorie
Belcher (who later became well known as dancer and choreogra-
pher Marge Champion), and the character was voiced by Adriana
Caselotti, the youngest daughter in an opera-singing family. Disney
had advertised for a "fourteen-year-old voice," and Caselotti, who
was eighteen at the time of the audition, told the casting agents
she was seventeen and purposely made her voice sound more juvenile for the part. This age ambiguity formed an important aspect
of Snow White's character, as she appears caught in that liminal
space between childhood and adulthood. There is in this ambiguity
a psychosexual allurement that presents an industry dilemma for
animators. As Grant notes,

> Animation has always had great difficulty with the characterization
> of young women. On the one hand it realizes that sexually attrac-
> tive females are good for the box office; on the other it wants to
> ensure that the heroine is of an age that the supposedly juvenile
> audience can identify with . . . The Disney approach has been to
> produce the heroine who has many of the attributes of a beddable
> young woman, and has a stated age accordingly, but who is, in
> most regards, a 14 year-old girl . . . This may not be confusing for
> the kids in the audience, but it most certainly is for their dads. The
> moviemakers are quite consciously using two different channels
> through which to cast their heroines' spell over the audience, and
> the two do not mesh well. (2001, 40)

Caselotti altered her voice enough to support the duality of Snow
White's character, a little girl/woman whose apparent innocence
and naïveté covers over a range of complex sexual responses. Snow
White's "art deco plasticity, yellow dress, puffed sleeves and bright
red hair ribbon match the round baby-face and wide-eyed look of
the [presexual] all-American child innocent," argues Robin Allan,
"yet [she is] guided by adults to be consciously imitative of sex"
(1999, 59). It is an interesting footnote that Grim Natwick, who
had co-created and animated the voluptuously feminine caricature
Betty Boop for Fleisher Studios, was hired specifically by Disney
to work on the contrastingly demure Snow White. Developing her

character was a touchy process. "Natwick's Snow White could not have helped knowing how much power her beauty gave her," argues Michael Barrier. "It was that awareness—sexual at its core, and certainly consistent with the Grimms' story—that made her so dangerous" (1999, 200). Supervising animator Hamilton Luske, under Disney's direction, prevailed upon Natwick to tone down Snow White's sexuality. These polysemous suggestions of her character notwithstanding, in the interest of furthering the film's romantic formula Disney significantly refashioned his version of the fairy tale with respect to Snow White's character and the domestic scene at the dwarfs' cottage. Instead of a prepubescent girl living with fully grown, albeit diminutive, men, Disney's dominant vision transformed Snow White into a nubile woman and the dwarfs into comical children.

When she enters the dwarfs' disheveled cottage (which in the Grimms' version is described as "dainty and neat"), Snow White speculates that the inhabitants are unkempt orphans in need of a mother. "Just look at that fireplace," she says. "It's covered with dust. And look, cobwebs everywhere! My, my, my! What a pile of dirty dishes! And just look at that [cobweb-covered] broom. Why, they've never swept this room! You'd think their mother would— [*gasp*]—maybe they have no mother!? Then they're orphans? That's too bad!" And conveniently, there she is to function in that capacity. The maternal theme becomes heavy-handed as Snow White cleans up after the dwarfs, disciplines them, insists they wash up for dinner, and even enforces a bedtime (seeing the dwarfs' names carved on their beds earlier, she had mused, "What funny names for children!"). Peter Brunette claims that Disney "simply translated the Grimms' German paternalism into American 'Momism,'" so that "the utterly pure Snow White [could] have the best of both worlds by becoming a mother without having to give up her virginity" (1980, 72), what Eleanor Byrne and Martin McQuillan consider a kind of "maternal haunting" (1999, 62). Reviewers in popular media generally saw the character of Snow White as immanently chaste and innocent, sometimes cloyingly so, as in John Canady's derisive commentary describing her as a "mawkish, vapid, gooeyvoiced, rubbery-bodied specimen of animated vanilla custard . . . [who is]

smug and prettified, appealing to every debased concept of virtue and beauty that has somehow become instilled into the popular mind" (1973). That is not to say that the film is devoid of sexual energy. To the contrary, we observe the dwarfs compete for kisses from Snow White; they ask her to tell them a love story; and they sigh longingly as she sings about Prince Charming. But since they are "freaks" in Disney's corporo-normative world, despite their cuteness, they cannot be considered serious contenders for her sexual affections (see Solis 2007, 126–27; Brunette 1980, 73; Ayres 2003, 44–45). At the same time, that understood prohibition complicates their relationship and renders it psychologically enticing.

JOKING RECEPTION

Jokes about Snow White in oral tradition, a more subversive form of reception, certainly seem to have picked up on the sexually charged complexity of the tale, and they are directed precisely at that fascination, imagining a scenario in which Snow White and the dwarfs actually might couple. One example is the short riddle joke that asks: "What's red and has seven dents in it?—Snow White's hymen." Steven Swann Jones (1985) analyzes a variant, in longer narrative form, located in a familiar joke setting at the Pearly Gates:

> Well, Snow White finally died, and she went to heaven, and when Saint Peter met her at the gates, he said, "Welcome, we have all been anxious to meet you. We hear that you have been an incredibly good girl, but before you can pass through the gates I have to run a quick check on your Maidenhead." Snow White said, "Sure" and she laid down, and St. Peter checked her out and said, "Well, you certainly do you still have your Maidenhead, but there seems to be seven little dents in it."

Jones sees the joke—rightly, I think—as a condensation of the fairy tale's underlying theme of sexual maturation, uncovering "Snow White's precarious intermediary position, half-way between being a girl and becoming a woman" (107). Jones argues further that the joke derives its humor from the revelation that "underneath Snow

White's demur façade . . . lies a sexually aware, interested, and active young woman" (108) and that "Snow White is in reality just like one of us" (109). While these revelations do signal deeper meanings of the joke, they are not particularly funny. Jones comes closer to identifying the real source of the humor when he explores the dwarfs as "underdeveloped forerunners of the prince" (108–9). The funniness lies partly in the unexpected suggestion that Snow White would have engaged the dwarfs sexually—but more so in the imagined incompatibility with regard to genital size. This sort of comic denouement is not uncommon in the world of sexual jokes. Gershon Legman's *No Laughing Matter*, for instance, devotes an entire subsection to the topic of what he calls "mutual mismatching" (1968, 534–44). This notion is also given some attention in the age-old wisdom of the Kama Sutra, which describes the sad realities as metaphorical elephants are irreconcilably coupled with pint-sized partners like rabbits. Related jokes are most often chauvinistic, portraying the woman as being too large for her companion, a perspective that in fact contemptuously projects onto the woman the common male fear of having an undersized penis. I am reminded of a comment jokingly attributed to Grumpy, who announces to Snow White, "We're going to give you seven inches of cock—but only one inch at a time." Within a chauvinistic worldview where bigger is somehow always better, these jokes in social performance may reflect male worries about phallic proportion. Grumpy's palpable sexual aggression appears as a reaction formation stemming from the anxiety of undersized masculinity. In this neurotic chauvinistic vision, Snow White naturally has no say in the matter; she functions only as receiver of the phallus. A sexual predator in this instance, Grumpy often assumes a prominent role in Snow White jokes, in a sense asserting himself as an ambassador for his fellow dwarfs, usually with lewd intentions. Actually, that portrait of him follows logically from the film, as Grumpy is perhaps the most fully developed character, partly due to his central role in the narrative but just as much from his depth of emotion and dramatic nuance as conveyed through the drawn renderings of master animator Bill Tytla, who was assigned to all sequences involving Grumpy (Barrier 1999, 207–10). From his initial warning about the dangers of Snow

White's visit to his stern interdiction about allowing strangers into the house to his curt annoyance at Snow White's orders to wash to his leading the climactic chase against the evil queen and his emotional breakdown after Snow White's death, Grumpy is a narrative focalizer and shown to be the "true hero of the film" (Davis 2013, 93).[7] And so he naturally becomes the protagonist or—in many of the circulating jokes about Snow White—the raunchy exponent.

Doe-eyed and sighing like schoolboys with crushes on their teacher, Disney's dwarfs vicariously participate in Snow White's wishing song about Prince Charming. In fact, their questions are borderline voyeuristic: "Was he strong and handsome? Was he big and tall? Did he say he loved you? Did he steal a kiss?" It is telling that the dwarfs ask about love and physical affection in conjunction with the prince's tallness, for the height differential is one attribute that makes Snow White unattainable for them; she is almost literally out of their reach. And this battery of questions immediately follows the party scene in which Dopey climbs onto Sneezy's shoulders so that together they can dance with Snow White as one full-sized man. If, like Bettelheim, we grant that the dwarfs themselves signify a phallus, then two of them stacked together as one may suggest an erection.

The revels become more and more frenetic, and at the climactic moment, Sneezy delivers a violent sneeze that propels Dopey upward like a cork from a bottle; the long coat then collapses limply onto the floor. Whatever Disney and his animators may have had in mind, it is difficult to see this as anything but an ejaculation scene (Brunette 1980, 73)—a symbolic wish fulfillment for dwarfs who fantasize about an existence beyond the restrictions of their height. One joke speculates on what sort of advantage they might gain by *all* standing together:

> One day, the seven dwarfs were coming home from work at the mine. And they approached the cottage, they hear these sounds coming from the garden. They're naturally curious, so they stand on each other's shoulders until, finally, Grumpy climbs on top and can see over the garden wall.

So he sees Snow White and the prince sitting and talking in the garden. He says to Happy, whose shoulder he's standing on, "Snow White is with the prince."

This in turn gets passed down, dwarf to dwarf, "Snow White is with the prince." "Snow White is with the prince." "Snow White is with the prince." "Snow White is . . ." (and so on) until it reaches all the dwarfs.

Then Grumpy says: "They're kissing." And then the chain starts again: "They're kissing." "They're kissing." "They're kissing." "They're . . ."

"He's taking off her clothes." "He's taking off her clothes." "He's taking off her clothes." "He's taking off . . ."

"They're both naked now." "They're both naked now." "They're both naked now." "They're both . . ."

"They're about to screw." "They're about to screw." "They're about to screw . . ."

At this point the prince hears a sound near the wall and he gets up to investigate. Grumpy sees this and says, "Oh my God, he's coming." "So am I." "So am I." "So am I." "So am I." "So am I." "So am I."[8]

What we are never told in the course of the joke, and what we can infer only after the punch line, is that the dwarfs are masturbating all the while. In a very literal sense, they are able to visualize a sexual fantasy only after they rise above the height barrier. On that account, Grumpy commands the privileged position on the totem pole. Not only is he exempt from bearing the weight of others on his shoulders, he is able to engage the subject visually. And with the gaze comes some power and agency (Sturken and Cartwright 2018, 93). For the dwarf to be tall and to watch is a close approximation to the act itself. Furthermore, he gets to manage the "narrative," while the others must rely only on second-, third-, fourth-, fifth-, and sixth-hand reports. More symbolically, the dwarfs' collective efforts can be seen as coitus itself, as Jones argues: "When these stunted and divided figures become excited, they figuratively unite and grow to become, appropriately enough, a giant erection that 'comes,' too, becoming in the joke what they could never be in the fairy tale" (1985,

107). I should point out that Jones's "Joking Transformations of Fairy Tales" does not bend its analysis to Disney film adaptations. But, like Gary Alan Fine's proposition of the "Goliath Effect" in mercantile legends, whereby the largest, most dominant corporation signifies the totality of a given market (1985), Disney versions have come to represent the entire culture industry of fairy tales. Therefore, as Zipes argues, "If children or adults think of the great classical fairy tales today, be it *Snow White*, *Sleeping Beauty*, or *Cinderella*, they will think Walt Disney. Their first and perhaps lasting impressions of these tales and others will have emanated from a Disney film, book, or artifact" (1995, 21; see also Griffin, Harding, and Learmonth 2017, 873–74). Any educator who has taught fairy tales can attest to this, as students invariably are surprised, sometimes astonished, at discovering divergent versions of the tales, versions that have been pushed to the margins by Disney's gargantuan marketing machine. This aggressive branding across media—and the exclusivity it creates—got its start with *Snow White*. David McGowan observes:

> Alongside toys and musical scores, the studio also released several story book adaptations, each presenting the film's events, including elements that deviate from earlier versions of the tale. The pervasiveness of the Disney branding—to the point of extending back into print—can potentially serve to diminish knowledge of the original adapted work(s). (2016, 9)

By its enormous influence and popularity, Disney's film stands as a monolith, perceived generally to be *the* definitive version of Snow White, to the obscurity of all others; therefore, we can reasonably regard any jokes about Snow White to be de facto jokes about the Disney Snow White.

CLEAN AND DIRTY

The sexual tensions embedded in the fairy tale and Disney's film adaptation have created a platform upon which audiences can construct their own subversive meanings. But I am not suggesting that Disney necessarily tapped into any of these ideas knowingly. In fact, the film is superficially keen on sanitizing the tale's sexual overtones. To wit, Disney expurgated two important scenes from the tale that point up Snow White's sexual interest and maturation—the temptations of the corset and comb—and he replaced those with two routines about cleaning—the extended bit on the dwarfs washing for dinner and the well-known housekeeping sequence that gave us "Whistle While You Work." These modifications are in keeping with Disney's dominant outlook; as he declared outright, "I don't like depressing pictures . . . I don't like pestholes. I don't like pictures that are dirty" (Schickel 1997, 354).

Excerpts from an October 31, 1935, story conference (with Disney, Hamilton Luske, and staffers Harry Reeves and Charles Thorson) provide insight into the production process as they discussed possibilities for the housecleaning scene.

> WALT: Her thought would be: "We'll get this all cleaned up before they get home and surprise them . . ." We could have squirrels washing the dishes . . . roll the plates along. Snow White catches squirrels sweeping stuff under the rug—corrects them. Squirrels could get plate to deer who licks it dry and shiny . . .
>
> HAM: Turn the plate and the reflection of the deer would show in the plate.
>
> WALT: Snow White sees that—says "That's no way to do it" and puts plate back in the water . . .
>
> HAM: Find something for every animal accompanying Snow White to do, adapted to the animal . . .
>
> HARRY: Raccoon would make a good duster.
>
> WALT: Have some birds up in the rafters getting cobwebs around their tails. One gag—birds get hold of spider asleep in web—spider wakes up, wants to know what it's all about—birds throw web right into tree—spider sees where it is and says, "o.k.—it's all right with me."
>
> HAM: Different tails could work like different kinds of mops—washing windows—one long tail would slap the water on, and another animal would squeegee the water off.
>
> HARRY: As she picks up sock, nuts fall out and squirrels make a scramble.

HAM: Dish-tub as well as table should be piled with dishes as if the dwarfs had all kinds of dishes but never got around to washing them.

WALT: Dish washing could be more or less a team work plan . . .

HAM: These are such little animals that most of the work has to be done in teams—two or four to carry things.

CHARLES: Would a long shot of the outside of the house work well there—with dust coming out of the windows, etc.?

HAM: Also possibility of animals who finish their jobs coming up waiting in line for something else—Snow White tells them of something else to do—or she inspects what they have done . . . rubs finger over dusted furniture—finds it still dusty and her finger black.

HARRY: And the animals must do it over again. (Holliss and Sibley 1987, 18–20)

The scene in its finished form shows us how the nascent ideas from the story conference years before had flowered. In an elaborate set piece, Snow White cleans the dwarfs' cottage with the help of a host of squirrels, rabbits, chipmunks, and deer, all of which—notably—bring their tails vigorously into the service (this kernel concept expressed during the initial discussion expanded significantly in later months of development). A cartoon animal tail can be viewed as a symbol of the animator's pen, which itself may be symbolic. As "almost all the early animators were men," Zipes argues,

> their pens and camera work assume a distinctive phallic function in early animation. The hand with pen or pencil is featured in many animated films in the process of creation, and it is then transformed in many films into the tail of a cat or dog. The tail then acts as the productive force or artist's instrument . . . a phallic means to induce action and conceive a way out of a predicament. (1995, 29)

Regarding the frenetic housecleaning scene in *Snow White*, the animals' tails also become a means of effecting symbolic order. The phallic innuendoes appear hardly sublimated in one sequence when we see a deer insert its tail into the decorative hole on the back of a carved wooden chair and then suggestively whirl it around. All this anal-obsessive washing and organizing is an apt metaphor for Disney's strict control of the film's production. For all his efforts at sanitizing the tale, though, Disney's film contains (and inspires) lots of sexual innuendo, regardless of what he may have intended. (This makes sense psychologically given that the impulses we most aggressively attempt to whitewash or repress tend to find exaggerated expression in some other form.) Such is the case with the film's most famous scene dedicated to cleaning and a cheerful work ethic ("Just whistle while you work / And cheerfully together we can tidy up the place"), which is filled with suggestive Freudian imagery, and bears out Richard Schickel's observation that the Disney Studio found in the backsides of humans (and anthropomorphized animals) "not only the height of humor but the height of sexuality as well" (1997, 241).

With so much of Disney's film fixated on cleaning, it shouldn't surprise us that the theme of cleanliness appears also in a Snow White joke. One circulates strictly in the UK as it is tied to a specific British laundry detergent called Daz, a brand unknown in North America, whose advertising campaign claims it produces "the whitest of whitest of whites." The joke asks: "Why did the seven dwarfs use Daz? They wanted their little things to come up Snow White!" More than just a droll pun on a popular detergent ad campaign, the joke perceptively affirms that the act of cleaning itself can telegraph sexuality. As with the images we've seen, the joke renders a world spotless on one level and graphically dirty on another—simultaneously both clean and obscene. Notably, the film *reifies* the multivalent inferences when Grumpy warns his cohorts that the unexpected cleanliness of their cottage is a sign of "dirty work afoot."

That is not to say that Disney himself enthusiastically embraced gymnastic interpretations of his work. To the contrary, he sometimes took an aggressively anti-intellectual stand in that regard. Karen Klugman argues that this is the very essence of Disneyfication—the application of a simplified intellectual standard "to a thing that has the potential for more complex or thought-provoking expression" (1995, 103). Schickel's polemical biography *The Disney Version* is more biting: "[Disneyfication is] that shameless process by which everything the studio . . . touched, no matter how unique the vision of the original from which the studio worked, was reduced to the limited terms Disney and his people could understand" (1997, 225). Upon the release of *Snow White and the Seven Dwarfs*, Disney was asked about the meaning of the film. He replied, apparently with some disdain, "We just try to make a good picture. And then the professors come along and tell us what we do" (Dorsey 1937, 21).[9] This speaks to that disconnect between the film's micro-managed production, where Disney held untrammeled authority, and the public reception, which obviously lay beyond his control.

Shortly after he died in 1966, Walt Disney would have had good reason to spin in his grave when Paul Krassner, editor of the counterculture magazine the *Realist*, commissioned Wally Wood (an artist at *Mad* magazine) to draw a montage of Disney characters memorializing their creator. The result was an irreverent inked illustration called "The Disneyland Memorial Orgy." The way Krassner saw it, Disney had repressed all of his characters' baser instincts, and now that he had died, the characters could "finally shed their cumulative inhibitions and participate together in an unspeakable Roman binge, to signify the crumbling of an empire." Disney, Inc. initially pondered a lawsuit but, considering that the magazine had a relatively low circulation, they withdrew to avoid further publicity. Poetically, that issue of the *Realist* turned out to be one of the most popular ever, and a year later Krassner reproduced the drawing as a poster that became an underground favorite. Krassner, who died in 2019, made the poster available on the internet as soon as the statute of limitations expired (Krassner 2012, 147). The drawing is an astonishing exhibition of sexual and scatological deviance: in the foreground, Pluto urinates on a sign bearing the image of Mickey Mouse, while Mickey himself, unshaven, is nearby injecting heroin into his arm; Goofy copulates with Minnie Mouse while Mickey's nephews look on with curiosity; Donald Duck shakes his fist angrily at Dumbo, who, flying overhead, has just defecated on him; the three little pigs are linked together in a sexual daisy chain; Cinderella, naked below the waist, hoists her leg seductively as Prince Charming slides the glass slipper onto her waiting foot. Positioned prominently at the center of the sketch, Snow White is being assaulted by Happy, Sleepy, Grumpy, Sneezy, and Bashful, all clutching and groping her in an apparent gang rape. A little to one side, otherwise occupied, Doc sodomizes Dopey.

Our own voyeurism at this prurient spectacle is mocked in the image showing Tinkerbell perform a striptease for Captain Hook, Peter Pan, the Lost Boys, Jiminy Cricket, and Pinocchio—who sports an elongated nose that assuredly is not the result of a recently told fib. The phallic impression of his nose is unmistakable, an "involuntary erection" that "makes manifest that of which he is ashamed and wishes to hide (the penis, the lie)" (Forgacs 1992, 372), and it brings to mind another joke about Snow White: "Did you hear that Snow White was expelled from Disney World? Yeah, she was caught sitting on Pinocchio's face and making him tell lies." If the fairy tale is, at its core, about sexual maturation, this joke makes it clear that Snow White has fully blossomed in that department. In this scenario, Disney's darling has fallen precipitously from innocence to become a libidinous sexual aggressor. The consequence, even within the universe of the joke, is institutional sanitation: she is branded as a deviant and then banished from the Magic Kingdom by the corporate authority that would police behavior, and meaning.

Fact is, before Pinocchio, Disney's *Snow White* had already given us plenty of reason to associate the nose with the penis. I've already discussed the phallic suggestions of the dwarfs themselves (by synecdoche) and the tails of animals, by downward displacement. Additionally, the nose, by upward displacement, is another classic Freudian phallic symbol. There are no fewer than eleven nose gags in the film. Not all of them are salacious—but enough of them are to indicate something of a fixation. When Snow White first meets the dwarfs, they are peeping up at her from the collective foot of their beds. As they do so, in a visual gag conceived by animator Ward Kimball, their noses pop over the footboard in contagion like so many miniature erections.[10] The image becomes even more evocative in the character of Grumpy, who among all the dwarfs sports the most prominent nose; Grumpy's nose is "large, rubbery, vulnerable, and an obvious target for slapstick gags," observes J. B. Kaufman (2012, 61). Walt Disney conceived of Grumpy's proboscis as "a gag license," and writers developed comic bits accordingly. At one point Grumpy's nose becomes wedged into a knothole right after he has been kissed by Snow White. The idea had come from Disney himself in a January 1937 story conference: "You follow [Grumpy—after the kiss] on a pan and show that he liked it. As he looks back, get a flash of her where she catches him looking and winks to him. He comes out of it, and sticks his nose high and smacks into the tree. Right up in close-up—his nose in a knot-hole. You hear her laugh, and he pulls out [!] indignantly."[11] By far the most suggestive, however, are the recurring sneeze gags with Sneezy, voiced by comedian Billy Gilbert, who by the 1930s was known for his comic sneeze routines. Sneezy is nasally explosive, ready to blow at any moment; in fact, it his eruptive sneeze that initiates the dramatic—and symbolic—climax of the dancing scene in the dwarfs' cottage. Alfred Kinsey claimed that sneezes and orgasms are physiologically analogous in terms of their "summation and explosive discharge of tension" (Kinsey et al. 1998, 631); there's a folk belief that says a certain number of sneezes is the bodily equivalent of an orgasm; and some even refer to sneezes as mini-orgasms. In any case, the two certainly are symbolically interchangeable. The visuals in the animation of the dance scene in *Snow White* resonate with this figurative reading: as the two dwarfs are stacked one on the other, Sneezy's bulbous nose protrudes precisely where a full-sized man's genitals would be located. That may or may not have registered with Disney, but the earlier scene in which the other dwarfs try to restrain Sneezy seems to bear it out. They capture him mid-sneeze and, in a struggle that looks strangely like a hazing ritual, they tie off his nose with a tourniquet. We would be hard pressed to find a clearer depiction of suppressed impulses. This, along with the other images we've seen, gives us a picture of Disney himself. That is to say, these are markers of his role as creative authority of *Snow White*—and whether or not we see him as a "twentieth-century sanitation man" effecting "prudish changes" on his source material (Zipes 2006, 67), his vision of

Snow White does seem fundamentally driven by an imperious urge to clean and contain. Just as Snow White herself, through jaunty singing, domesticates the wild animals in the forest, who then provide collective labor to clean the dwarfs' cottage, Disney spent significant resources corralling natural, untamed impulses and sanitizing untidiness (Byrne and McQuillan 1999, 62).

There were moments when, like Sneezy's unpredictable expulsions, the repressed sexuality of the *Snow White* project erupted unexpectedly into the working environment of the studio. The animator Shamus Culhane, who had drawn sequences of Pluto in earlier Disney shorts and was responsible for the famous scene of the dwarfs marching home from the mine singing "Heigh-Ho" in *Snow White*, remembered the grueling pace of work as the Christmas 1937 deadline approached:

> Suddenly, near the end of the picture, the tension in the studio was too much. To relieve it, there was a spontaneous avalanche of pornographic drawings from all over the studio. Drawings of Snow White being gang raped by the dwarfs, and mass orgies among the dwarfs themselves. Even the old witch was involved.
>
> Some of the drawings were about comic sexual aberrations that Kraft-Ebing would never have dreamed of. This mania went on for about a week, and as suddenly as it started the whole thing stopped. It must have been a form of hysteria brought on by fatigue and the relentless schedule. As far as I know, Walt never heard about it. (1986, 180)

These extracurricular sketches among the Disney animators in 1937, by Culhane's description, were not too different from the sort that Wally Wood would draw for the *Realist* in 1966. Animator Ward Kimball reasoned that the irreverent sketches provided much-needed release for the staff at a particularly arduous moment in the production schedule—a way, he said, "to challenge the suffocating perfections of Walt Disney's world" (Gabler 2006, 264). This supports Krassner's more general observation: "The more repression there is, the more need there is for irreverence toward those who are responsible for that repression" (Kupfer 2009).

There was constant pressure on writers and animators to generate ideas that would help amplify Disney's vision into a feature-length film. Taking a lead from screwball comedies, which were just getting a popular foothold in the early 1930s, Disney insisted that his animators infuse the film with sight gags and comic routines. With that, it became clear that the dwarfs would carry the story—and the studio became a joke factory. (It is telling that most of the Snow White jokes in folk tradition involve the dwarfs in some manner.) Disney began compensating employees on the spot for the jokes they contributed, creating a sharply competitive atmosphere in which every writer and animator was vying for the next bonus. It became codified as the "$5 a gag" policy (equivalent of about $90 today). This demonstrates a fundamental component of the Disney ethos—that jokes (like toys, books, films, or ideologies, for that matter) are commodities to be bought and sold. With *Snow White*, Disney was taking his first steps down a long, lucrative path; it was the first feature film that opened with an accompanying merchandising blitz and soundtrack recording album, "marking the start of an elaborate nexus of entertainment and advertisement that would eventually become a model for the American marketplace" (Telotte 2008, 98–99; see also Pallant 2011, 22–23).

MONETIZING CUTENESS

In order to facilitate the continual flow of gags, the animators highlighted the comical cuteness of the dwarfs, using drawing techniques that were well practiced in the studio since the Silly Symphony cartoons, rendering large eyes relative to head size and large heads relative to body size—"all round and cute and solid," according to Luske.[12] Early sketches had followed European influences and depicted the dwarfs as gaunt, elderly, and gnarled figures, but in the process of their development, argues Barrier, "the dwarfs went through a neotenic evolution, growing younger (despite their white beards and jowls), cuddlier, and more immediately appealing" (1999, 202). In visual terms, roundness is a key marker of juvenilization; accordingly, in Disney's master vision, the dwarfs were drawn with rounder heads, cheeks, limbs, and plumper bodies

(Lawrence 1986, 67–68). Canady (1973) regarded the little men contemptuously as "cutesy-pie dwarfies straight out of a Bavarian souvenir shop." Similarly, David Forgacs likens the dwarfs to toys or dolls. Morphologically, the chubby-cheeked, pot-bellied dwarfs were reminiscent of kewpie dolls, which were extremely popular in the 1920s and 1930s. There was during that time a general move toward cuteness in the Disney studio (1992, 364–65). Zack Schwartz, onetime animator and art director at Disney, later commented, "That word 'cute' used to drive me crazy, it was all over the studio" (Frayling et al. 1997, 5). And Disney was said to have pinned memos over all of the animators' desks reminding them to "Keep it cute" (Bailey 1982, 75).[13] It was a natural commercial extension, then, when Disney licensed cherubic little dwarf toys (and scores of other items) with the release of the film (Forgacs 1992, 370).[14]

WHAT'S IN A NAME?

Besides their cuteness, the dwarfs' individual names and temperaments contributed to the overall comic value, and Disney exploited them to the fullest. Often, all seven of the dwarfs appear on the screen together, and they are differentiated by the actions emanating from their defined personalities, providing an unprecedented degree of comic action on the full animation screen, "unlike anything moviegoers had seen before" (Inge 2004, 138). From a practical standpoint, Disney developed the dwarfs into individuated characters as a way to hold the film together. "The seven dwarfs, we knew, were 'naturals' for the medium of our animated pictures," he observed in 1937 after production ended. "In them we could instill humor, not only as to their physical appearances, but also in their mannerisms, individual personalities, voices, and actions" (1937, 7). Bettelheim sharply criticized Disney for this, arguing that naming the dwarfs and assigning them distinct personalities "seriously interferes with the unconscious understanding that they symbolize an immature pre-individual form of existence which Snow White must transcend. Such ill-considered additions to fairy tales, which seemingly increase human interest, actually are apt to destroy it because they make it difficult to grasp the story's deeper meaning" (1989, 210). But Disney was not the only one—or even the first—to apportion separate sobriquets for the different dwarfs. A number of theatrical adaptations of Snow White had done so earlier. In 1877, German American Henriette Kühne-Harkort penned a children's stage play, the sort popularized by the Kindergarten movement in Germany, based on the Grimms' tale. Her dwarfs carried the names of various minerals and elements: Granite, Sodium, Carbon, Iodine, Soda, Sulfur, and Quartz.[15] Ames's 1912 play identified the dwarfs with the names Blick, Flick, Glick, Plick, Whick, Snick, and the smallest one Quee, who may have been a prototype for Disney's Dopey. And in 1921, English artist John Hassall illustrated an edition of *Snow White* that labeled the dwarfs separately with the embroidered names Stool, Plate, Bread, Spoon, Fork, Knife, and Wine on their breeches, reminiscent of the episode in which the lost Snow White wanders into the dwarfs' cottage, sits at their table, and consumes their food and drink (Hassall 1921). Still, none of these dwarfs, though individually named, had differentiated personalities; they more or less behaved as a collective. It was Disney who developed the dwarfs' separate temperaments and caricatured them as universal traits, comparable in their way to the allegorical characters in European morality plays (Allan 1999, 58). Only after extensive conferences with his production staff did Disney settle on the personalities and seven monikers that are so familiar now.[16] For instance, some of the staff opposed the name Dopey, claiming it seemed too modern or that "it would sound as if the dwarf was a hop head," but Disney convinced them that the word *dopey* appears in Shakespeare (it doesn't) and that it was the perfect appellation for "somebody who's a little off-beat" (Holliss and Sibley 1987, 15). Among the rejected dwarf names were: Jumpy, Baldy, Sniffy, Stubby, Lazy, Puffy, Stuffy, Shorty, Wheezy, Burpy, Dizzy, Tubby, Deafy, Hoppy, Weepy, Dirty, Hungry, Thrifty, Shifty, Woeful, Doleful, Soulful, Awful, Snoopy, Blabby, Neurtsy, Gloomy, Daffy, Gaspy, Hotsy, Jaunty, Biggy, Biggy-Wiggy, and Biggo-Eggo.

The writers devised scenarios by which the individual dwarfs could be introduced; even before the dwarfs appear onscreen, Snow White discovers their beds with the unusual names carved into them, and she later matches the dwarfs to their names by way of introduction. Animating the long, dialogue-heavy bedroom sequence was a laborious task, but necessary, Disney felt, to establish the dwarfs' personalities. "We've got to take the time to have [Snow White] meet each dwarf individually, so the audience will get acquainted with them," he later explained to Bob Thomas. "Even if we bore the audience a little, they'll forget it later because they'll be interested in each individual dwarf" (Thomas 1958, 53).

This sort of character development was a calculated strategy of Disney's production, and to the extent that their singular dispositions advanced the comic possibilities of the overall narrative, the dwarfs became gags in and of themselves—the cute, diminutive embodiment of sleepiness, grumpiness, bashfulness, and so on. Comic bits in the film based on the dwarfs' personalities have their subversive counterparts in jokes from folk culture, and they depict a contorted erotic version of Disney's "clean and separate" fairytale universe (Croce 1991). Apart from Doc, the dwarfs' names designate emotional, mental, or physiological states that can be experienced (or *felt*); therefore, prurient jokes emerged that played with the double meanings of "feel," as in (1) to experience an emotion or sensation, or (2) to touch (sexually). So, Snow White creates resentment among the dwarfs with her sexual exclusivity: "Snow White always goes to bed at night feeling sleepy. Apparently the other six dwarfs are really jealous." Or she freely replaces one partner with another: "Snow White was in the bath feeling sleepy. He got out, so she felt Grumpy instead." Or the dwarfs all share a homoerotic wash, excluding Snow White altogether: "The seven dwarfs were in a bath all feeling happy. Then Happy got out so they all felt grumpy." Or Snow White swaps one inadequate partner for a more exciting ménage á trois: "Bad sex with Doc left Snow White feeling bashful and grumpy." Taken together, the jokes depict a debauched sexual free-for-all at the dwarfs' cottage and, according to another riddling jest, the erotic familiarity apparently breeds contempt: "Why is Snow White angry with the seven dwarfs? Because of the way they always greet her: 'Hi ho, hi ho, hi ho . . .'" In 2009, advertisements for Jamieson's Raspberry Ale in Victoria, Australia, struck a similar note. The campaign, whose rallying message was "Anything but sweet," featured illustrations of Snow White, reconceived as a bordello mistress and renamed "Ho White." Crowded in bed with seven lecherous-looking, half-naked dwarfs—three on one side of her, four on the other, she lies naked herself with a postcoital ciga-rette between her fingers as she casually blows smoke rings into the air (Byrnes 2009; Johnston 2009). The heavy carved Bavarian décor, the red ribbon in Ho White's hair, and the dwarfs depicted with differing personalities (renamed Ugly, Freaky, Dirty, Dodgy, Filthy, Smarmy, and Randy) all betray the illustration as an unblush-ing send-up of Disney's film. The risqué campaign disappeared right after its initial launch, under threats from Disney for copyright infringement, but not before it had already circulated widely around the globe on Web news sources and blogs. "As an ad, it's horrible," reported *CBS News*, "As a PR stunt, it's magnificent" (Edwards 2009). Like the other jokes we've seen, the ad was psychologically enticing because it comingled the seemingly antithetical: in a single image Disneyesque notions of the cute, innocent, and wholesome are uncomfortably yoked with their X-rated opposites.

Similarly, the women's activist/cosplay/craft group called Nerds with Vaginas creates and markets, among other items, wom-en's panties with the phrase "Someday My Prince Will Cum" and the silhouette of an apple silk-screened onto the seat. The song title (with its ribald homophone) and the image of the apple are sugges-tive enough, but the object of the satire is absolutely clear with the words printed in the unmistakable Disney company logo script.[17] One advertisement for the underwear shows Disney's Snow White asleep on the bier, awaiting the magical kiss from Prince Charming, and floating above her head, as in a dream, is an image of the slo-ganized panties.

WISHES, SEX, AND DEATH

There was considerable deliberation among writers and animators as to how the film's final sequences might be executed. During a December 7, 1936, story conference, the discussion turned toward the mourning scene in the final act, when the attending dwarfs and animals believe the unconscious Snow White to be dead:

WALT: There's not much light except around her. She's got to be beautiful as she lays there. Sort of like Juliet . . . When someone good dies there is always a question why. So many bad things in the world that go on . . . Remember Romeo and Juliet? How pretty Juliet looked? They had her so she looked very beautiful there.

DICK CREEDON (STORY ADAPTER): When it's over (the Queen's death) the rain drops like tears (mourning Snow White).

WALT: Sad—yes—sort of steady. You could work that in like the rain symbolizes tears. (Allan 1999, 61)

Fully produced, the scene became a tableau of transcendent sadness. The dwarfs and animals weep bitterly, and the universe commiserates as the beautifully rendered falling rain and dripping wax of vigil candles form sympathetic tears. The cutting-edge animation and heart-wrenching pathos of the scene are the handicraft of Disney's artistic sensibility, careful planning, and clarity of purpose.

It was in that same conference that Disney, contemplating how they would handle Snow White's awakening, reaffirmed his underpinning conviction for the entire project: "I believe any fairytale can have wishing things . . . I believe in fairytales" (Allan 1999, 61). Indeed, from the initial scene in which Snow White sings "I'm Wishing (for the One I Love)" and then meets the prince at the wishing well to the enticing magic *wishing* apple that precipitates her presumed death, wishing is employed in the film as a device to carry the plot to the ultimate conclusion of Snow White's return to life. Wishing, as we know, was to become one of the pillars of the Disney ethos. "When You Wish upon a Star," originally recorded for *Pinocchio* (1940), effectively became the company's theme song, used in the opening credits for the Walt Disney anthology television series and since the 1980s as accompaniment to the opening logo of Disney films. When ships in the Disney Cruise Lines sound their signal horns, passengers recognize the blaring melody as the first seven notes of "When You Wish upon a Star." If Walt Disney was a fairy godfather, as he seems to have self-identified, then he was a strict one. He built a company that, through "the pleasures of wholesome entertainment," ostensibly offers young people the promise of wish fulfillment—while at the same time it asserts significant political, economic, and ideological control within the culture industry (Giroux 1999, 26). Fantasy, wishing, and magic abound at the Happiest Place on Earth, but they are contained within a particular (corporate) worldview that has historically challenged disaffection. At Disney, the creative vision is engineered to reflect a singular dominant design that leaves little room for variance, such that the viewer of a Disney film or visitor to a Disney theme park "will only dream Disney's dreams" (Croce 1991, 95; Sklar 1980, 63). As onetime Disney president Michael Ovitz observed, "Disney isn't a company as much as it is a nation-state with its own ideas and attitudes, and you have to adjust to them" (Bart 1996, 1). Though Disney Studios was promoted as something of a dream factory, Walt managed it like a "benevolent and paternal [dictator]," according to animator Ward Kimball (Mosley 1992, 188) or, as Croce puts it, as "an odd combination of the entrepreneurial arch-capitalist and the virtually pre-modern patriarch" (1991, 99).

As for Snow White, the unflagging wishing (and hoping) for the one she loves is rewarded in the end when the princely kiss revives her and she (eventually) ascends the throne. In what surely is one of the most dramatic emotional reversals in cinematic history, the dwarfs, who moments before drooped with crushing grief, dance and frolic about with the animals in exuberant joy at Snow White's awakening. The final good-bye is moving for the dwarfs (and the audience), and—as with the prior scenes we've discussed—it was carefully supervised by Disney in terms of its narrative effect.[18]

Allan reflects on the closing moments of the film in sentimental, even ethereal, terms: "We identify with the dwarfs, while [Snow White] goes on to marriage and sexual fulfilment in a Maxfield Parrish landscape of trees, sunset and castle in the air . . . We and the dwarfs are left behind to grow old and die; Snow White, resurrected, moves towards everlasting life" (1999, 61). There is no disputing that romance is the overriding sensibility, but folk humor gives us another viewpoint on the same sequence: "What did Grumpy say when Snow White rode off with Prince Charming?

Ok, fellas, now it's back to masturbating." Here, Grumpy reduces the princess/dwarf relationship solely to base carnality, although he does share some fraternity with his compatriots for their mutual loss; all of them face the same sobering reality—the party is over now that sexual privileges have been commandeered by a taller, more eligible rival. Another rendition with just slight variance creates a substantially different meaning, its implications much graver: "What did Grumpy say when Snow White woke up? I guess it's back to masturbating." The sexual encounters in this case end abruptly not because a princely paramour has insinuated himself into the scenario but by the simple fact that Snow White regains consciousness. If we accept that the dwarfs believe Snow White to be dead until that awakening, then this joke makes them out to be necrophiliacs. At the very least, it seems, they are serial rapists, having had their way repeatedly with Snow White's unconscious body. These perverse little deviants of joking tradition are the furthest imaginable from the cute amiable dwarfs that Walt Disney produced.

❊ ❊ ❊

For a film whose plot was advanced largely through gags and jokes—jokes also became an important part of its reception. This collection of jokes in bold strokes bears out what Huimin Jin (2012) asserts as a fundamental proposition of reception studies, that "the audience is never as innocent as what the [media] text hopes" (40–41). We might well imagine Disney's vexation to find Snow White reentering the folk tradition in the form of joking allusions that highlighted the very elements he had sought to bowdlerize, consciously or otherwise. These jokes, which continue to circulate, remind us that even amid the sprawling tentacles of the Disney Corporation's material and ideological power, there remains space for resistance.

3

Haunting Visitors

Tourism, Narrative, and the Spectral

ON THE NORTHWEST END OF THE ISLAND OF Jamaica, about ten miles east of Montego Bay along the coast, stands the Georgian mansion called Rose Hall. Completed in the 1770s as the Great House for a 6,000-acre sugar plantation, it is perched atop a rolling hill and enjoys a panoramic view of the azure Caribbean Sea. British architect James Hakewill's 1825 volume *A Picturesque Tour of the Island of Jamaica* includes an aquatint drawing of Rose Hall, with this accompanying description:

> Rose-Hall, the property and residence of John Rose Palmer, Esq., is situated on the sea-side, at nearly equal distance from Montego Bay and Falmouth. The house of which we give a view is justly considered as the best in Jamaica, and was erected about fifty years since by the uncle of the present proprietor, at the expense of £30,000 sterling. It is placed at a delightful elevation, and commands a very extensive sea view. Its general appearance has much of the character of a handsome Italian villa. A double flight of stone steps leads to an open portico, giving access to the entrance hall; on the left of which is the eating-room, and on the right the drawing-room, behind which are other apartments for domestic uses. The right wing, fitted up with great elegance, [is] enriched with painting and gilding . . . and the left wing is occupied as

DOI: 10.7330/9781607329909.c003

FIGURE 3.1. Rose Hall Great House, 2015. (Photograph by Curtis Nelson.)

servants' apartments and offices. The principal staircase, in the body of the house, is a specimen of joinery in mahogany and other costly woods seldom excelled, and leads to a suite of chambers in the upper story. (93)

Despite a distressing history, the house survives today and remains among the finest buildings in Jamaica (see figure 3.1); but it has also become—through the interplay of oral history, pop culture, and tourism—an emblem of Jamaica's troubled past.

THE BACKSTORY

Legends about Rose Hall abound, and they are centered on the one-time proprietress Annie Palmer, born Annie Mae Patterson in 1802 to an English mother and Irish father who moved to Haiti when she was ten years old. Orphaned shortly after when her parents both died of yellow fever, the legends say, Annie was raised to adulthood by her Haitian nanny, a voodoo practitioner who instilled in the young girl a keen interest in the magical crafts. At the age of eighteen, just about the time that Hakewill was making his Jamaican sketches, Annie moved to Jamaica in search of a rich husband. Said to have been beautiful and petite (around four feet eleven), she met and married John Palmer, the owner of the Rose Hall estate, which included the Great House and a vast sugar plantation with some 2,000 slaves. Just months into the marriage, Annie grew discontented with her husband and began taking slave lovers into her bed. One day her husband caught her with a lover and beat her with a riding crop. Annie didn't like that, so she murdered him by poisoning his coffee; she then inherited Rose Hall and became its sole overseer. Thus began a decade-long reign of terror on the estate. Occasionally, as she sipped breakfast tea on the balcony, for amusement she had slaves whipped and tortured in the courtyard below. Bear traps were secreted around the plantation to keep slaves within property lines; some defiant slaves who strayed lost a foot, snapped clean off. Any slave who displeased her—for whatever minor infraction—was precipitously killed. But all the while, she entertained a succession of slave lovers, none of whom lasted very long as she would murder one as soon as she grew tired of him, and then move on to the next.

Annie married twice more, and murdered those partners as well, one by pouring poison into his ear while he slept. She boasted on one occasion, "If I survive, I'll marry five" (Rattle and Vale 2005, 69; Morris 1985). The bodies of the unfortunate husbands were carried from the house by slaves through a secret passageway, and then buried close to the sea. And no one ever heard from those slaves again, as Annie had them killed by overseers before they returned to the estate. The endless string of murders, along with her brutality and association with voodoo, earned Annie the moniker the White Witch of Rose Hall.

Some slaves on the plantation revolted in 1831, led by her slave lover Takoo, and put an end to the cruelty by strangling Annie to death in her own bedroom. She was immediately buried on the estate, and the slaves burned her possessions, fearing that they were tainted by her spirit. An obeah ritual was performed to seal Annie eternally into her grave but, the legend goes, the ritual was not fully completed. As a result, her restless ghost haunts Rose Hall to this day, with all the accompanying signs—reports of inexplicable voices, screams, and hurried footsteps in the empty Great House; shadowy figures on the balcony and roaming the grounds; ineradicable bloodstains; and the like.[1]

It is said that the White Witch—the last, worst, and most famous mistress of Rose Hall—is the one ghost known to everyone on the island of Jamaica. The house itself seems to have been tormented by the horrors of its past, to the point that it became uninhabitable, standing derelict and unoccupied for more than 130 years. Over that time, naturally, it fell into sad disrepair. Architect Tom Concannon described the condition of the house in 1961: "[It had deteriorated into] a gaunt, forlorn rotting pile of masonry and timber . . . the haunt of bats, owls, and—who knows?—spirits of the past. What little was left of the roof timbers fell to the ground, window openings became gaping gashes in the walls, giving the building an eerie, ghost-like appearance in keeping with its sinister reputation as the home of Annee Palmer, the legendary mistress of bygone days" (*Rose Hall, Jamaica* 2004, 9).

In 1965, the Great House, nearly rubble by then, and the surrounding plantation were purchased by American entrepreneur John W. Rollins, a former lieutenant governor of Delaware. From 1966 to 1971, Rollins financed a massive, multimillion-dollar renovation of the property, restoring the house and furnishings to period splendor. Today, the refurbished Great House overlooks the Caribbean Sea as it did 200 years ago; it stands as a material reminder of slavery, colonialism, and the plantation, but it signifies much more than that. In its contemporary function as a touristic site, the Great House is at once both alluring and menacing, inspiring polysemous participation from a wide range of agents—tour guides and visitors, locals from the island and foreigners, blacks and whites. There are a number of complications, we'll see, among the producers and audiences of performed history at Rose Hall.

The legend derived from the oral culture of slaves (Lomas 1994), but its continued proliferation owes much to early literary adaptations, which over time shifted the emphasis and dramatis personae of the story. The first written account was James Castello's 1868 pamphlet *Legend of Rose Hall Estate in the Parish of St. James, Jamaica*, which set the story in the eighteenth century, attributing the lurid murderous exploits to Mrs. Rosa Palmer (the titular Rose of Rose Hall, who died in 1790)—"her nights spent amid drunken orgies, scenes too disgusting to describe," her days "spent in inflicting the most tyrannical cruelties and dreadful tortures upon her slaves, who were alternately the companions of her evening orgies and the victims of her morning remorse" (9). M. C. De Souza's 1891 *Tourist's Guide to the Parishes of Jamaica* also vilified Rosa, claiming that she had murdered *five* husbands before she herself was strangled. A statue of her was erected in the St. James Parrish Church in Montego Bay, and De Souza alluded to supernatural signs at the site that were presumed to be corporeal postmortem clues of Rosa's nefarious deeds: marks appearing around the statue's neck such as those that would be made by a hangman's rope, and blood oozing from the nostrils (Robertson 1968, 8).

An exchange of letters in several 1890s issues of the Jamaica *Daily Gleaner* attested to the sensational local appeal of the legend, but the incongruent details and contradictory evidence served only to perpetuate public confusion. For instance, after searching archival records at Spanish Town, an E. N. McLaughin concluded that the whole story was a "myth . . . aided by the threads of some forgotten tale of the blood shedding days of Jamaica." He added, "I am quite convinced that the legend has no more connection with the Palmers of Rose Hall and Palmyra, whose history I have tried to trace, than it has with the man in the moon" (Robertson 1968, 9).

More to the point, extant versions of the legend at that time did not sit well with high-ranking women of Jamaica, who perceived such acts of debauchery and violence as unbefitting a woman of station like Rosa. (Most notably, Lady Blake, the governor's wife, protested the legend on these grounds.) The ensuing public debate in the pages of the newspaper did not erase the powerful image of a ruthless white slave mistress but, framed as it was as a sort of class argument, it did effectively shift the blame from the honorable Rosa Palmer to the less prestigious Annie Palmer from a half century later (Rosenberg 2007, 82).

The public perception of Annie as the malefactor narrowed further with Joseph Shore's confidently titled "The True Tale of Rose Hall" in 1911, which positioned itself as the definitive and "well-authenticated" account of the Rose Hall legend (1970, 51–52). Shore alleged that the same Annie (Patterson) who married into the Palmer family in 1820 was irrefutably the perpetrator of all the rumored ghastly misdeeds at the Great House. His assertive claims, amplifying and expanding on Castello's tale but blaming someone else, did much to sway subsequent oral historical accounts, and as a result Annie Palmer's singular infamy increased in following years.

To a greater extent, though, it was the sensationalist historical novel *The White Witch of Rosehall*, by well-known Caribbean editor/writer Herbert G. de Lisser (2007), that permanently etched a particular version of the lurid story into the narrative consciousness of Jamaicans. The editor of Jamaica's most influential paper, the *Daily Gleaner*, for forty years until his death in 1944, and founder of the annual magazine *Planter's Punch* in 1920, de Lisser held "a near monopoly on the manufacture of public opinion" (Rosenberg 2007, 63). The novel was published originally as *The Witch of Rosehall* in the 1929 issue of *Planter's Punch*, reaching an audience of approximately 50,000 Jamaicans (Carnegie 1973, 162). Reissued in numerous editions since then, the novel remains in print today, widely available in Jamaica and beyond. De Lisser drew upon, stylized, and liberally embellished earlier written and circulating oral versions of the Rose Hall legend. Although the book jacket advertises the novel as "a very striking and curious story, founded on fact," many of the plot details are de Lisser's own fabrications—not least the driving narrative structure of a fictionalized romantic triangle between Annie Palmer, the overseer Robert Rutherford, and the mulatto housekeeper Millicent. De Lisser also originates the character of Takoo, a local voodoo practitioner (and grandfather of Millicent) who, at the novel's conclusion, strangles Annie to death, while Jamaica's 1831 slave rebellion erupts as a dramatic backdrop. There is no question that de Lisser's *White Witch* further popularized the already familiar story of Annie Palmer, and though based only loosely on "a sub-stratum of fact" (Lomas 1994, 70), it became, in a sense, the authoritative account of the legend, infiltrating an oral tradition whose variant details had been inconsistent and somewhat sketchy. Today, word-of-mouth transmission of the Rose Hall legend remains as vibrant as ever, but de Lisser's famous novel—popular, commercially sanctioned, and peddled widely by touristic vendors across Western Jamaica—insinuates itself into those oral narratives.

Recent pop culture has played a role as well in propagating the legend of Annie Palmer. For example, the Travel Channel's *Ghost Adventures*, Fox's *The Scariest Places on Earth*, and SYFY's *Ghost Hunters International* have all dedicated full episodes to the Rose Hall hauntings. The story has enjoyed countless treatments in popular ephemera like newspapers, magazines, brochures, travelogues, and even postcards, where Rose Hall is often touted as "the most haunted house in the Western hemisphere" (e.g., Holzer 2004). In 1969, the psychedelic American rock band Coven recorded the song "The White Witch of Rose Hall," the second track on their brazenly titled album *Witchcraft Destroys Minds & Reaps Souls*. (The band is credited with having introduced the "sign of the horns" into early rock and metal culture, and they reportedly signed their Mercury Records contract in blood.) Apart from its driving emphatic rock beat, the song's lyrical rendering of the legend bears a distinct de Lisserian influence:

> The white witch of Rose Hall,
> The devil she could call.
> Mister Rutherford came one day,
> Into Montego Bay.
> The Great House,
> An accountant man.
> Annie Palmer had to have this man.
>
> The white witch of Rose Hall,
> A beauty above all.
> The slaves out in our fields
> Had brothers who were killed.
> This Obeah made the spirits rise,
> Destroying the unwanted with her eyes.
>
> By night in the black
> When she did rise,
> Anyone in her path would die.
> Robert met Millicent one fine day,

Now the girl stood in Annie's way.
Her life meant nothing without his love.
But she couldn't bear the evil of . . .

The white witch of Rose Hall
The devil she could call.
Robert's love then died.
The blame Annie denied.

But the father
Of this dead slave girl
Casted Annie from his world.

The white witch of Rose Hall.
The devil she could call.
The white witch of Rose Hall.
The devil she could call. (Coven, 1969)

A little later, in 1973, Johnny Cash, who for decades owned a vacation home adjacent to the Rose Hall property, released a more tranquil song titled "The Ballad of Annie Palmer." He references a commonly recurring motif in the legend, that a certain number of palm trees (usually three, but sometimes as many as five) remain as natural seaside grave markers where Annie's murdered husbands were deposited by slaves.

On the island of Jamaica
Quite a long, long time ago
At Rose Hall plantation
Where the ocean breezes blow
Lived a girl named Annie Palmer
The mistress of the place
And the slaves all lived in fear
To see a frown on Annie's face

Chorus:

Where's your husband Annie
Where's number two and three
Are they sleeping 'neath the palms,

Beside the Caribbean Sea?
At night I hear you riding
And I hear your lovers call
And I still can feel your presence
Round the Great House at Rose Hall

Well, if you should ever go to see
The Great House at Rose Hall
There's expensive chairs and china
And great paintings on the wall
They'll show you Annie's sitting room
And the whipping post outside
But they won't let you see the room
Where Annie's husbands died

Chorus repeat (Cash, 1973)

Now, every day from 9:00 to 6:00 packs of visitors shuffle through the Great House, led by tour guides in period dress who enumerate gruesome details of the debauchery and death that supposedly occurred there. The tourists are escorted through the estate's halls and hidden passageways; they view the separate bedrooms where Annie's husbands met their fate and the balcony from which she ordered her slaves tortured; they wander through the stone basement—the so-called dungeon—which displays one of the infamous bear traps and has been transformed now into a tavern called Annie's Pub, where patrons can sample the house specialty, a rum cocktail known as Witch's Brew. And the tour concludes on the grounds behind the house where Annie is buried in a limestone crypt, imprinted with crosses on three of its four sides (Annie's spirit reportedly travels in and out of the grave through the "permeable" side with no cross inscribed on it; see figure 3.2). As an epilogue, docents sing a verse from "The Ballad of Annie Palmer," sometimes identifying Cash as the composer but other times reciting it as if it's an anonymous traditional air, creating a more somber effect as it seems then to carry the weight of a long history with it.

Nighttime tours are available as well, publicized on the official Rose Hall website with spooky images and this accompanying text:

FIGURE 3.2. Stone burial vault on the grounds of Rose Hall, purported to be the resting place of Annie Palmer. (Photo by Curtis Nelson.)

> At night, Rose Hall is not for the faint of heart! Experience the Rose Hall Plantation's dramatic past as you venture into the world of the White Witch as she roams this Eighteenth Century sugar plantation seeking the love and fortune that first lured her here. But be warned legend holds that no one who crossed her survived to tell the tale!! This promises to be the encounter of a lifetime.[2]

The legendary horrors of Rose Hall promulgated through these different communicative platforms—oral narrative, literature, historical tourism, theatrical performance, television, popular music—coalesce to form a striking example of transmedia story-telling (see Jenkins 2006, 97–98).

Here's the rub: regarding the lechery, violence, and murder that are said to have vexed Rose Hall—none of these things happened. On several fronts, the details of the legend of Rose Hall recounted above have been soundly—publicly—discredited. In 1965, the same year that John Rollins purchased the plantation, Jamaican archivist Geoffrey Yates, through painstaking analysis of municipal documents and other archival evidence, pieced together the verifiable history of Annie Palmer and her relationship to the estate (1965a, 1965b). It is unsubstantiated that she was orphaned or that she dabbled in voodoo, but in 1820 she did indeed marry John Rose Palmer, the nominal owner of the plantation. Theirs was not a life of luxury, however, but rather one filled with money worries as the property was already in receivership at that time. He died in 1827 at the age of forty-two (probably from yellow fever; but in any case, he wasn't murdered) some £6,000 in debt. At that point, "Annie had no money, no real claim to the estate, no slaves, nothing" (Yates 1965a, 7). In 1830, she sold whatever rights she may have had in Rose Hall for £200 sterling to a Dr. Bernard in Bristol. And then she left. The estate quickly fell into disuse. A Presbyterian missionary, H. M Waddell, who held services at the Great House on three Sundays in August 1830, described it as "unoccupied save by rats, bats, and owls" (1863, 42).

Annie never remarried. Nor was she murdered in 1831; rather, she died some fifteen years later in 1846 in Bonavista, near Anchovy, and was buried in the churchyard at Montego Bay by the Reverend T. Garrett on July 9. Her supposed "tomb" at Rose Hall is in fact not a grave at all but an empty touristic prop (Radford 2010, 282). There is no real proof, archival or otherwise, linking Annie Palmer with any form of crime, depravity, or unnatural death. (John Roby's reputable *The History of the Parish of St. James*, printed in 1849, makes no mention of anything nefarious regarding either Annie or the Rose Hall Plantation house.) Over time, the literary sources amplified and further popularized the already-disturbing oral legends of Rose Hall, and the aftereffect, according to Jennifer Donahue, was a "wholesale defamation" of Annie Palmer (2014, 244).

The archivist Yates was hoping perhaps to extinguish conclusively the outlandish and unsubstantiated tales that had been circulating for more than a century. After all, the two installments of his report, appearing in the November 21 and December 5, 1965, issues of the *The Kingston Gleaner*, were titled "The True Tale of the 'White Witch of Rose Hall': Death of a Legend" and "The Rose Hall Legend: Was It Really Annie?" One can understand how an information professional whose interpretation of history relies on archived records and documentary evidence might think this way.

Still, though the persistent misinformation was to him an annoyance, Yates demonstrated some awareness of the processes of
oral tradition:

> Legend grows rapidly, smothering facts and attaching itself like a
> vine to places where it does not belong . . . Somewhere, a far-off
> tale of murder has become attached to Rose Hall and Palmyra and
> to the two Mrs. Palmers who lived there. Hearsay rumours were
> taken as gospel truth, and once the legend was given currency, by
> Castello in his pamphlet of 1868, it stuck. Because it was in print,
> it became believed as true and then people started to look for
> blood stains and ghosts and saw them. De Lisser gave the legend
> far wider currency . . . The legend throve, the facts disappeared.
> Now it has become so firmly established—and I frankly admit it is
> a good story. (1965a, 7)

More recently, the contemporary skeptic Ben Radford (2010), in
his book *Scientific Paranormal Investigation*, devoted an entire chapter
to Rose Hall and handily debunked the legend, motif by motif.
There is much work to be done by professional debunkers, but
my interest leads elsewhere. In fact, if we engage a doubt-centered
approach to the touristic legend of Rose Hall, rather than a conventional truth-centered approach of the sort that would energize
debunkers, our emphasis shifts toward the more slippery issue of
audience reception (see Mould 2018, 418). It's intriguing that—even
in the face of so much indisputable evidence to the contrary—the
legend of Rose Hall continues to flourish. Moreover, authenticity
itself—tangled up as it is in complex political, economic, and social relations—remains an elusory notion (Douny 2017, 141; Taylor
2001, 8–9; Bendix 1997). We must conclude that the Rose Hall
narrative and touristic performance serve psychological or social
functions beyond just reportage of verifiable historical fact. And
therein lie deeper meanings.

First, from an economic standpoint, violence and murder sell.
Tourism to destinations where death and tragedy have occurred is
not a new phenomenon.[3] But now such tourism is big business—and
scholars have suggested a number of labels for this fascination:

"negative sightseeing" (MacCannell 1989), "black spots tourism" (Rojek 1993), "tragic tourism" (Lippard 1999), "thanatourism" (Seaton 1996), "necrotravel," and "grief tourism." Presently, the most commonly used term, coined by Lennon and Foley (2000), is "dark tourism." Countless tourist attractions fall into this category: like New York City's National September 11 Memorial & Museum, guided excursions through World War II concentration camps, ghost walks in New Orleans, the Lizzie Borden Bed & Breakfast in Fall River, Massachusetts, and the Jack the Ripper tours in London, which were recently enhanced with images from handheld projectors, what they call "ripper vision."

So it is with Rose Hall. A heritage house that has historical significance is made all the more fascinating by adding and emphasizing elements of the abject and the macabre. Tour operators and local guides "reengineer" the local narrative tradition, converting it into a commodity to be bought and sold. The tours cost US $20, plus any optional gratuity for the tour guide.[4] But for these native Jamaicans, the exchange value of the Rose Hall tourist experience is more than just monetary. To that point, it is no coincidence that the Rose Hall legends have well settled on 1831 as the year that Annie Palmer was killed by rebelling slaves (even though it is known that Annie had already left the plantation well before then and that she died years later). There was indeed a slave rebellion in Jamaica that year, from Christmas 1831 into 1832, generally acknowledged as one of the most significant slave uprisings in global history. It came to be known as the Christmas Rebellion, the Great Jamaican Slave Revolt, or more commonly as the Baptist War because it was led by the educated and charismatic Baptist preacher Samuel Sharpe, a native Jamaican slave born in the same parish where Rose Hall is located. Sharpe was attuned to the abolitionist movement in London, and at the crucial moment of the laborious sugarcane harvest in December, when many slaves worked overtime, he organized a peaceful general strike across several estates in Western Jamaica. But things quickly turned violent on the night of December 27 and the strike escalated into full-on rebellion, with sugarcane fields and hundreds of plantation houses being set afire. That the plantation houses themselves should be attacked by slaves makes symbolic sense, as the buildings were the functional material appendages of the Jamaican body politic and vital organs of the whole plantation system.[5] In the end, around 500 protestors and fourteen plantation owners had been killed in the conflict.

It was the largest—and would be the last—slave uprising in the British West Indies. Though colonial forces and the plantocracy quelled the rebellion in January 1832, the event was to be a clarion call for emancipation across the empire: British lawmakers began to view the whole system as unsustainable, leading them ultimately to pass the Slavery Abolition Act in August 1833. The rebellion is celebrated as one of Jamaica's most important historical moments—and Sharpe, who was executed for his part in it, is credited as a forerunner of the labor movement and honored as a national hero. A statue in downtown Montego Bay commemorates Sharpe and the uprising; in the ultimate veneration, his picture appears on the Jamaican $50 bill.

Back to Rose Hall. Some versions of the legend say that the Great House escaped the conflagration of the Baptist War because protestors feared that the White Witch might retaliate from beyond the grave. (We know that's impossible given that Annie was not even deceased yet.) More likely, Rose Hall was spared because it was irrelevant; it was not a viable plantation, for there were no overseers, no slaves, and no crops there at the time. In any case, it is notable that this Great House survived the conflict while others in Western Jamaica did not. And for well over a century, it stood as a decaying, hollow relic of a bygone era (see figure 3.3). Now, after costly restoration, and through touristic performance and manipulation of local legend, it has been transformed into something of a *tableau vivant* of Jamaica's historical struggle—one version of the national narrative of emancipation.

What worked for de Lisser as a dramatic literary device—coupling the legend of Annie Palmer with the 1831 rebellion—also makes for good tourism at this site, for the profusion of alleged sadism and killing is salable, and figurative of a grander story about the endemic brutality of a slave society. Annie's mythologized reputation as the cruelest proprietress at the most feared plantation in 1830s Jamaica has metaphorical weight: she embodies the

FIGURE 3.3. Postcard showing Rose Hall Great House in ruins, circa 1960. C7042, distributed by the Novelty Trading Co., Kingston, Jamaica. (From the author's collection.)

"voracious lust and uncontrollable brutality . . . of colonial and plantation rule" (Paravisini-Gebert 1990, 28). Her murder at the hands of slaves in December 1831, then, is the symbolic first act of the Baptist War and the death knell for the plantation system.

Tours at heritage sites like Rose Hall are mediated performances of history, and if we accept that all tourism is transactional (Nash 1989, 44–55; Harmes-Liedtke 2012, 48), that is, an exchange between guest and host, then the question arises: what do the tourists get from all this? In the multivalent complexities of touristic discourse and performance, there is no single easy answer.

LEISURE MEETS THE NEOCOLONIAL

On one level, the guests may experience a feeling of superiority. Theorists analyzing tourism in developing countries have noted the social construct that "reawakens memories of race and labor relations of the colonial past and so perpetuates resentments and antagonisms" (Gmelch 2003, 35). The host's difference in culture, in this view, is typically perceived (by tourists) as inferior, thus reinforcing hegemonic Western values (Wearing and Darcy 2011, 19; Williams 2012, 194–96). In that light, one doesn't have to read too deeply to see tourism at Rose Hall as a neocolonial exercise: a significant number of the guests are white, affluent tourists from North America or the Commonwealth, many on day excursions from all-inclusive luxury resorts or from cruise ships docked nearby at Montego Bay. Meanwhile, the docents are Jamaican locals, dressed in period folk dress, which, whatever may be intended, is sartorially emblematic of early nineteenth-century plantation slavery (I discovered a number of reviewers on travel websites who referred to the tour guides at Rose Hall as "slaves"). And the glue that holds this social enactment together is a sensational local legend about an imperious British landowner, whose whiteness becomes both her name and her notoriety. Visitors experience plantocracy for a day.

Perhaps the conventional touristic ethos of Western superiority is subverted somewhat, when, in the epilogue of the tour, the narrative turns to the slave rebellion and the murder of Annie Palmer. But the vindication is only fleeting and illusory if we read de Lisser's *White Witch* (and by extension the touristic legends derived from it) as supporting rather than undermining the empire. The debasement and collapse of the plantation are ascribed to Annie's Irish heritage, her upbringing in Haitian voodoo practices, her gender—but, strikingly, not to colonialism itself. As Erin Mackie notes, the story projects "a vision of colonial corruption that identifies and disowns corruption as foreign (Irish, Haitian, female) to the very English colonial powers culpable for it" (2006, 204). We can compare a correlative American legend about New Orleans Creole socialite Delphine LaLaurie, notorious for allegedly torturing and murdering slaves in her now-famous French Quarter house, which caught fire in 1834. Frank de Caro argues that the oral tradition vilifying this creolized woman similarly absolves the culpable patriarchy: "By shifting the blame for cruelty to a woman, who might be thought deviant anyway, the story [tends] to relieve the burden of guilt from the white men who were actually most involved in slavery" (2015, 44).

Although nineteenth-century Jamaican slave rebellion and emancipation provided a contextual backdrop for de Lisser's novel,

as an anti-nationalist writing in the late 1920s he was more immediately concerned with the historical legacy and legitimacy of British
colonialism in the West Indies (Mackie 2006, 206). In penning what
remains the most recognizable and repeated version of the legend
of Annie Palmer, de Lisser has in effect perpetuated these colonial anxieties. (It is worth noting that neither Emancipation Day
[August 1] nor Jamaican Independence Day [August 6], national
holidays commemorating, respectively, the Slavery Abolition Act
of 1833 and Jamaican independence in 1962, is observed in any
institutional way at the Rose Hall Great House.)

More broadly, the various performances of history at Rose
Hall continually stage local culture for commercial consumption,
and the inexorable forces of capitalism—what Hilary Beckles calls
the "new plantocracy" (Pattullo 2005, 64)—are never too far in
the background (see Adler 1989, 1384). As in the days of old, the
Rose Hall estate is in the business of production that depends on
foreign control and investment. But now, instead of sugarcane,
the chief commodity is tourism—in the form of Great House
tours, special events like weddings, relaxation at the Rose Hall
Hilton Resort and Spa, nineteen holes of golf, and other commercial and residential real estate ventures (all on plantation grounds).
Specifically, all operations are administered by overseers of a different sort, executives at the American-owned company Rose Hall
Development Ltd.

The heritage experience at Rose Hall follows a familiar pattern. As Barbara Kirshenblatt-Gimblett notes in *Destination Culture*,
"Locations become museums of themselves within a tourism
economy. Once sites, buildings, objects, technologies, or ways of
life can no longer sustain themselves as they formerly did, they
survive—they are made economically viable—as representations of
themselves . . . Dying economies stage their own rebirth as displays
of what they once were" (1998a, 151). Given that Kirshenblatt-
Gimblett refers elsewhere to this economic reincarnation of tourism
sites as "afterlives" (1997, 4), haunting becomes an apt metaphor
for the process. History is imprinted on place (Ironside 2018, 110),
and there are multiple levels at which Rose Hall materializes the
bedeviled spirits of its past.

As part of an enterprise with vested economic interests in the reputation of haunting, the spirits at Rose Hall—of murdered husbands, tortured slaves, rejected lovers, and Annie herself—are exemplars of what Dennis Waskul categorizes as "commercial ghosts" (2018, 59). Certainly, the business of ghosts at the Great House reminds us of the well-established principle that a good supernatural story can be marketed for profit (Clarke 2012, 286; Ellis 2003, 94). Even the narrative substance of the ghost legend itself has been commercially co-opted: one of the three award-winning golf courses on the property, managed by Ritz-Carlton, is called "The White Witch." The tenth hole is alleged to be haunted by the ghost of Annie Palmer, whose chief spectral activity appears to be disrupting golfers' games: inexplicable hooks and slices and errant putts are explained away with the common refrain, "The witch got you" (Holstein 2004, 60). The legend becomes part of the marketing strategy; as course designer Robert Von Hagge affirms, "Like Annie Palmer, the legendary 'White Witch of Rose Hall,' the course is alluringly dangerous and unpredictable . . . Just as her personality might shift without warning, so do the winds, turning a six-iron shot in the morning into a five-wood late in the day" (Curley 2018). Annie Palmer ("no relation to Arnold"), writes golf editor Robert Fagan (n.d.), reviewing the course, "makes for a good story and if you are not on your game, the White Witch will certainly devour you!" The environs are maintained primarily by local black groundskeepers whose hard manual labor cultivates pristine landscapes for the enjoyment of affluent, foreign—and predominantly white—patrons. Thus, vacationers at the Rose Hall plantation participate in a convergence of aesthetic, cultural, and corporate interests—and by that measure the historic Great House, symbolically and practically, is not too far from the clubhouse (see figure 3.4).

The quasi-historical narratives of daytime tours at Rose Hall parse these issues somewhat as they retell the past (guides talk freely and soberly about slavery and the wretched conditions of plantation life), but neocolonialism is not the only lens through which we might examine the touristic practices at Rose Hall. Considerations of performance, heritage studies, and audience reception open up a wider range of emergent meanings.

Figure 3.4. Directional sign on Rose Hall Plantation grounds.
(Photograph by Curtis Nelson.)

TOURISTIC PERFORMANCE AT ROSE HALL

The haunted house and estate grounds are located within an
enclave, that is, within a supervised space designed to "create and
control a cultural as well as physical environment" (Freitag 1994,
541). Enclave tourism is a kind of stage management that leads
consumers toward rehearsed, prefabricated themes and experiences; it flourishes only within the boundaries of superintended
spaces, which, typically removed from social contact with the
local populace, delimit which activities may occur and who may
be admitted (Edensor 2000, 328). The process relies heavily on
containment and control: tour guides as directors deliver fixed
scripts to tourists, whose movements are carefully choreographed
through hermetic stage-managed sites. Underneath it all is the
desire to minimize disorientation and direct the touristic gaze
(Urry and Larsen 2011). Tourism at Rose Hall can be approached
in terms of narrative reiteration and as nuanced cultural theater.
The social enactments at the site are managed performances on
a stage, with tour guides and tourists—producers and consumers
of culture—bound together as partners in those performances,

although not necessarily cooperatively (Maoz 2006, 225). In order to observe these touristic dynamics directly, I conducted field-work at Rose Hall in July and August 2015, digitally recording both daytime and night tours in the house, as well as interviewing tour guides and administrators for insights into the "directorial" manipulation of the legendary material.

For visitors to Rose Hall, it commences on the A1 highway below the plantation. Turning off, they must first stop at a guarded checkpoint with an electric gate along the driveway leading up to the Great House. Once admitted onto the property, they wind their way uphill to the site 600 yards farther. Adjacent to a small paved parking lot, tourists find the Rose Hall gift shop, a mod-est air-conditioned structure crowded with knickknacks for sale: carved and painted animal figures, jewelry, scarves, coffee, baskets, postcards—as well as books and pamphlets about Annie Palmer, Johnny Cash CDs, and White Witch brand perfume and massage oil. This is where Rose Hall tours proper begin and end. Guests buy their tickets here and then browse about until the tour starts, when the guide leads them up the front walkway to the Great House. Institutional arrangements join together the separate activities of shopping and house tours under the aegis of one enclavic attrac-tion, creating, as Tim Edensor notes, "a single-purpose space that delimits economic and social activities which diverge from the ser-vicing of tourists and their designated practices" (2000, 329). The guide shepherds guests through the main entrance into the front ballroom, the largest open space at Rose Hall, and from there he or she launches into the scripted historical legend, taking the visitors through room by room.

In a sense, the house *is* the story, as the narrative is manipulated to follow the floor plan. Each room unfolds more details in the cumulating tale of death and debauchery; the tour guides appear to be mindful of the relationship between narrative, place, and artifact as they describe curious objects and architectural features along the way. The dining room on the first floor, for example, displays an ornate Sheraton knife box with a locking device, which on the tour becomes a material emblem of one of Rose Hall's legendary themes. As one guide describes:

Now this is a Sheraton knife box and each box would have knives in it, lots of knives [*demonstrating*]. So open it up. There are two strips, one to the left and one to the right. So face the sides, go along and lock the key here. Now I think Annie locked the knives in here at nights from slaves because she was afraid while she was sleeping they would come and kill her. She wasn't nice. [*laughter from guests*]

Another guide related the information with some variance:

Directly below is an inlaid sideboard with a Sheraton knife box. Knives are kept in this box here and locked away with a key. Rumor has it that this was done so that the slaves wouldn't harm themselves. However, we really believe that the slaves would harm Annie. They would have more reasons to harm Annie, right?

And a third guide added a sarcastic tone:

Directly below is an inlaid sideboard and on top is a Sheraton knife box. Oh, this is where Annie would store and lock away all the knives with a key. Her theory was, she's preventing the slaves from harming themselves. Yeah, right.

In this way, although the guides work from established scripts, there is ample latitude for variable emphasis and individual performative styles. The explanation of the knife box, however delivered, paints a picture of uneasy slave/master relations at Rose Hall and prefigures the *specific* revenge killing of the Annie Palmer legend.

Similarly, throughout the tour, explanations about the history of the house and its furnishings are framed in rhetoric that animates the overriding master narrative about the White Witch. So an ordinary fixture like a chandelier, for instance, that may appear to us barely worth mentioning, takes on special meaning when described like this:

Above here we have a chandelier from France. This is made of crystal. Photographs have been taken by guests of the chandelier. When the photographs were developed, bat-like images appeared in them. Now bats in Jamaica represents [*sic*] the ghost. Out here in Jamaica we call them duppy, D-U-P-P-Y. So while you're here

in Jamaica and you see a bat coming in your room, then you know
that's a ghost visiting you—duppy following you. [*uncomfortable
laughter from guests*]

Such commentary is unexpected and invites the guests to ruminate
on the supernatural, setting the stage early in the tour for the pervasive spectrality of their visit to Rose Hall.

In every room on the first floor, connections like these are
made—in the reception hall there hangs a painted portrait of
Annie, and her eyes mysteriously follow guests as they walk by; the
breakfast room displays antique pewter tableware in a cabinet, and
the guides suggest that Annie's psychopathy may have been the
result of prolonged exposure to lead in the dishes. A heavy wooden
bucket on the floor becomes a prop for elaborating on the dreadful
conditions endured by slaves in the household:

> Now, folks, I'm about to pass around [this] wooden pail. I'll start
> with you, Marvin, just send it around that way. Careful not to drop
> it on your toes, though. It weighs fifteen pounds when empty
> and it would be double that in weight whenever it was filled with
> water. Now, children between the ages of five and nine years old
> were required to fetch water in buckets like those from a mile and
> a half. Oh, you think that's bad? If they spilled any of the water
> on their return journey they would be whipped. By the time they
> were ten years old they were deemed fit enough to work on the
> sugarcane plantation. So I guess that was a form of training or
> muscle building for them, but it was horrible.

In keeping with its relation to architectural space, the legend ascends to its next gruesome level when the tourists climb the wide
mahogany staircase to the second floor, where, guides say, "all the
loving and killing took place." There is the balcony where Annie
perched to watch slaves being tortured and killed below; the crewel room, named for the hand-embroidered fabric lining the walls,
where Annie strangled her third husband (most guides make a playful reference to the word "cruel"); the toile room, named for the
ornate French fabric on the walls, where Annie stabbed her second

husband in his sleep; Annie's bedroom, appointed throughout in deep crimson to match her hot temper and passion for blood. Here in the heart of the house, and at the heart of the legend, guides slow their narrative pace. They become more deliberate, more dramatic, as they chronicle the tangled relations between Annie, Rutherford, Millicent, and Takoo, and elaborate on the lurid goings-on within the bedroom, the very spot where Annie "lived, loved, and died."

In the adjacent sitting room, tour guides point out a gilded Chippendale mirror hanging between windows on the north wall, recounting the experience of a Canadian tourist who years before photographed the mirror and subsequently discovered ghostly forms in the pictures, as with the photographed chandelier downstairs. The difference in this instance is that the guests will have the opportunity to examine the photo itself, displayed inside a glass case in the dungeon. This kind of discourse echoes throughout the tour as guests are frequently presented with physical "evidence" and anecdotal corroboration of the supernatural.

The so-called gentleman's room follows, where Annie is alleged to have killed her first husband by pouring arsenic in his coffee. This is the murder that initially set her up as the wealthiest, and most-feared, plantation owner in Jamaica. (It is worth noting that as it touches on Annie's reputed crimes, the tour upstairs is structured as an inverse chronology, taking guests through a backward narrative arc, one murder and one room at a time.) In the gentleman's room, the guides relate a summary abstraction of Annie's lethal modus operandi:

> GUIDE: [Annie] cleverly blamed the death of each of her husbands on the dreaded yellow fever virus because it was very prevalent back then. What she would do is lock their bodies away in the room, claiming that it was contaminated. She would then order a slave to have that body removed and buried by the ocean. Now, the slave that got that unpleasant task was killed on his way back as she would tell her overseer to be on the lookout for runaways and that's how she covered her tracks. She was married to her first husband seven years. The second husband two years. And the last husband?

GUEST: Fifteen minutes? [*laughter from group*]

GUIDE: You know, man, I'll give you A for effort. Because she did really get better at the killing thing. I don't think she was *that* good. Actually six months . . . Now, there are three palm trees located at the Palmyra today. They indicate where each of those husbands were buried. It is about two or three minutes' drive away from here.

The summary serves as a preliminary coda to the core legend of the White Witch and points to physical evidence on the present-day landscape attesting to the grisly past of Rose Hall. But then the tour enters a different narrative space with its last stop on the second floor, the guest room. There are no more details of murders or Annie's abuses and debauchery; rather, the focus shifts to the supernatural encounters of contemporary visitors to the site. One such encounter, reported as a "very true" occurrence, is a modern variation of classic tales about individuals testing their courage by spending the night in a haunted house:[6]

This is the safest room in the house. We're safe, guys. We're safe. Are you guys familiar with the TV series *The Love Boat?* Right. Now the writer, Dana Franklin, she and her husband, they came here. They didn't believe the house was haunted, so they got special permission to spend the night here. While they were here having coffee at this table, they heard the sounds of [a] baby crying coming from the crewel room, which is the room across the hall.

Now, they felt brave so they went in search for the baby. They didn't find any baby, however, so they came back with the intention of completing their coffee, only to find that their mugs were missing. Now, at that time I would have just left. But they became investigators. They went in search for their mugs. They did find their mugs in Annie's room, smashed to pieces. So they took this as a message that they were not welcome here. So they came back and hurriedly packed their stuff and left. Since then, no one was ever brave enough to sleep here. I don't know if you guys feel brave tonight, do you wanna spend the night here? No? . . . Alright. Let's go downstairs to where it's nice and safe.

The repeated use of the word *safe* is striking as a rhetorical transition into a different facet of the Rose Hall experience. As at most heritage sites, the guides' rehearsed—and sometimes improvised—spiels are descriptive, informative, and, in this case, morbidly provocative. But the added feature of haunting compels tourists differently. A haunting, by supernatural means, coalesces the past and present in a single moment—a palpable joining together of history with the here and now—and pushes the tour in the direction of the experiential. Ghost tourism provides a different way of knowing the past, a "dialectical tension between experience and knowledge" that constitutes a kind of "haunted heritage" (Hanks 2015, 15). And to the extent that tourists are encouraged to have supernatural experiences of their own at the site, belief itself is commodified. One tour guide invited visitors to "take a photo of the mirror and see if you capture any ghosts," and the official website of Island Routes Caribbean Adventures entices potential guests with the claim that "you're sure to feel goose bumps as these eerie tales come to life in this grand estate, where ghost sightings have been reported over the years."[7]

BELIEF TOURISM

The commercial structures at Rose Hall have created an elaborate staging area for what Diane Goldstein has termed "belief tourism, . . . the marketing of the experiences of cultural 'others,' but with a particular focus on the images and traditions associated with spiritual, metaphysical, or paranormal values" (Goldstein, Grider, and Thomas 2007, 194). It culminates as the tour group descends the back stairs of the house, down into the dungeon, where a number of artifacts are exhibited in a long glass display case. There are various photographs with inexplicable hazes, auras, and fuzzy images taken by guests years ago, many with attestations of authenticity, like affidavits, and separate written accounts of paranormal occurrences on the property. One is the often-repeated report about the Chippendale mirror in the sitting room that has been codified as part of the official tour script:

The enclosed photograph was taken at Rose Hall Great House on November 21, 1989, at approximately 1 to 1:30 p.m. Both my wife and myself have been at a loss to explain the woman in the mirror, as she was not with our tour group. Looking at the picture logically, I was slightly to the left of center, so the woman would have to have been to my right and behind me. However, if she was so placed why did the sofa in the foreground of the picture not show up across her waist? If you look closely at the mirror on either side of the woman, it appears to show the top of the couch. To add further to the mystery, while on tour I commented several times to my wife and the guide that I felt the presence with us. On another occasion while waiting to view the last bedroom (undergoing renovation), I asked my wife to stop crowding me; however, when I turned to give her hell for pushing me, there was no one around me! I cannot explain any of the above logically but maybe someone there can help. If you have any further questions, comments or explanations or require copies of my other photos please do not hesitate to call.

Another message, typed onto a torn and yellowed sheet of paper without a date, is secured on the counter under a rock about the size of a small apple. More than just a paperweight, the rock sits there as physical evidence corroborating the story, an artifact of the "material record" of the legend (Holly and Cordy 2007, 347):

To whom it may concern:

Please return this rock to the Rose Hall Great House's retaining wall behind Annie Palmer's crypt, where the tree roots grow through the wall from above. My family and I vacationed in Jamaica a few weeks ago and while on the house tour I felt compelled to have this rock, so I put it in my pocket, and didn't really think about it. Since I have been home I have been plagued by bad dreams, bad luck, and bad nausea. My wife complained of this also until I removed the rock from our home. I brought the rock to work and issues spread there. So I am returning this to its origin, with my sincerest apologies for having removed it in the first place, in hopes that the situation will end. Maybe it's my imagination, maybe it's something else. Either way, I feel better returning this.

Thank you very much for your time and help; it is greatly appreciated.

> Sincerely,
> J. Grandrimo

Guests are given free time to peruse the materials themselves and, as the tour guides say, "come to your own conclusions." In this way, audience reception becomes an important component of the negotiated theater that is a Rose Hall tour, with guests performing their identities as believers, disbelievers, or any of the gradations in between (Hanks 2015, 74, 83). As Dégh and Vázsonyi observed of traditional legend encounters, responses range from belief to indifference to skepticism to nonbelief to opposition—but these are all part of the dialectic process of legend formation (1976, 117). Just so, the guests' "own conclusions" regarding the legend complex around Annie Palmer and her plantation house are agentic evaluations on their part, and they are encouraged. This is a familiar practice in the commoditization of narrative, Regina Bendix observes, as tourists strive "to wrest a personal experience and an individual memory from the thick offering of fabricated or suggested memories for sale" (2018, 81). At Rose Hall, those who claim their own supernatural encounters at the site effectively form their touristic experience into the folk process of a legend trip.

LEGEND TRIPPING AND PARTICIPATION

A ritualized performance designed "to introduce the uninitiated to the realm of the supernatural," the legend trip transpires in three phases (Thigpen 1971). First, before the uninitiated have a chance to visit the legend scene, the story is shared "in a manner that will heighten the anticipation of uninitiated and initiated alike, thus enhancing the receptive psychological state of all involved, so they will be more likely to perceive the 'supernatural' occurrence" (205). This happens in different ways for tourists to Rose Hall. Guests who grew up in Jamaica have seen the ominous mansion on top of the hill and heard versions of the legend all their lives. The story is for them "invasive," a permanent curio in the local oral tradition (see Thomas 2015, 51). (Our taxi driver remembered his second-grade teacher scaring the class with a particularly graphic version of the Annie Palmer legend.) Alternately, foreign tourists may pick up the story through popular culture or just as likely from Jamaican travel guidebooks, which are replete with lurid details designed to entice prospective visitors. Through whatever means, locals and vacationists are exposed to the legend and their curiosity lures them to the site.

The second phase transpires as participants perform certain activities at the site or interact with the legend in some manner. With contemporary legends, this may involve such specified acts as rubbing one's hand across a cursed gravestone (e.g., Clements 1980, 259, 261), or parking in the middle of a haunted bridge and blinking the car lights a prescribed number of times; but the action may also entail "merely being in a certain place at a certain time" (Thigpen 1971, 205). A tour at Rose Hall, especially a night tour, as we'll see, immerses the visitors in the setting and circumstances of the legend. As a re-creation, an acting out, of the conditions of the legend, a visitor's trip to this legend site is an instance of ostension—a self-conscious fusion of narrative and action (Holly and Cordy 2007, 345; Lindahl 2005, 178–81; Thomas 2003, 16–17; Meley 1990). It is a performance on the part of the audience, driven by a "sustained effort toward heightened awareness: straining to hear or see something out of the ordinary, reacting to phenomena that just might be otherworldly, and maintaining the sense that the supernatural [is] *supposed* to be present" (Kinsella 2011, 31). A self-aware playfulness emerges as part of a larger ritualized folk drama, in which participants purposely suspend disbelief and actively cultivate the *possibility* of supernatural happenings in order to enhance the spooky mood (Ellis 2003, 173; Hall 1973, 170–71).

The third stage of the legend trip plays out as participants retrospectively process their encounter, emphasizing not the past events of the legend but rather the fresh personal experiences of the participants. Here, the memorate—the first-person experience narrative—is the benchmark. Like participatory fandoms that "poach" and expand upon their favorite media texts (Jenkins 2013), some visitors to Rose Hall augment the legendary lore with their own supernatural addenda: personal tales about mysterious images in photographs; cursed objects taken from the plantation grounds; episodes of clairvoyance, telepathy, and other heightened sensory perceptions. Interacting with the site and tuning into the supernatural possibilities, tourists amend a long-standing narrative tradition with stories of their own (Goldstein, Grider, and Thomas 2007, 225). These are audience interventions, social enactments of what Scott Magelssen (2011) calls "visitor performance" (175) or "second-person interpretation" (177). For example, after one night tour, a guest from Australia approached me and asked about the nature of my research. He identified himself as a psychic medium by profession and told me that he had visited Rose Hall because of its reputation for paranormality. (Later, I learned from a manager that Rose Hall has over the years attracted many such individuals—psychics, occultists, ghost hunters, and the like.) The psychic proceeded to tell me about spirits he sensed in the house and about revelations that had come to him during the tour. He offered up an account with significant detail about a young girl who had drowned at Rose Hall and whose body, unbeknownst to the managers and staff working there, is still buried somewhere on the grounds. He also described a negative presence in the house that touched him on the shoulder during the tour, an incorporeal being whose name begins with the letter K.

Although at times they may be framed as such, tours at Rose Hall are by no means unilateral reproductions of "truth"; they are, rather, communicative acts involving multiple social actors who interact but do not necessarily collaborate in the production of meaning. The varied ways that tourists respond in belief (or disbelief) and inject their own expressive behavior into existing tradition are performative choices. As Athinodoros Chronis observes of "co-constructed" narratives at Gettysburg:

> The resulting narratives are contested by tourists and become
> subject to negotiation. During the performance of the story,

tourists are not passive readers of the text. Rather, they are actively engaged by using their prior background, negotiating, filling gaps, and imagining. Hence, service providers do not simply teach history and tourists do not only learn about the past. Rather, through their interaction, marketers and tourists perform history by means of negotiation, narrative completion, and embodiment. (2005, 400)

Thus, as they reinterpret, reformulate, and augment the encoded texts delivered to them, tourists act as producers as well as consumers of culture (see Du Gay et al. 1997). And, as Urry and Larsen explain, "Tourists do not only decode past texts, but are part of creating new ones through ongoing interactions and performances with other tourists, guides, discourses, buildings and objects" (2011, 206). It is worth noting here that in addition to these multiple levels of encoding and decoding, tourism as an enterprise adds a fourth segment to the established tripartite structure of legend tripping—the purchase. The touristic event is pitched in terms of experience and the accompanying paraphernalia that can be bought and sold (Thomas 2015, 67).

THEATRICS AND POST-TOURISM

The evening tours at Rose Hall are explicitly dramaturgic events that offer tourists a different experience altogether, and to which the tourists bring a different set of expectations. In 2011, Rose Hall management contracted actor and director Douglas Prout, founder of the performing arts company Bay Vibez, to produce an interactive theatrical variation of the tour for nighttime audiences. Fully redesigning the tour, Prout adapted the existing script and introduced an array of stagecraft: props and scenery; lighting and sound effects; a cast of hired actors in makeup and costumes playing designated roles.

At night, a good portion of the house's history is related by tour guides outside the building itself, eerily lit by an arrangement of kerosene lanterns fashioned from old Red Stripe beer bottles on bamboo posts along the front walkway. The façade of the house is bathed in moody light, and visitors, if they are observant, will catch a brief glimpse of a silhouetted female figure, Annie, in one of the upper windows. Groups are led inside and through the house room by room, as in the daytime tours, but the altered staging creates a different atmosphere entirely. Actors enter the performance at key moments along the tour, mostly silent in the background but theatricalizing key motifs of the narrated spiel.

While some tourists find the period dress of daytime guides suggestive of colonial slaves, there is no question that the actors at night are playing the part. The women wear bonnets or kerchiefs on their heads and roughly woven plain cotton dresses, the men ragged cotton pants and loose-fitting shirts or no shirt at all. Some of the characters have iron bands and chains around their necks. All of them don pasty pale theatrical pancake, with ghoulish highlights of stage blood and scars and dark cavernous eyes. These are the ghosts of slaves haunting Rose Hall. Meanwhile, the evening tour guides wear contemporary attire that distinguishes them from the historical specters.

As guests file into the main entrance and ballroom, a ghost slave appears in the adjacent staircase hall, walking backward while whistling ominously. These cryptic actions make sense once it is known that in Caribbean ghostlore "duppies" are believed to walk backward in the afterlife, and once the guides point out in the dining room that slaves were required to whistle while serving meals to their masters to prove that they were not sampling the food.[8]

Sometimes the ghostly slaves appear without warning, startling the guests—always at some pivotal moment in the overall narrative. A door swings open suddenly to reveal a ghost behind; another ghost rattles and peers through a window to give guests a good fright; yet another appears out of nowhere and trails the tour group through the house for a time. By far the most electrifying scare of the house occurs when the guide is showing guests the small door leading to the secret passageway. It is through that portal, the guide explains, that Annie's murdered husbands were carried to the seaside, and where Takoo gained access to the Great House before he climbed the stairs to strangle her in her bed. Just as the narrative reaches that dramatic pitch, the door slams open and an actor dressed as the slave Takoo scrambles onto the main floor, then runs frenetically upstairs, yelling indiscernible patois all the while. Audience reactions are predictable: screams and recoiling, followed by uncomfortable laughter and chattiness. On one evening I observed a crowd of eighteen guests at this point suddenly stumble backward en masse, as if choreographed, one of them falling against the window and then onto the floor. If, as I've suggested, the house is an embodiment of the legend, then the hidden passageway becomes all the more significant as a liminal "administrative boundary" on plantation grounds (O. Davies 2007, 46), a portal of egress and ingress: murdered husbands and slave lovers are secretly transported from the house, Annie's responsibility for the crimes ostensibly carried away with them; but the passageway is also the conduit by which the slave rebellion spills into the material environment of the house itself, where the proprietress is killed, poetically, in her own transgressive bed (see Pettitt 2005, 48–52).

Upstairs, when the door to the toile room is opened, an actor/slave hurries out, carrying over his shoulder a stage dummy, reenacting the hasty disposal of one of Annie's newly murdered husbands; inside that room, a slave girl falls from behind the dresser and immediately begins scrubbing the floor with a dried coconut brush, attempting to scour away the indelible stains of blood (several of the guides allude to real bloodstains on that spot that were allegedly expunged during the 1965 restoration); and in Annie's crimson-hued boudoir, the audience is jolted again when the Takoo character suddenly leaps up from behind the bed and bolts out of the room. Supporting stagecraft includes dramatic lighting, furniture mysteriously sliding across the room on its own, flickering lamps, stage fog, and inexplicable eerie sounds throughout the house. The experience of the nighttime tour is modeled somewhat on North American Halloween haunted houses, with fright gimmicks and cast members jumping out from the shadows at opportune moments to surprise guests.

But, from a production standpoint, the scares at Rose Hall, coordinated with an existing legend tradition as they are, appear more strategic and purposeful. When I interviewed Prout, he reflected, "I didn't want to do too much of the [actors] running out from cupboards. We have to have that for the hook, to let people laugh and [maybe even] embarrass themselves." The gimmicked surprises are not just frights for fright's sake, he added, but rather in service of a higher design:

> I wanted to keep a sense of authenticity, a sense—the integrity of what actually happened. Slavery was real, but it really happened right there. People were killed and worked and maimed right there in those walls that you walk, so that's not a joke. So I used the script, the existing script, but I broke it into the rooms now, and I wanted a bit of interactivity to help enhance, transport . . . What I wanted to do was to enhance the entertainment value, taking you back into time, to make it come alive. I wanted to make it come alive. So here we are in present day. There's a tour guide, they're in present day, talking to you, but while they're talking to you, there's this relic, this historical thing where a time machine takes us back. We see glimpses of what could have happened back in 1820s. So that's what I tried to do, and to get authentic like that.

Although the nightly reenactments at Rose Hall capitalize on and magnify a legend whose veracity is apocryphal (and easily debunked), Prout thoughtfully points out the larger—verifiable—historical truths at work in his production, which actually have little to do with Annie Palmer and her alleged crimes, as he made clear in our interview:

> KELLEY: So you've given theatrical expression to a hard, a sad reality about [Rose Hall]?
>
> PROUT: Exactly, exactly. What helped is the authenticity, the relevance that it happened right there. This building is standing and it was a plantation house in [the]1820s, and they really had slavery here, they had people whipped. So that's undeniable, and you are now part of that. When I go to that building and I kneel and I put my hand on the floor and on the walls, my ancestors were here, 100 years ago, they walked through, and that's real. So how I embellish, or how I tweak, or take artistic license to those very basic facts is another matter.

By Prout's own analysis, the White Witch legend functions as a metaphor; his staged adaptation is, he says, a theatrical vehicle for a broader message about slavery and emancipation in nineteenth-century Jamaica.

Designed as a participatory theatrical experience, the nighttime tour creates a more ludic atmosphere than does the daily tour. It is especially conducive to visitors who are looking for active—and interactive—fun (a remarkable thing, given the historical subtext of the site). Consider the introductory comments from Curley Roberts, one of the livelier tour guides at Rose Hall, which set the tone for the evening:

> CURLEY: [I need someone] to ward off the evil spirits.
> GUEST 1: Yes.
> GUEST 2: I will attract them. [*group laughter*]
> CURLEY: Do we have another brave person? Everybody else has just volunteered other people. [*group laughter*]
> CURLEY: Who says, "I'm brave"? Who's the brave person here?
> GUEST 3 [*an eight- to ten-year-old boy*]: I'm a brave person.
> CURLEY: You're a brave? And what's your name?
> GUEST 3: Morgan.
> CURLEY: Morgan.
> MORGAN: Uh-huh.
> CURLEY: Alright, Morgan. I got me two brave persons. Just take care of the coward guy. Okay? [*Curley shakes Morgan's hand*]
> MORGAN: Okay.
> CURLEY: Alright. Now listen. Everybody else, we work together as a team. Alright? Anything spooky happens—you scream, I run. [*group laughter*]

Curley continues with the scripted biography of Anne Palmer but injects his own idiosyncratic performative style and rhetoric to engage the audience:

> CURLEY: When Annie was only ten years old, her parents moved with her to Haiti. Shortly after, they contracted the yellow fever virus and died. She was then adopted by her nanny [*claps his hands loudly and jumps at audience*], a voodoo priestess. [*group laughter*]

> She taught her, I mean, everything she knew about witchcraft.
> Oh, by the way, folks I'm also working on my scary voice, okay?
> So feel free at any point in time to say, "Oooo." [*group laughter*]
> When she was eighteen years old her nanny died, so she left
> Haiti and came here to Jamaica in search of a wealthy husband.
> GUEST: Oooo. [*group laughter*]

Later, inside the house, Curley leads guests in a rotating path past
the large portrait of Annie, inviting them to witness for themselves
her mysterious wandering gaze:

> CURLEY: There is something interesting, but I'd rather say spooky,
>   about it. See, if you happen to walk along this pathway—follow
>   me—while staring at it, you will notice her eyes and head seem
>   to follow you wherever you go. Don't take my word for it. You
>   see it, John?
> JOHN: Yeah, I see it, man.
> CURLEY: Please tell me I'm not the only crazy person in here.
> JOHN: Yeah, man, it's real.
> CURLEY: And I know she seems to be looking at me, but I hope
>   she's looking at you, sir. [*To entire group*] Alright now, if you're
>   not seeing it happening, continue walking like that for the rest
>   of the tour. [*group laughter*] Alright, just kidding.

And in the commotion of screams and laughter following Takoo's bursting forth from the secret passageway door, Curley self-
deprecatingly says to the group, "Come on in. I don't feel so badly,
I'm not the only one that peed in my pants." The group laughs.

Framed in this way, the Rose Hall night tour offers the perfect
milieu for the "post-tourist," a visitor who playfully embraces the
negotiated experience of tourism in a postmodern world. A concept originally conceived by Feifer (1985) and developed further by
Rojek (1993), Ritzer and Liska (1997), and Urry and Larsen (2011),
post-tourism is marked by: (1) a recognition, and playful handling,
of the commodification of tourism; (2) an attraction to touristic
experience as an end in itself, rather than as a quest for education
or self-development; and (3) an awareness that the representations
of tourist sites are as meaningful as the sites themselves (Rojek

1993). Post-tourists are freed from the constraints of seeking only high cultural or only purely pleasurable touristic experiences; in fact, they move comfortably between the two and even draw amusement from the contrasts. They are fully aware of themselves as tourists, and they know that "tourism is a series of games with multiple texts and no single, authentic tourist experience" (Urry and Larsen 2011, 114).

Accordingly, at Rose Hall, whereas the day tour is suited to curious history buffs who are looking to learn something about the heritage site and its legendary background, the less conventional night tour presents itself as a venue for those seeking spirited, unpredictable, historically based fun. For tour guides and visitors alike, there is considerable room for improvisation. What evolves is a nuanced and fluid relationship between narrative authority and creativity, between the predetermined and the emergent in this interactive cultural performance. In terms of audience reception, the touristic pleasures of the night tour come as much from the playful consumption of the experience as from the production of it. The participatory energy of the performance is tangible: guests touring through Rose Hall at night are significantly more boisterous and convivial, frequently responding to comically scripted lines from the guides with improvised jokes of their own. There is a kind of frenetic electricity that overtakes the group members after frightening moments, and they become increasingly physically raucous as they make their way through the house. On more than one occasion, I observed visitors grabbing and scaring each other as the tour moved along, effecting shrieks and nervous giddiness. So the guests can be regarded as active agents and co-producers of the nighttime touristic experience at the Great House.

The guide leads visitors finally along a crushed coral walkway behind the house to Annie's tomb, lit dimly by a single flickering flame. By that time, after repeated cycles of escalating anxiety and sudden frightening release, the guests appear somewhat relieved to have exited the house; they let down their guard a bit and stop looking for danger. But the tour is not over, and the dénouement of the narrative, about Annie's ghost passing through the unmarked façade of the tomb, initiates one last trick of scary stagecraft: a heavy iron chain skitters cacophonously across the rough stone, causing the audience to jump with fright. This hair-raising moment is the dramatic finale of the tour, and it has symbolic significance, says Prout. One association is with the rolling calf, a ghostly bovine creature in Jamaican folklore whose body is wrapped in chains that clank in the nighttime. It's an apt connection in this case, as the local tradition holds that the rolling calf was first brought to Jamaica from Haiti by Annie Palmer herself. More poignantly, the clattering length of chain signifies the shackles of slave bondage being shattered. In that instant of the tour, there is a semiotic convergence: the storied rationale for Annie's haunting and the symbolized emancipation of a nation coalesce in a single moment of performance. It is no wonder that Jamaica's prime minister Hugh Shearer, in a speech celebrating the opening of the refurbished Rose Hall in 1971, proclaimed the story of Annie Palmer as "a treasure in our history" (*The Daily Gleaner*, February 27, 1971).

* * *

It is debatable whether Rose Hall is inhabited by ethereal spirits that might be documented by ghost hunters or contacted by psychics, but there is no denying the site's *haunting presence* as a place of national and ethnic heritage. Since the Rollins family purchased and renovated the house in 1960s, it has stood, for better or worse, as an imposing material reminder of Jamaica's plantation past. But its appeal as a touristic site has been sustained largely through the marketing of a culture of memory—through oral history and legend.

4

"That's What She Said"

Folk Expression Meets Media Meme

RICHARD DORSON, LONGTIME CHAIR OF Indiana University's Folklore Institute, repeatedly lamented the popularization and commercialization of folk material. He spent considerable energy in the 1960s and 1970s defining and protecting the borders of *authentic* folklore, as differentiated from what he considered commercialized "fakelore" in the popular press (1977; 1976; 1973, 201). Since then, scholars have come to recognize generally that the folk and the popular are not neatly discrete and separable realms. There is a fluid interconnection and extensive cross-pollination between the processes of face-to-face, oral communication and mediatized popular culture. In what Foster and Tolbert have termed the folkloresque, there are perceptions and performances in popular culture "[giving] the impression to the consumer (viewer, reader, listener, player) that they derive from existing folkloric traditions" (2016, 5); moreover, folkloric expressive behavior often imitates, varies, or otherwise manipulates circulating media forms. So, in terms of media production and folk reception, each feeds and also feeds on the other. Within that larger constellation, audience intervention and participation is not an isolated or new phenomenon, as we have established; the *opportunities* for intervention, however, have increased exponentially with the advent of digital communication and social media. New technology offers consumers more

DOI: 10.7330/9781607329909.c004

conduits and resources by which they can create their own reactive content as "co-producers," often altering, and sometimes hijacking, the communications of corporatized and institutional media. Thus, meaning and cultural value have essentially become crowdsourced in a hybridized blending of folk and virtual digital culture. Media consumers now have numerous channels through which they "speak back—and for themselves," observes Trevor Blank. "The widespread acceptance of the Internet as a communicative tool has only further demonstrated the behavioral hybridization of face-to-face and virtualized folk processes . . . Such a merger supports the notion of a 'folk' web but, more important, demonstrates how analog and digital hybridization shows users' agency rather than passive consumption" (2013, 19). Australian media scholar Axel Bruns coined the portmanteau term *produsage* to describe this interrelationship between corporate production and grassroots consumer use in the digital age. "The creation of shared content takes place in a networked, participatory environment which breaks down the boundaries between producers and consumers and instead enables all participants to be users as well as producers of information and knowledge," he argues (2008, 21). Media consumers, then, are avid *produsers*, who continually access, combine, remix, and mash up available media, retooling broadcast content to create new forms of expressive communication (275). We can see these forces all at play in the social and mediated workings of one jocular folk expression with a long history that was adopted and adapted in popular culture and then launched back into widespread folk circulation through the participatory practices of audiences.

"THAT'S WHAT SHE SAID"

The hit NBC sitcom *The Office*, which ran from 2005 to 2013, featured manager Michael Scott, played by Steve Carell, frequently employing a particular verbal quip that hinges on double entendre. He would add the suggestive rejoinder "That's what she said" (hereafter TWSS) to perfectly innocent comments uttered by coworkers, or even himself. Effectively recasting the innocuous into the salacious, the tagline is an exercise in semantics and points up the ways in which context constitutes meaning. The first three of the series' many instances of the joke appear in season 2, episode 2 (2005), entitled "Sexual Harassment," which centers on the office's review of workplace sexual harassment policies. Early in the episode Scott delivers the TWSS line on two separate occasions in response to innocent comments uttered by coworkers: "No thanks, I'm good," and "My mother's coming." These instances establish precedent and anticipate the center-piece joking exchange later in the episode, when Scott, mandated by human resources and the corporate office, makes a general announcement to his employees:

> MICHAEL SCOTT: Attention, everyone. Hello. Yes, I just want you to know that, this is not my decision, but from here on out, we can no longer be friends. And when we talk about things here, we must only discuss work-associated things. And you can consider this my retirement from comedy. And in the future, if I want to say something funny, or witty, or do an impression, I will no longer ever do any of those things.

Jim Halpert, played by John Krasinski, takes the opportunity to coax Scott into violating his new pledge right away, baiting him with setup lines in what clearly is already institutionalized as an of-fice joking practice:

> JIM: Does that include "That's what she said"?
> MICHAEL: Mhmm. Yes.
> JIM: Wow, that is really hard. You really think you can go all day long? Well, you always left me satisfied and smiling, so . . .
> MICHAEL: That's what she said! [*laughs uproariously*]

At play is an analogical mapping between two conceptual do-mains: the terminology of the literal, innocent source domain also describes situations and objects in a nonliteral, erotic target domain (Kiddon and Brun 2011, 89). The lewd suggestions were considered graphic enough that the episode originally aired with a warning about adult content and subject matter, a rarity for a network comedy.

PROTOTYPES

The rhetorical device appeared well before *The Office* debuted in 2005. Danish teenagers had been saying "Det sagde hun også igår" (That's what she said last night) since the 1990s, as the form had seeped into common usage in the decade after its first appearance in the 1980 comedy film *Kaptajn Klyde og hans venner vender tilbage* (*Captain Klyde and His Friends Return*); there's an instance of the joke in the 1992 film *Wayne's World*; and Chevy Chase purportedly inserted the one-liner into a Weekend Update segment on *Saturday Night Live* in 1975, what some claim is the first occurrence in American pop culture. Fact is, the joke has roots in an earlier humorous trope from the UK, "as the actress said to the bishop." Eric Partridge, an authority on British slang, explains how the idiom operates similarly to TWSS: "As the actress said to the bishop—and vice versa—is an innuendo scabrously added to an entirely innocent remark," he says, "as in 'It's too stiff for me to manage it—as the actress said to the bishop' or, conversely, 'I can't see what I'm doing—as the bishop said to the actress'" (1977, 31).

Drawing upon well-trafficked idioms like "as the man in the play says," which occurred regularly in eighteenth- and nineteenth-century farces as a way to "[lend] humorous authority to a perhaps frivolous statement" (Partridge 1977, 32), the more suggestive actress/bishop expression most likely originated around Edwardian times, fed by popular attitudes about the English theater, in which actresses were often thought to have loose morals, supplementing their meager income by prostitution (Pullen 2005). That perception, coupled with the age-old image of the lascivious clergyman, created an unlikely comical pair.

But even the actress/bishop one-liners are indebted to a much older form, the well-studied Wellerism—traditionally a three-part proverbial expression in which a statement, an identified speaker, and some attributed action are combined for humorous effect ("'I've gotten a little behind in my work,' said the butcher as he backed into the meat grinder"). A literary form dating from classical Greek, appearing in sixteenth-century European proverb collections and in the work of such notables as Sir Walter Scott, Jonathan Swift, and Shakespeare (Baer 1983, 173; Mieder 1997), the Wellerism later became immensely popular. It was so named for Sam Weller, the comically exuberant Cockney bootblack in Charles Dickens's *Pickwick Papers* (1868) who has a particular penchant for this verbal construction. Weller frequently erupts with commonplace but quotable phrases that he then ascribes to peculiar sources, accompanied by actions outrageously incongruous to the conversational context. A few examples:

> "He wants you particklar; no one else'll do," as the Devil's private secretary said ven he fetched avay Doctor Faustus. (vol. 2, 8)

> "Business first, pleasure arterwards," as King Richard the Third said wen he stabbed t'other king in the Tower, afore he smothered the babbies. (vol.2, 209)

> "It's over, and can't be helped, and that's one consolation," as they always says in Turkey, ven they cuts the wrong man's head off. (vol.3, 88)

In fact, Dickens owes his early fame to the character Sam Weller. The first three installments of the serialized *Pickwick* did not sell well, only around 400 copies; but once Weller was introduced in the fourth installment, sales increased exponentially, to 4,000; then, after Weller had become a regular as Pickwick's hired valet, 40,000 of each monthly number by the end of the serial's run in 1837. As Nina Martyris (2015) observes of the phenomenon she calls the "Sam Weller Bump,"

> Everyone up and down the social ladder began to devour *Pickwick*, from butchers' boys to John Ruskin, who read *Pickwick* so often he claimed to know it by heart. Copies were passed from hand to hand and read aloud as family entertainment. The critics effused with praise. Dickens, who was twenty-four and expecting his first child, had become a household name.

Proffering homespun proverbial wisdom as he does in his distinctive idiolect, "Sam Weller introduces the English people," G. K. Chesterton (1911, 21) extols. And the bootblack's signature rhetoric was widely understood to signify the "genuine mother-wit and unadulterated vernacular idioms of the lower classes" (*Quarterly Review* 1837, 507).

With nearly fifty instances appearing in the novel, eclectic Wellerisms became emblematic logos of *Pickwick*; they were themselves popularized and actively commodified as their own brand of humorous traditional apothegm (Pollack-Pelzner 2011, 537–43). The quotable, and portable, sayings—transformed into folksy citations from bizarre sources—were decontextualized and inserted ready-made into a wide variety of popular literature and entertainment—newspapers, joke books, theatrical performances, and the like. Accompanying this was an aggressive merchandising campaign that included playing cards, cigars, Sam Weller puzzles, candy tins, and china figurines. *Pickwick* was to be the most popular book of Dickens's career, selling 1.6 million copies, due in no small part to the incorporation and manipulation of traditional material in the form of the Wellerism, which captured the early Victorian popular consciousness as "a national mania" (Baer 1983, 173). Here, we have the jocular attribution of a quote, what may be the taproot of the TWSS joking form, but also an early model of interactive exchange between folk culture and popular entertainment, something ancestrally akin to a contemporary media meme, albeit long, long before the digital age.

By the turn of the century, Wellerisms had seeped like water into everyday idiomatic speech on both sides of the Atlantic; in one variety, for instance, the monkey, which in English slang often figured as a "witty, pragmatically wise, ribald simulacrum of unrestrained mankind" (Partridge 1977, 32), appeared frequently as the vocalizer with a scatological fixation. As in: "'You must draw the line somewhere,' as the monkey said when peeing across the carpet"; "'A little goes a long way,' as the monkey said when he pee'd over the cliff"; "'All is not gold that glitters,' as the monkey said when he pee'd in the sunshine"; and "'That remains to be seen,' as the monkey said when he shat in the sugar bowl."

The structure of the more recent TWSS jokes is analogous to these literary and folk prototypes: someone proffers a "host" statement, whose meaning alone is unremarkable—but then ancillary information about the speaker and circumstances places the original utterance in a new humorous light. Through the painstaking efforts of scholars like Mieder and Kingsbury, the Wellerism has been thoroughly documented, historicized, and catalogued (Mieder and Kingsbury 1994; Mieder 1997). We know what Wellerisms look like and where they come from, but there is still much to learn about how they are actually used rhetorically in social life. For instance, it is generally assumed with the Wellerism proper that the quote and accompanying attribution are uttered as a single phrase by one speaker, a ready-made piece of proverbial wisdom with a comical twist. But on occasion the attribution is introduced unexpectedly as a punch line by a second speaker, as is typical in the actress/bishop and TWSS rejoinders.

Actress/bishop jokes (and their variations) might not be traditional Wellerisms, strictly speaking, because they don't supply the third module of the customary tripartite pattern; that is, they don't describe any actions of the couple. But the form certainly is Welleristic, we might say, and the jokes do conjure up something of an *implied* micro-narrative just by the dramatic tension that arises when these two antithetical character types are cast together—a dramatic tension well appreciated by British comic artist Brian Bolland, who authored a series titled "The Actress and the Bishop." The pair, he said, "[looks] like the punch line of a smutty joke" (2006, 202). (With the verbal TWSS joke, on the other hand, we know nothing about the nondescript hypersexualized "she" whose lewd talk—upon reiteration—renders nearly all language as potentially obscene.) Variations on the actress/bishop include the actress and soldier, the girl and sailor, the vicar and the tart, the art mistress and gardener, the windmill girl and stockbroker (this last one still denotes an actress, referencing the Windmill Theatre in Westminster, which was a variety and revue playhouse famous for its nude fan dancers and for never closing its doors throughout World War II).[1]

By the late 1920s, jocular phrases in the form of "as the *x* said to the *y*" appeared often in everyday parlance. As an example, in a rare surviving sound test from the 1929 film *Blackmail*, director Alfred Hitchcock tried on the set to embarrass his female lead, Anny Ondra:

A.H.: Now, Miss Ondra. You asked me to let you hear your voice on the talking picture. [*unintelligible*]

A.O.: But Hitch, you mustn't do that.

A.H.: Why not?

A.O.: Well, because I can't speak well.

A.H.: Do you realize the squad van will be here any moment?

A.O.: No, really? Oh my gosh, I'm terribly frightened.

A.H.: Why, have you been a bad woman or something?

A.O.: Well, not just bad, but . . .

A.H.: But you have slept with men?

A.O.: Oh, no [*blushing and turning away*].

A.H.: You have not? Come here! Stand in your place. Otherwise it will not come out right—**as the girl said to the soldier**. [*laughing and signaling to the cameraman*] That's enough.

The actress/bishop quip became widely popular through the detective fiction of Leslie Charteris, most famous for his novels of the 1930s chronicling the adventures of Simon Templar, "the Saint" (some readers may remember the later British television series starring Roger Moore in the title role). The catchphrase circulated extensively among the Royal Air Force by the end of World War II, and became well established generally in the 1950s.

THE OFFICE BUMP

Ricky Gervais did occasionally invoke the actress/bishop line in the British *Office* (2001–3), but not nearly to the extent that TWSS became a part of the fabric of the American spin-off—and the British catchphrase certainly didn't activate the profuse imitation across media as did TWSS in the American version. The phrase became viral through its repeated use on *The Office*. In the seven seasons that featured Carrell (who left the show in 2011), the TWSS joke appeared no fewer than forty-four times (more than one fan website has compiled and catalogued them all).

Carrell's acceptance speech for the 2010 People's Choice Award for Favorite TV Comedy Actor was delivered as an extended TWSS bit:

S.C.: Ladies and gentlemen, if you would repeat after me: That's what she said [*gestures to audience*].

AUDIENCE [*in unison*]: That's what she said. [*laughter*]

S.C.: Wow, I cannot believe it [*handling award*]; this is much bigger than I thought it would be.

AUDIENCE: That's what she said.

S.C.: You know what I'm going to do tonight? I am going to go home and I am going to find a special place to put this.

AUDIENCE: That's what she said.

S.C.: I'll be completely honest with you. I wanted this so bad I could taste it.

AUDIENCE: That's what she said.

S.C.: Thank you, this is a true honor. And I am glad I came.

AUDIENCE: That's what . . . [*tapering off as Carrell's interrupts*]

S.C.: No! no! [*walks off stage*].

Thereafter, any mention of the TWSS joke became a shorthand marker for the show. In 2013, one entertainment website heralded the finale of the series with the headline "Last Call for 'That's What She Said' Jokes: *The Office* Is Closing" (Adams 2013). And another recapped the last episode with the derivative title "That's All She Said" (Tedder 2013). Carrell returned for the finale, and not surprisingly his first line in the episode was "That's what she said."

Beyond the show, the number of allusions and oblique TWSS references in other TV programs and film is astounding. Here is just a sampling:

Family Guy, *"Emission Impossible" (3.11, 2001)*

BRIAN [*constructing a cradle*]: OK, insert rod support A into slot B.

PETER: **That's what . . .**

BRIAN: If you say "That's what she said" one more time, I'm gonna pop you.

Frasier, *"War of the Words" (9.18, 2002)*

FRASIER: Frederick, aren't you gonna say something?

FREDDIE: Talked to Mom today.

FRASIER: You're a bigger man than I am.
FREDDIE: *That's what she said.*

Without a Paddle *(Steven Brill, 2004)*

TOM: This could lead out of here. Dan, you're the only one small
     enough to go through.
JERRY: *That's what she said.*
DAN: It's . . . it's a mine shaft. They had to get the ore out somehow.
TOM: It's our only chance, Dano.

Gilmore Girls, *"Fight Face"* (6.2, 2005)

LORELAI [*while looking at Twykham house*]: It's big.
SOOKIE: *That's what she said.*
LORELAI: Good one.
SOOKIE: Hey, I'm still twelve.
LORELAI: But I meant the house. It's very big.

Larry the Cable Guy: Health Inspector
(Trent Cooper, 2006)

AMY: It's right in front of your face, and you don't wanna see it. You
     wanna close your eyes and pretend it's not happening.
LARRY: *That's what she said.*

Veronica Mars, *"Weevils Wobble but They Don't Go Down"*
(3.19, 2007)

MAC: I feel so bad for Wallace. He needs more thrust.
LOGAN: Don't say it.
DICK: *That's what she said.*

One Tree Hill, *"Screenwriter's Blues"* (6.16, 2009)

BROOKE: I slept with Julian.
PEYTON: Come again?
BROOKE: *That's what she said.* She being me . . . it's a joke.
PEYTON: I know. I get it.

Two and a Half Men, *"Good Morning, Mrs. Butterworth"* *(6.23, 2009)*

ALAN [*with puppet named Danny*]: Howdy-do, Charlie.

CHARLIE: Get that ugly thing out of my face.

ALAN: ***That's what she said.*** Oh, Danny! Danny, you're horrible.

Extreme Movie *(Adam Jay Epstein and Andrew Jacobson, 2009)*

MR. MATTHEWS [*addressing students entering the classroom*]: Bring it on in! We got a lot to do and a little time to do it! Wanna make sure we can cram it all in. ***That's what she said***. Ha ha ha! You guys know what I'm talkin' about.

Rules of Engagement, *"Indian Giver"* *(4.7, 2010)*

RUSSELL: I wanted to tell you that . . . God, this is harder than I thought.

SUNEETHA: ***That's what she said*** [*laughs*]. I got that from you. It makes me laugh every time.

RUSSELL: Yea, well, it's solid. It's one of the classics.

Peace, Love & Misunderstanding *(Bruce Beresford, 2012)*

ZOE: Stop it, or I'm gonna throw it out the window. God, I swear that thing's like your third arm.

JAKE: ***That's what she said.***

ZOE: Seriously, it's obnoxious.

JAKE: Well, Zoe, you never know when life is gonna happen.

Face Off [*competition reality show about makeup artists*], *"Subterranean Terror"* *(5.4, 2013)*

CONTESTANT 1: So I'm definitely going to get this thing molded today.

CONTESTANT 2: Oh my gosh, that's going to be so big.

CONTESTANT 1: ***That's what she said***. It's starting to set up, so I know that I can come in first thing in the morning.

Faking It, *"Remember the Croquembouche"* (1.5, 2014)

FARRAH: Both of you, to your rooms, now!

LAUREN: This isn't gonna come out of my hair until I shower.

AMY: **That's what she said.**

LAUREN: Classy. Are you adopted? Because you are nothing like
     your mother.

Palo Alto *(Gia Coppola, 2014)*

APRIL: Wow, it's kind of hard.

LUKE: **That's what she said.**

TEDDY: It's cool looking.

LUKE: Ted, check this out.

Rush, *"Don't Ask Me Why"* (1.2, 2014)

RUSH [*sewing up a hand wound*]: You're probably gonna feel some
     pressure, but it shouldn't hurt.

VICTORIA: **That's what he said.**

RUSH: [*after she winces*]: Sorry.

VICTORIA: No, you're not.

Unbreakable Kimmy Schmidt, *"Kimmy Has a Birthday!"*
(1.9, 2015)

DONG: . . . stealing parts from other delivery guys' bikes.

LILLIAN: Yeah, okay, I'll help you get it in. **That's what she said.**

The Night Shift, *"Back at the Ranch"* (2.2, 2015)

PAUL: So, um, my trick is that, uh [*giving ball to patient*] here you
     go . . . that I have them squeeze the ball . . .

DRUNK PATIENT 1: **That's what she said.**

DRUNK PATIENT 2: No, you mean "That's what he said."
     Dumb ass.

DRUNK PATIENT 1: No, that's not what I . . .

MICHAEL: Hey, we're trying to work here.

DRUNK PATIENT 1: **That's what she said.** [*laughs*] Oh, that one didn't
     make sense.

This sort of joke is the red meat of slob comedies, and an aggregate of examples like this accrues a sort of punch line fatigue. I include the list to demonstrate just how widespread the joke had become into the 2010s. Sometimes a self-referential awareness of the popularity of the joking form is scripted right in:

Rules of Engagement, *"Jeff's Wooby" (1.7, 2007)*

RUSSELL: Come on!

ADAM: You know how some people make double-entendres and they go . . . *"That's what she said."*

RUSSELL: Yeah, I did go to junior high school.

ADAM: I think Jesse is "she." I mean, she's the "she" of "That's what she said."

Raising Hope: *"Everybody Flirts . . . Sometimes" (1.20, 2011)*

JIMMY: Wow, this is harder than I thought.

BARNEY: *That's what she said.*

JIMMY: What?

BARNEY: That's just a joke a guy on a TV show I used to watch says.

Two and a Half Men, *"What a Lovely Landing Strip" (9.11, 2011)*

WALDEN: I think this could get serious.

ALAN: Wow, you're moving pretty quick, aren't you?

WALDEN: *That's what she said.* [*Jake laughs*]

ALAN: What are you laughing at?

JAKE: He did a "That's what she said" joke.

WALDEN: Because that's what she said.

JAKE: Oh, that's not funny.

30 Rock, *"TGS Hates Women" (5.16, 2011)*

ABBY: I don't know where you found that, but I am taking it down. [*laughs*] *That's what she said!*

LIZ: Hey, first of all, Steve Carell owns "That's what she said." He owns it.

30 Minutes or Less *(Ruben Fleischer, 2011)*

TRAVIS *[cleaning a pool]*: Where do all these leaves come from?
DWAYNE: Where the hell do you think, dude? From fucking trees.
TRAVIS: ***That's what she said.***
DWAYNE: No, "That's what she said" jokes don't work with that. It
    has to be in a sexual reference.

In the wake of wide popularity of TWSS jokes, there was a proliferation of virtual communities assembling TWSS straight lines from
all sorts of media (TV, film, video games, lectures, song lyrics, book
titles, even city council meetings)—and *Star Wars* seems to have been
one of the favorites here: an alliance pilot, upon seeing the Death
Star for the first time, says, "Look at the size of that thing"; Han
Solo says to Chewbacca before their escape into the trash compacter,
"Get in there. I don't care what you smell." And countless others.

    In simply doing his job, one frenetic sports announcer call-
ing a horse race in 2009 broadcast unintentionally—but enthusiastically—a sustained TWSS gag:

> Around the turn, a length and a half on top Speak Peace.
> Between horses second and the outside Run, Mama Bear, Run.
> That's What She Said now coming through along the inside, and
> now veers to the outside for racing room. Inside the final furlong,
> Shake N Quake the leader—That's What She Said starts to reel
> her in on the outside. A sixteenth to go. Shake N Quake digging
> down. That's What She Said coming to her; it's down to these
> two. That's What She Said on the outside! Getting up—That's
> What She Said![2]

The owners of the horse no doubt anticipated the string of innuendoes that would result as race announcers repeatedly shouted
TWSS interspersed with other unusual horse monikers. The inferences assuredly did not go unnoticed by those who commented on
the YouTube video of the race, which is titled *Michael Scott Buys a
Horse.* One person recalled seeing this same horse in a close race
with another one by the name of "you-make-me-thor." One can
imagine the endless potential for lewd overtones. A 2010 posting

of outrageous high school detention notices included an example from Redmond Junior High, where one teacher, not amused with a pupil named Dalton Duncan, writes: "Another student made the comment 'you need to push it in further' (innocent comment) and Dalton added 'that's what she said.'" Earlier, at another school, a Ms. Friedrichs had sent Richard Avis to detention, reporting: "After a student said 'can it be that big?' his comment was 'that's what she said.'" And in a distinctive teacherly idiom, she adds, "These inappropriate comments are made too often."

Sometimes graffiti completes the thought. A number of photographs have been posted online of signs with the phrase TWSS graffitied below or to the side, including: a warning to employees in an office restroom—"The sink is loose. Please be gentle"; a posted sign in a driveway—"Pull out"; a billboard advertising vitamin-enhanced water—"Easy to swallow"; a cautionary road sign "Slippery when wet"; and a notice in a billiard hall—"Please do not switch balls between tables." A few websites simply collect images under the banner TWSS, and we are left to connect the dots from there, including: a billboard for the Newport aquarium—"Guess What's Coming?"; directions at a loading dock—"EZ In"; a notice on a glass door at a convenience store—"Pull Out"; a posted directive for cyclists—"Please dismount"; a church marquee—"He is Coming Again"; and the sign for a British Columbia store selling furniture for tiny apartments—"OMG It's Small." There are more than a dozen TWSS apps available for iPhones and androids. Most of them will play recorded male and female voices uttering the phrase in a variety of inflections, some clearly in tones suggestively lewd. With these apps, stripped away from any surrounding verbal context, the punch line becomes pure commodity. They appear to be marketed to individuals who have the urge to insert the phrase TWSS into conversation, but who don't have the chutzpah to say the actual words themselves.

In 2011, the joke became the subject of an academic study at the University of Washington. Researchers Chloé Kiddon and Yuriy Brun set out to develop a computer program to identify sentences that would potentially elicit the TWSS punch line. The study examined the ways in which humans recognize and employ double entendre, and whether machines could be programmed to do the same. Attempting to formularize in computer code the semantic and cultural understandings implicit in the joke, Kiddon and Brun identified necessary lexical markers—the presence of nouns that are often euphemisms for more sexually suggestive nouns (like banana) and syntactical structures common to X-rated literature.[3] To train the computer program, which they named DEviaNT (for Double Entendre via Noun Transfer), the researchers assembled 1.5 million sentences from erotic literature and 57,000 from more mainstream texts, drawing from *The Brown Corpus* of American English (Francis and Kučerna 1979), including exceedingly unerotic entries like the annual report of the Carnegie Foundation and Barry Goldwater's 1961 essay "A Foreign Policy for America." Analyzing large batches of lexical content, DEviaNT began to recognize which terms often appear together in bawdy contexts, thus indicating potential TWSS opportunities, and which tend to accumulate in more conventional and modest discourse. The program then processed more than 2,000 sentences from t-w-s-s-stories.com, an online forum for TWSS jokes.

DEviaNT utilized an "adjective sexiness function" and a "verb sexiness function" to gauge the likelihood that a given sentence would work as a TWSS joke. For example, *suck, ride, lick, bang, eat, come, blow,* and *squeeze* all have high verb sexiness functions, while *call, promise, gather, visit, walk,* and *sweep* have low ones. Kiddon and Brun created the functions by studying the modifiers and verbs that typically circulate around an aggregation of seventy-six explicit, predetermined nouns, most of which describe sexual objects or body parts. Trained in a sense to be raunchy (Weems 2014, 112), the program identified TWSS setups with about 70 percent accuracy and achieved, writes culture blogger Katy Waldman, "the same dirty-joke-telling ability as a 12-year-old boy" (2011). This sort of metaphorical mapping, useful though it may be in the field of computational linguistics, is a bit quantified for folklorists, perhaps (see Oring 2019, 165–68); but the study does demonstrate an applied clinical interest in the processes of this pop culture phenomenon.

MEME-ING TWSS

Google searches for the phrase TWSS spiked notably in 2009–10, corresponding almost exactly to the run of season 6 of *The Office*, and I think we can extrapolate that the show's accumulation of TWSS references over the years reached a sort of tipping point by then that launched the phrase generally into the popular consciousness. That, and the extensive repetition of this folklore form across the digital landscape, sent it on its way to becoming a bona fide media meme. The application of biological meme theory to folkloristics is certainly not without its quandaries. In the fullest scholarly treatment on the subject, Elliott Oring (2014a, 2014b) thoroughly interrogates precedent studies of memetics and folkloristics by Pimple (1996), Zipes (2008, 2011b), Ellis (2003, 75–97), and Heath, Bell, and Sternberg (2001). Oring is especially critical of earlier tautological formulations claiming that memes demonstrate "fitness" simply by dint of their continued replication; in the end, he remains skeptical as to the value of memetics theory for cultural analysis because, he argues, the operative principle of selection in cultural dissemination has not been *conclusively* demonstrated.

Oring's discussion focuses primarily on nonmediated cultural forms, however. Once the consideration broadens to include the wider expanse of electronic communication—broadcast media, the internet, digital social networking—the possibilities for proliferation, and therefore evolutionary selection, would seem greater, albeit still difficult to measure. While descriptions of media memes as "self-replicating" are flawed, as they fail to account for human agency in the production and dissemination of culture, the conceptual notion of the meme does provide "a compelling way to understand the dispersion of cultural movements," Jenkins, Ford, and Green accept, "especially when seemingly innocuous or trivial trends spread and die in rapid fashion" (2013, 19). Complexities arise when the supposed replicating "selfish genes" meet social selves (Haig 2020). Within those larger questions about why certain instances of folklore (face-to-face, mediated, or otherwise) multiply while others go extinct (Oring 2014a, 473), I would suggest that the TWSS joke replicated effusively, and remained robust for a period, partly as a function of its brevity and relatively stable form.

It should be noted here that there is a distinction to be made between virals and memes. The difference lies in variability, notes Limor Shifman. Virals are single cultural units (videos, photos, or jokes, e.g.) that proliferate in numerous copies, while internet memes are comprised of collections of remixed, mashed-up, and repurposed texts (2014, 56). In that regard, then, TWSS jokes qualify as both virals and memes. The four-word TWSS text presents low variability, disseminated virally as it is in a consistent, compact verbal form. But the truncated (and therefore easily transmitted) jocular phrase is embedded in wide varieties of conversational and/or visual contexts, whose meanings then shift toward the salacious as a result. So as a rhetorical device, the TWSS tagline is transformative, retroactively refiguring benign antecedent discourse into extended dirty joke telling. There is something of a balancing act here, struck between adherence to the established patterns of the meme and creative innovation in novel expressions of it (see Nissenbaum and Shifman 2017, 493–94; Milner 2013). The memetic quality stems from the variously adapted *uses* of the joke, employed socially and across digital media in myriad ways. Furthermore, the TWSS joking complex demonstrates several of the factors that Shifman says contribute to (both) viral and memetic success: simplicity, humor, and the opportunity for audience participation (95).

All of this imitation is curious—given that the television show appears to hold up the joke as an example of *inept* humor. That is, at its core, *The Office* is about social clumsiness, and an important depiction of that is Michael Scott's particular brand of humor—almost always awkward or desperate and rarely funny. The show's overuse of the hackneyed TWSS retort is satirical—in a sense showing just how stale the joke had already become. As comedian Dave Hill said, "They brought [the joke] back from the dead and then shot it in the face" (Official Comedy, 2:42). Many of the folk and pop culture imitations seem to miss the irony—propagating the form without realizing that it is being lampooned as a model of the unoriginal, the banal, and the sophomoric. But all satire has multiple meanings that collide in a variety of possible audience responses. We should consider how the show's representations of workplace gender politics—and the memetic TWSS joke rippling outward from it—reinforce or controvert patriarchal hegemony.

CRITIQUE OR AFFIRMATION?

Birthisel and Martin find that while the gender hierarchies represented on *The Office* affirm established male-dominated workplace stereotypes, the mockumentary production style (with interspersed talking-head interviews that allow coworkers to voice their disapproval of Michael Scott's behavior) and the lack of a prerecorded laugh track (which allows the audience to find its own laughing points) "opens more possibilities for oppositional readings" (2013, 75). In many ways *The Office* presents a model for laughing at and mocking others, but it remains unclear from the show's positioning whether we are invited to laugh "at" or "with" the misogynistic humor. "Satire's calling card," argue Gray, Jones, and Thompson, "is the ability to produce social scorn or damning indictments through *playful* means and, in the process, transform the aggressive act of ridicule into the more socially acceptable act of rendering something ridiculous" (2009, 12–13). The key is ludic hyperbole. The success of comedic satire rests on the audience's recognition that the outrageous behavior of an offensive character is not real but performed; it can be laughed at more easily when perceived to be a *burlesque* of the socially unacceptable. Actors who perform caricatured versions of intolerance, for instance, in what Fiske (2011) calls "excess as hyperbole," lack realism and approach a kind of self-awareness typical of camp. *Mock* offensive behavior is more comedically comfortable (and safer for producers as audience polarization is diminished) (Thompson 2009, 41). But audience response defies oversimplification. With regard to *The Office*, Michael Scott's unrealistically hyperbolic, and therefore mockable, office antics paired with the quasi-realistic documentary production style of the show muddy the waters of reception. Furthermore, excess itself provides for contradictory meanings: "There is a straight meaning which is borne by the face value of the words and fits the dominant ideology, and there is an excess of meaning left over once this dominant meaning has been made that is available for viewers to use to undercut the straight meaning" (Fiske 2011, 91).

Ambiguities abound for diverse readers/viewers of *The Office*, which both dramatizes sexism and simultaneously critiques it. The satirical posture of the production does not ensure any one particular audience response, whether hegemonic or resistant. John Hollon, a columnist for *Workforce Management*, sees the program as a "just-barely warped reflection" of workaday office existence. "The big joke of *The Office*," he writes,

> isn't that it's about such an off-the-charts dysfunctional workplace,
> but rather, that so many of us can so closely identify with the
> issues, the situations and the personalities in the show. Actually, it
> isn't much of a caricature at all—just a slightly juiced up depiction
> of the real workplace craziness that we all deal with on more days,
> and in more ways, did we ever care to admit. (2007, 34)

To date, there is no quantitative study analyzing audience reception of *The Office*. But we can draw some correlative inferences from two important audience studies of *All in the Family*, Norman Lear's 1970s sitcom whose central character Archie Bunker lampoons working-class bigotry. Neil Vidmar and Milton Rokeach's "Archie Bunker's Bigotry: A Study in Selective Perception and Exposure" (1974) found a significant measure of selective perception among viewers of the show: that is, viewers' prior attitudes effectively predicted their reactions. Progressive viewers perceived the show as a clear satire of bigotry, while other viewers, who through empirical means were determined to be ethnocentric, prejudiced, or intolerant, identified with Archie Bunker as someone who "tells it like it is." Different frames of reference among the viewers ascribed different meanings: some applauded Archie for his racist viewpoints (which rationalized their own), while others praised the show for mocking racist attitudes. The show's creators had asserted that the character of Archie Bunker was purportedly a "means by which bigoted television viewers would perceive the absurdity of their opinions, beliefs, and values," but Surlin and Tate (1976) interrogated the widely held critical concern that Archie was normalizing rather than diminishing bigotry. Their study accorded with earlier findings that the disposition of individual viewers shaded whether they would perceive the satirical humor as critique or affirmation.

And so it may be with *The Office*. Birthisel and Martin's unsubstantiated claim that "it is highly unlikely that audiences would interpret [the show's] workplace behavior as acceptable" (2013, 76) offers no evidence beyond just their *belief* that that is the case; without empirical audience research, we are left to speculate as to how viewers might perceive the show's chauvinistic focalizing character Michael Scott, who could be viewed as an awkward but harmless buffoon with an offbeat sense of humor or derided as a misogynist whose sexist jokes create a miserable predatory work environment for women.

Similarly, TWSS, the signature joke that *The Office* catapulted into wide popularity, carries with it a wide range of applied meanings depending on circumstances and social use. We can analyze the most common folkloresque instances of the joke (that is, performances of the joke in popular culture). The joke is typically gendered in its application, spoken almost exclusively by males. When delivered male to male, it smacks of blustery locker room talk in which men competitively assert heteronormative masculinity by boasting about sexual exploits that routinely objectify and demean women. In its extreme, this sort of male repartee is a rhetorical underpinning of rape culture. But sexist language, as we know, is not exchanged only fraternally. Nor is the TWSS joke, for that matter. When a male injects the TWSS tagline into discourse with women, which occurs more commonly than male/male iterations, the implications are more outwardly aggressive and predatory. The semantic maneuver denies women (and antecedent "actresses," "art mistresses," "windmill girls," and so on) the agency of determining the meaning of their own speech; their own communication is sexualized without consent. Couched as it is in the language of a suggestive joke uttered typically by men in the company of women, TWSS in use sometimes appears as a jocular rhetorical version of the widespread sexist ethos "No means maybe."

TWSS IN USE

These observations pertain to the joking form as it appears in TV
and film and is repurposed by media consumers across digital conduits. There is scant ethnographic information, however, on uses
of the joke in the unmediated vernacular. While real-life detention notices or the occasional graffito, as mentioned above, provide
hints, we lack data on the folk *performance* of the joke. A Reddit
thread from 2011 asks users, "What's the best 'that's what she said'
moment you've ever witnessed?" Here are a few representative
examples from among more than eighty responses:

UNNAMED
We were peer grading our math papers in 10th grade. Mine was
being marked by a guy friend a few rows away. When we finished
grading we were told to put them in a folder in the front of the
room. My friend yelled from a ways away "Do you want to see it
first or do you want me to just put it in?" There was probably a
good 20 seconds of silence throughout the entire room, which
is unusual for a sophomore class. The silence was followed by 4
people saying "that's what she said."

TICK_TOCK_CLOCK
I went on a backpacking trip in Boy Scouts. Spending several
days in the wilderness, we tended toward cruder humor, including a "that's what she said" contest among the Scouts. On the
second-to-last day, it had rained, and my friend noticed a path
with sunken-in footprints. [He said,] "That's going to look
interesting when it dries." And it was the grey-haired, grizzled
Scout leader who called him on it [with a "that's what she said"].
Everyone burst out laughing.

MINDBODYPROBLEM
Two summers ago I tried to pay for a soda and some snacks with
a $50 bill at the Grand Canyon gift shop. It was about 8 a.m.
While her male co-worker watched, I tried to hand the $50 bill to
the girl behind the counter to pay for my few snacks.

> GIRL: "I can't take anything that big this early."
> ME: "That's what she said."
> GIRL: [*stares blankly*]
> MALE CO-WORKER: [*laughs out loud*]

PLASTICPLAN

I was in my criminal law class last year. We were covering the rape cases and the professor asked a student to present defense counsel's arguments. The guy he chose was wearing a pink shirt with "that's what she said" on it.

KEEPCALMANDCARRYON

I tried to enter through the rear door on a bus and the driver goes "please don't use the back door," and I blurted out "that's what she said." The cadre of middle-aged women on the bus were not amused.

Although they affirm the diffuse popularity of the TWSS joking trope in 2011, truncated and decontextualized entries such as these offer us little insight into performative features or the ways in which the joke works as social action.

Luckily, my research uncovered a 2009 post from the personal blog of Isley Unruh, who at that time was a librarian in Kansas. The blog, still active, is self-described as "focused on film, heavy metal music, Tolkien, board games, and general silliness (and not necessarily in that order)."[4] Unruh's post abstracts the "Top Five Classic TWSS Moments" from his own experience. He considers himself "a master of sorts of the [TWSS] phrase," and asserts winkingly that "TWSS never really gets old no matter how many times you inject it into conversation." Usefully, Unruh documented actual situations in which the joke appeared, with contemporaneous notes on attendant contexts. Like the Reddit entries, some are banal or predictable applications, as in the reported instance of Unruh watching the film *Dark Passage* with his father and introducing the joke in response to a line spoken by Lauren Bacall: "I wish I knew of some way to break it off without hurting him, but all I can do is wait for him to get tired of coming." On another occasion, Unruh dispenses the tagline after his friend Brenda consoles the pet dog that is begging for extra rib bones in its bowl: "Sorry dog, there is already a bone in there."

But two others of his recorded examples give us real insight into more nuanced social uses of the TWSS joke. In one instance, Unruh is at the gym weight training with his friends Carol and

Dillon. Between lifts, they fall into a discussion of each other's preference for lowering the weight after a particular behind-the-neck weight-training maneuver.

> UNRUH: I'd rather catch on the front of my shoulders since I some-
> times miss the sweet spot when I drop it behind my head.
> DILLON: I prefer to take it from behind . . . uh . . . crap . . . that's
> what she said!
> CAROL: You can't do yourself!
> DILLON: Well, I figured I better get on in there before Isley did!
> UNRUH: That's what she said!

Here, Dillon appears to make the joke reluctantly but with some sense of social obligation to preempt Unruh, who was not likely to miss the TWSS opportunity of such a ripe setup line. Carol's interjection "You can't do it yourself" identifies a generic expectation of the joking form, which typically dictates that the setup line and the punch line be delivered by different parties. Dillon's explanation becomes itself an unwitting setup for Unruh's final TWSS callback.

Another exchange, reported secondhand from Unruh's friends Cori, Nadine, and Shena after a lunch outing, becomes a metacommentary on the whole TWSS joking enterprise.

> CORI: This sausage is too big for my buns.
> SHENA: I'm not even going to make the obvious joke right now.
> NADINE: It's a good thing Isley isn't here.
> SHENA: Now THAT'S what she said!

Shena's recognition that there is an "obvious joke" to be made points up the common frame of reference among these women. For them, the TWSS wisecrack is floating in the ether. Nadine is convinced that their mutual friend Unruh, had he been present, would have chimed in with a resounding TWSS tagline to the invitingly suggestive setup about sausage and buns; and, as in the preceding example, her evaluative comment "It's a good thing Isley isn't here" is reconceived as an opportune straight line in its own right. Shena's final TWSS rejoinder is refreshingly feminist in this instance, contravening the typical masculinist posture of this over-worked joking form. Further, Unruh's highlighting this exchange on his blog, wherein he is the butt of the joke, self-deprecatingly *confronts* chauvinistic readings of the TWSS "text."

At the time of Unruh's post, the TWSS joking form had entered the working repertoire of his friends and was well trafficked among them. The transcriptions suggest that the participants in these situations were all in on the joke, that no one was wholly surprised when it was injected into conversation. Together the individuals formed a localized mode of social interaction that Gary Alan Fine terms idioculture, "a system of knowledge, beliefs, behaviors, and customs shared by members of an interacting group to which members can refer and employ as the basis of further interaction" (1979, 734). The viability of a given expressive form (like a recurrent joke) within an idioculture, Fine theorizes, depends on the degree to which the form is (1) *known* to the group members, (2) *usable* (suitable for group interaction), (3) *functional* (generally believed to support the interests of the group and its members), and (4) *appropriate* (consistent with established patterns of social interaction). A final overriding criterion, which incorporates the others, is the *trigger*, the mechanism by which an individual, through voice or action, brings a particular cultural item into group life and promotes its use (Fine 2012, 40–49). When the item persists, with the help of the promoting agent, it may become for the group something of a "super tradition," frequently invoked or mentioned in social life; the group's collective recognition of the expressive form and its reiteration in social practice is one means by which members develop a shared past and by which their everyday talk is transformed into culture (Fine 2012, 48, 40). Thus, Fine's theory of "Tiny Publics" illuminates what developed among Unruh and his friends regarding TWSS jokes. For Unruh and his cohorts, as within any idioculture where the sharing of jokes—especially frequent inside jokes—is always meaningful, the TWSS joke appears to have been stitched into the fabric of their social discourse.

Unruh positioned himself as the chief sponsor of the joke within the group. In an interview, he kindly elaborated on his original post and further reflected on the use of the TWSS joke among his friends. The group consisted of about twenty individuals—whom he remembers as an eclectic assortment of nerds, jocks, and intellectuals, with an even split of men and women, who shared a common appreciation for *The Office*. Once the program became popular, Unruh said, "TWSS jokes just kind of started happening." He is reluctant to call TWSS his "signature" joke, but he does admit, "I probably did take it a bit further than some of my friends, causing it to be more 'my thing.'" Unruh, who now holds a master's degree in media and film studies from the University of Kansas, has some insight into how the joke operated in social practice:

> Kind of the whole point of TWSS is that it's a shit joke. There's a reason Michael Scott loves it so much: his sense of humor is awful. So a reaction to TWSS should range from "Oh, goddammit, that was awful" (in the sense of a stupid joke) to "Oh, goddammit, that was awful" (in the sense of the recontextualization of the words bringing truly horrible images to mind). I would say we all said it quite a lot. Everyone knew to just use the abbreviation TWSS in [text] chat, after all. As for pushback, it's a fine line—it's a stupid joke rooted in sexist mindsets, so you obviously don't want to overdo it, and you don't want to use it for just regular situations like "That was really hard," or "Put it in there." It became more of an intellectual game where points were rewarded for the most creative recontextualizations, rather than simply throwing the joke out at every possible situation.

I queried Unruh as to his view of the gender politics of the joke:

> KELLEY: What about gender issues? Is it ever "That's what *he* said"? If not, why not? How do your female friends feel about it?
>
> UNRUH: Obviously it is a sexist joke, the kind of thing that would have more appeal to frat boys, and I would guess in most groups, that is how it is used. We've used "He said," "X said," etc. They all work fine, sometimes even better if you can make a leap but hold it all together. "She said" is still the go-to; the restrictive nature of the joke breeds creativity in its use. As for people being offended, it all depends on the group. If you keep them self-deprecating (the best ones all involve things that one

would hope "she" would never say), self-aware statements, I've
found that it lessens the misogyny quite a bit. I'd say I have more
female friends than male, and most have embraced the joke.

Here Unruh considers how the joke worked specifically within
his idioculture, set apart from other, more typically chauvinistic
iterations in "most groups." Although the joke moves in that direction, sexism is not necessarily built into it; as always, meaning
is emergent in particular social use. TWSS jokes in pop culture
are sparser these days, certainly less frequent than they were years
ago when *The Office* was on the air and claimed a substantial fan
base. As a corollary, the joke has diminished among Unruh and
his cohorts as well, though it appears from time to time in a lin-
gering way, he says, demonstrating that "it [still] has legs for a
supposedly lame joke."

Popular though it was with North American audiences, *The
Office* was a heavy-handed, uninspired adaptation of the subtler,
funnier British original. Nevertheless, the American *Office* was
instrumental in propagating the TWSS joking form to a vastly
wider contemporary audience. Easily executed but rarely clever or
original, TWSS jokes and their prototypes are considered essentially *non-jokes* by some—like the sardonic anonymous writer in
Punch magazine who commented that "spoken English, having no
jokes of its own, turns ordinary statements into jokes by adding the
phrase 'as the actress said to the bishop' afterwards" ("Complete
Vocabulary of Spoken English" 1973, 511). As regards TWSS jokes
specifically, there is no question that they are sophomoric—and in
their ephemeral manifestation as a media meme, they were terribly overused. Those factors together well-nigh guaranteed the joke
fatigue that ensued.

In the 2009 slob comedy *Big Stan*, starring Rob Schneider, a
real estate con artist on his way to prison for fraud hires a martial
arts mystic to train him in fighting techniques before the incarceration. The film, which scores 11 percent on Rotten Tomatoes, is
essentially one tediously extended fear-of-sodomy joke. The Master
(played by David Carradine) insists on a peculiar liquid diet as part
of the discipline, and the following exchange ensues:

MINDY (STAN'S GIRLFRIEND): I blended all that gross stuff you
    wanted. I got it all in Koreatown. I didn't even know there was
    a Koreatown.
THE MASTER [*sniffs the concoction*]: Too many eggs. Fish oil is nice. Ox
    pancreas is good. Next time, use more tongue.
BIG STAN: That's what she said!
THE MASTER: [*punches Stan in stomach*]

The gut punch is a disapproving editorial on the hackneyed TWSS
joke, a curious gimmick for a film like this, whose stock in trade is
the basest level of lewd comedy. Vulgar and loutish as the humor
is elsewhere in the film, within its universe the overused TWSS gag
in this moment is shown to be beneath even those low standards.

❋ ❋ ❋

Lauren Bans (2010) penned a piece for *GQ* titled "That's What
She Said? Yeah, Give It a Rest." In it, she urged restraint amid
the memetic frenzy: "Please stop celebrating International That's
What She Said Day (yes, it exists). Don't make lists like 'The Best
TWSS Moments in *Ghostbusters*' and evangelically promote them
on your blog. Free up 16 characters by leaving #thatswhatshesaid
off your tweet. You are what you joke, and if what you joke has
unfortunately evolved into cliché, well, then, you become a cliché."
As memes, TWSS jokes have well passed their zenith, supplanted
by innumerable other visual and verbal gags that have come in and
out of fashion in the digital universe. Still, TWSS jokes, in their
various manifestations, have an extensive pedigree. As faddish and
then fleeting as they may have been in contemporary media culture,
in formal terms, they are situated in a long lineage of related traditional joking expressions. What we see here corroborates Blank's
observation that "people catch up and adapt to the progressing
culture by merging the old and familiar with the emergent capa-
bilities of a new medium" (2013, 21). The TWSS joke flowed into
digital culture from folk and literary origins, was transformed in
wide circulation as a media meme and, in turn, was reinvigorated in
folk culture; in terms of the broad communicative use of this joking phenomenon, media consumers became de facto co-producers
of the form.

5

"Your Kind of Place"

Brand Awareness and Intervention in Children's Culture

COMMERCIAL KIDS

Each winter semester, my students undertake a modest field project in children's folklore. Among recent collections was one twelve-year-old boy's ready-made insult to classmates: "Your mamma's so poor, she goes to Kentucky Fried Chicken to lick *other* people's fingers." A funny image, this—a woman scuttling about the KFC lapping up from diners' fingers greasy remnants of the colonel's secret recipe. Besides its humor, and whatever social business it may have accomplished for the informant and his peers, the invective reminded me just how much children's folklore draws from commercial culture, and how ready children are to adapt and repurpose popular advertisements.

Childhood and commerce do not operate separately but rather co-constitutively as each gives meaning and action to the other (Cook 2008, 201). While most consumption studies fail to consider childhood at all, those that do often fall into false dichotomies, seeing children *either* as pawns manipulated by media and marketing *or* as "agentic individuals who are able to resist their positioning as consumers" (Marsh and Bishop 2014, 89). Sparrman, Sandin, and Sjöberg (2012) mediate and contextualize such dichotomies with their notion of the "situated child consumer," and Gottzén further problematizes the knotty process by which children *become*

DOI: 10.7330/9781607329909.c005

consumers amid "complex relations to parents, money, commodities, and friends, as well as discourses on childhood" (2012, 104). The layered linkages between childhood and consumerism can be viewed as a function of what Daniel Cook terms "commercial enculturation," a transactional process whereby children "[engage] with goods, advertisements, brands and packaging—as well as with parents, peers, siblings and others" to "form and re-form meanings about the material-commercial world in ways that emplace products in social relations and social relation in products" (2010, 70–71). Growing up, children are programmed by the determined forces of capitalism, first as peripheral consumers (that is, as users of products bought by their parents or observers of commercial exchange) and then later as active customers with burgeoning spending power (De la Ville and Tartas 2010, 35; Buckingham 2011, 52). Given these social, semiotic, and material complexities, children's playground adaptations of commercial culture and consumerist messages are all the more meaningful.

Children occupy a subcultural niche wherein they often find themselves at odds with the social and political agendas of adult-dominated society. As with subcultures generally, children often gravitate toward geographical locations separate from home life, "territorialized" spaces where they congregate and affirm their social bonds (Gelder 2007, 2). We might think of these zones generically as "the playground." Not playgrounds literally, of course—they could be city parks, street cul-de-sacs, treehouses in the back yards of neighborhood friends—but, importantly, these are settings where children separate themselves from the authoritative watch of parents and teachers. And there, occupying a social position something comparable to that of a minority group (Oldman 1992), amid peer group play, the children develop elaborate practices of nonsense, parody, and secrecy that mitigate and undermine the power grip of dominant adult culture (Mechling 1986, 99–102). The playground—in this metaphoric sense—becomes for children a tiny island of temporary social control in the vast sea that is adult-dominated society. It is headquarters for children's folklore, which bends toward the subversive, and among the recurring topics and targets are brand name companies and their ads.

BRAND AWARENESS

Children's lives are infused with brands. Lindstrom and Seybold's extensive study of children from eight countries found that eight- to fourteen-year-olds are exposed to more than 8,000 brands a day, and "almost by force of circumstance they have developed an internal filter which absorbs, selects and adopts" corporate names and logos (2004, 6). Seven- to eight-year-olds, on the young end of Lindstrom and Seybold's subject group, are typically just beginning to develop an understanding of bias, promotional intent, and deception in advertising (Moses and Baldwin 2005, 192, 194). By age eleven, most children are able to recognize and attribute the persuasive design of advertising aimed at them (Young 2010, 120). Amid that developing awareness, children naturally incorporate popular commercial material into their ludic repertoires.

But brand names and ads saturating the lives and lore of children is not a new phenomenon. For instance, Peter and Iona Opie identified a corpus of "promotional skipping chants" dating back to the nineteenth century, like "Manchester Guardian, Evening News / I sell Evening News." Variants of the rhyme proliferated across municipalities as young girls skipped rope and effectively became publicists for their local newspapers. The prevailing version in Radcliffe, Lancashire, was "Manchester, Bolton Evening News, / I sell evening one, two . . ."; in Wellington, Shropshire, they chanted, "Wellington Journal, Evening News, / Ever see a cat in a pair of shoes?"; and in Shrewsbury it was "London Liverpool, Weekly Post, / I say number one, two, three . . ." (1959, 5). Additionally, the Opies' vast collection of children's ludic material included the game "Shop Windows," played in front of a store window display: one child studies items arranged in the window while her cohorts, some distance away, line up along the sidewalk. She shouts out initials as clues to which item she has in mind, and when it is correctly guessed by a peer, a race ensues, usually to the other side of the street and back. The Opies observed a variation called "advertisements," in which the clues announced by the caller are not initials but rather advertising slogans of products on display; the other players then identify the products by matching them with the proffered slogan (1984, 278–79).

Sometimes the brand names infiltrated children's lore not as part of a guessing game, like "shop windows," but by chance, as kids happened upon discarded packages littering the sidewalk. Discovering derelict packets of Black Cat cigarettes, for example, children devised this rhyming charm: "Black cat, black cat, bring me luck, / If you don't I'll tear you up." The chant was observed in Monmouth, Manchester, and Oxford with reference to "Willy, Willy Woodbine" cigarettes. In Ipswich, the locally manufactured Churchman's Tenner brand of cigarettes inspired "Red Tenner, Red Tenner, bring me luck, / If you don't I'll tear you up," which first appeared no later than 1910 (Opie and Opie 1959, 222–23). It may not surprise us that even crumpled cigarette packs would find their way into the panoply of found objects that figure into superstitious childhood play (e.g., coins, four-leaf clovers, buttons, horseshoes, feathers, sticks, rings, etc.), ludic customs that the Opies call "half belief." After all, children are acutely observant of their environs and they are always ready to exploit any available resource in the interest of play. But the cigarette chants also point up just how relentlessly brand names insinuate themselves into children's verbal lore, even apart from the calculated designs of advertisers and publicists.

That said, persistent and targeted advertising most definitely amplified children's general brand awareness, going back to the turn of the century and even earlier. The old children's racing game called "peep behind the curtain" included a variety of temporizing chants uttered by a single player as others sneaked up from behind. One informant recalled from her childhood in Bath, around 1905, that the favorite chant in her neighborhood was "Sunlight soap is the best in the World." (Sunlight was the world's first packaged and branded laundry soap, introduced in 1884 by the British company Lever Brothers.) "Advertisers were able then, as now, to have their slogans adopted by children," the Opies observed, adding that "in the period before the First World War, commercial advertisers had a number of amusing devices for attracting juvenile attention which are unknown today" (1984, 192n). While they do not elaborate on what those devices were, the Opies cede elsewhere that advertising jingles in particular, despite their catchiness, seldom had the right appeal or structure to enter into children's permanent verbal repertoires. They did observe one notable exception: a Murray mints television jingle from the late 1950s that appeared nearly verbatim as a child's skipping song in Edinburgh in 1975:

Murray Mints, Murray Mints
The too-good-to-hurry mints,
You buy the taste,
There is no waste,
For minty, minty Murray mints.

The Opies (1997, 213) posit that advertising forms like this one, performed essentially intact on playgrounds, rare though they were, "must surely be an ad-man's dream"; but even just the mention of a product name conjures a kind of brand loyalty, they suggest, as in the skipping rhyme: "HP Sauce, HP Sauce, / Mummy likes, Daddy likes, HP Sauce" (from Kent in 1934), observed later as "HP Sauce, HP Sauce, / My mother uses HP Sauce" (from Swansea in 1954).

Jackie Marsh and Julia C. Bishop's study *Changing Play* includes an exchange with one older informant named Beryl who remembered childhood chants from the 1950s based on contemporary advertisements:

BERYL: And I'll tell you another chant we had. Do you remember Andrews Liver Salts?
JULIA: Yes.
BERYL: Skipping to this: "Andrews, Andrews, Andrews for inner cleanliness. What a blessing Andrews, effervescent Andrews, Andrews. Andrews, Andrews for inner cleanliness."
JULIA: So did you sing that?
BERYL: You're actually skipping about going to the lavatory. Yeah.
JULIA: But that came off the wireless then or the TV?
BERYL: I think that came off the wireless, I can't swear to it. But it also appeared on TV that. And also an advert for Pepsodent, do you remember Pepsodent? . . . And I remember, I don't know whether we skipped to it but I remember us singing it, "You'll wonder where the yellow went when you brush your teeth with Pepsodent."
(2014, 81)

These games and rhymes incorporate brands simply, in terms of basic brand awareness and straightforward imitation of ads, as instances of what Rebekah Willett calls "onomastic allusion": "names, catchphrases, gestures, [and] musical utterances from media used in passing in play" (2016, 134). But in some other ludic forms children become active agents in the mimetic or mocking manipulation of the commercial material to which they are exposed.

INTERVENTIONS

The popular Pepsodent advertisement mentioned by Beryl, which aired for a full decade after its introduction in 1948, was reworked by other children in the UK as: "You'll wonder where your front teeth went when you brush your teeth with Earle's Cement." (G & T Earle Ltd. is an old and well-known cement company in the UK.) So, while parents and advertisers obsessed over proper oral hygiene, children responded with petrifying disdain through their folklore. Further parodies playfully described dental care in the 1950s as hazardous business: "You'll wonder where your teeth have gone when you brush them with an atom bomb." The rhyming parodies eventually became more political, reflecting the racism and militarism of the atomic age: "You'll wonder where the yellow went / When the H-bomb hits the Orient" (Andresen 2003, 187).

Likewise, consider the children's adaptations of PK chewing gum ads. Named after Philip K. Wrigley, CEO of the Wrigley Company from 1925 to 1961, PK gum advertised with the slogan "PK penny a packet." Children in North America and the UK picked up on the slogan and integrated it into a number of skipping and hand-clapping games; but it appeared most often as part of ball-bouncing game known as "two balls," or "balls on the wall." The chant specified a series of playful actions that one might perform in the process of chewing the gum:

> PK penny a packet,
> First you lick it,
> Then you crack it,

Then you stick it to your jacket,
PK penny a packet.

In the children's satirical constructions, "crack it" and "jacket" fell naturally into place as well-near inevitable rhymes for the beckoning "packet." Corollary gestures accompanied the chant, as one ten-year-old girl from London explained: "On the word lick you must put your tongue out, then when crack is said you must stamp your foot and on the word jacket you must quickly put your hand down your dress" (Opie and Opie 1997, 156). Later, in the 1970s, Wrigley's launched another ad campaign for PK gum with an infectiously bouncy jingle that became extremely popular:

PK chewing gum, gum, gum.
Carry the big, fresh flavor
Wherever you go, whatever you do
It's the finest pack of flavor
Wherever you go, whatever you do
It's the famous PK flavor
With great Wrigley's taste
Delicious to chew.

Drawn to the catchy repetition of the buoyant tune and the extensive possibility for rhyming fun, children generated parodies like this:

PK chewing gum, gum, gum.
Stick it up your bum, bum, bum
Pull it out with your thumb, thumb thumb,
Tastes good—yum, yum, yum.

And listeners were introduced to an increasingly aggressive and graphic catalogue of gum-related maneuvers:

If it doesn't stick, stick, stick
Stick it on your dick, dick, dick
If that doesn't work, work, work
You're a big fat jerk, jerk, jerk

Or the gum was disposed of altogether:

If it doesn't stay, stay, stay
Throw it away, way, way
PK chewing gum, gum, gum

In keeping with much of children's lore, we see here the experimentation with comically taboo language, a flouting of social convention, and a preoccupation with the body.

Pepsi Parody
Stateside, in the late 1930s amid the golden age of Madison Avenue advertising, this popular soft drink jingle swept the nation:

Pepsi Cola hits the spot
Twelve full ounces, that's a lot
Twice as much for a nickel, too.
Pepsi is the drink for you.
Nickel, nickel, nickel, nickel,
Trickle, trickle, trickle, trickle [*fades out*][1]

During that era of radio advertising, without accompanying visual imagery to hook consumers, it was essential that jingles be brief, memorable, and catchy. In that effort, the Pepsi jingle writers Alan Bradley Kent and Austen Herbert Croom-Johnson smartly revitalized a snippet of melody from a traditional Scottish air about fox hunting called "Do ye ken John Peel," which itself drew upon an older folk song—"Bonnie Annie"—with roots in the eighteenth century.[2] The jingle certainly stuck in the popular consciousness, making broadcast history as it was the first stand-alone advertising jingle played and heard coast to coast (Bird 1947, 230–31). *Life* magazine declared it "immortal" (October 7, 1940, 79), *Advertising Age* magazine ranked it among the top ten jingles of the twentieth century (March 29, 1999), and it has been trumpeted as "the most famous oral trademark of all time" (Louis and Yazijian 1980, 68). In 1941 alone, the jingle played 296,426 times on 469 radio stations—and countless other times on American jukeboxes, where it was also a favorite (Mack and Buckley 1982, 136). Within a year of that, according to one survey, the Pepsi jingle had become the best-known tune in the country (Louis and Yazijian 1980, 69).

The jingle had been played more than a million times by 1944, the *New York Times* reported, and was at that time still being heard regularly on 350 radio stations nationwide (Graham 1944, 26). Bob Garfield, co-host of NPR's *On the Media*, considers "Pepsi Cola Hits the Spot" to be the "granddaddy of all jingles"; he quips that "[it] embedded itself not so much in the nation's psyche as in its very nerve endings, like the Pledge of Allegiance, or—depending on your viewpoint—a case of shingles" (1999, 82). It continued to circulate for a few decades, through the war years, and was later updated and fully orchestrated for a 1950s audience.

A catchy jingle echoing in the ether for that long and at that level of popularity would naturally become a lightning rod for childhood parodies. In a 1959 live recording, Pete Seeger was in concert and talking to the audience about how songs can change over time. He recalled singing "John Peel" to a school group on one occasion, noting their *preferred* lyrics to the traditional melody:

> I was singing that to some kids in school, explaining that that came from an old English folk song,
>
> > Do you ken John Peel at the break of day
> > Do you ken John Peel when he's far away,
> > And so on . . . la dee da . . .
> > With his hounds and his horns in the morning.
>
> Oh, the kids say, you're not singing it right. This is the way we sing it,
>
> > Pepsi Cola hits the spot,
> > Ties your belly in a knot.
> > Tastes like vinegar looks like ink
> > Pepsi Cola is a stinky drink!
>
> Yep, you make 'em up all the time. (Seeger 1959)

Like Seeger's, all of the archived parodies of the Pepsi jingle corralled below duplicate the commercial's first line faithfully, exactly as it appears in the original ads; from there the variances proliferate—with all manner of intestinal and olfactory offense.

Here's one from South Carolina in the 1950s:

> Pepsi Cola hits the spot
> In your stomach it will rot
> Tastes like vinegar, smells like wine
> Oh my God, it's turpentine!

Another from the same era:

> Pepsi Cola hits the spot
> Smells like vinegar, tastes like snot
> Pour it in the kitchen sink,
> Five minutes later, it begins to stink.

A favorite rhyme appears to have been the culminating word *pot* in line 2, as in:

> Pepsi Cola hits the spot,
> Makes you vomit in the pot.
> Looks like water, tastes like wine
> "Oh, my god, it's turpentine."

And with the pot—the toilet—designated as the consummate rhyme, predictably the parodies spiraled into a scatological free-for-all.

> Pepsi Cola hits the spot,
> 'Specially when you're on the pot.
> Press the handle, pull the chain—
> There goes Pepsi down the drain.

> Pepsi Cola hits the spot,
> 'Specially when you're on the pot.
> Press the button, pull the chain,
> Out comes a little choo-choo train.

Once supplanted by the "Pepsi generation" campaign in 1963, the jingle no longer aired, but the parodies continued to circulate in oral tradition until well into the 1980s, some fifty years after the jingle was first broadcast on radio. As in:

> Pepsi Cola hits the spot,
> Makes you throw up in a pot.

Throw it up 'til your face turns green,
Drink 7-Up with no caffeine.

We know that this version appeared after 1982, when 7-Up initiated its "no caffeine" campaign (*Gainesville Sun* 1982) which, incidentally, led the cola giants to cry foul at the company for ginning up phony concerns over the supposed health risks of caffeine; not surprisingly, it became a nonissue once Pepsico acquired a significant portion of 7-Up's global rights. Seeger's ruminations on folk song alteration are well observed in this case: a bona fide folk song made its way into popular culture as an advertising tool and then was transformed back into genuine folk tradition through the parodies of children, who may well have never heard of "John Peel" or "Bonnie Annie"—or, for that matter, even the original ad that inspired the parody.

Toxic Bosco

Another brand from the same era, Bosco chocolate syrup, was heavily marketed to children and provides us with another case study. Bosco was first produced in 1928 and though its sales always ran a distant second to the more popular Hershey's brand of chocolate syrup, the company jingle "I Love Bosco" had real staying power in popular and then folk culture. Here's the original, sung in commercials by children:

Oh, I love Bosco!
It's rich and chocolate-y!
Chocolate-flavored Bosco
Is mighty good for me.
Mommy puts it in my milk
For extra energy.
Bosco gives me iron
And sunshine vitamin D.
Oh, I love Bosco!
That's the drink for me![3]

Written in 1955, "I Love Bosco" was broadcast widely on radio and television and provided rich material for the mischievous young

minds of the playground. The Bess Lomax Hawes Archive of
Student Folklore at California State University, Northridge, holds
eight versions of the "I Love Bosco" parody, collected between
1960 and 1968, located in a folder titled "Anti-parent rhymes." One
typical version is literally explosive:

> I hate Bosco
> It's full of TNT
> My mommy put it in my milk
> To try to poison me
> But I fooled Mommy
> I put it in her tea
> And now there's no more mommy
> To try to poison me.
> I hate Bosco
> It's not the drink for me.[4]

Much of children's folk culture, by principle, stands in opposition to
established adult social order (Mechling 1986, 97; Pellegrini 1995, ix).
And as a result, in their lore children will often resist—sometimes
aggressively subvert—the imposition of conventional adult authority. It's ponderable why that would be so graphically articulated in
the Bosco parodies, and I suspect that it has something to do with
the heavy-handed way the original ads present the custodial respon-
sibilities of mothers. The jingle and accompanying visuals in print
and TV ads appeal directly to women and imply that adding Bosco
to a child's diet is just an expression of good mothering. In one
print ad, a youngster enthusiastically hoists a glass of Bosco and
milk with a speech balloon that reads, "Mmm, that's swell chocolate
flavor!" His perfectly coiffed mother, in an adjacent panel, extols,
"Bosco makes Billy drink more milk—and it's rich in iron, too!"
Another stand-alone advertisement depicts a woman holding up a
jar of Bocso and saying, "He gets Bosco for being good . . . and
it's good for him, too. It's rich in iron." And the jingle positions the
child's point of view: "Mamma puts it in my milk for extra energy,
/ Bosco gives me iron, and sunshine vitamin D."

     If it's possible that the didactic maternalism was lost on some
consumers, it was labored in longer television commercials like

the full one-minute spot featuring talk-show personality Virginia Graham as the designated homemaker:

> Hi, everybody. I am Virginia Graham. Gosh, aren't children bounc-
> ing with energy these days?! And we mothers know that their bet-
> ter health is due to better foods, of course. And one of the most
> perfect foods is milk, and you can make milk even more perfect
> for your children by adding Bosco milk amplifier. This nutritious
> chocolate-flavored syrup adds iron and vitamin D, and actually
> increases the food value and digestibility of milk. Yes, Bosco and
> milk builds healthier bones, stronger muscles, better teeth. And it's
> so easy to use—just one tablespoon of chocolatey Bosco per glass
> makes children drink more milk and love it! And that's why chil-
> dren sing: "Oh, I love Bosco, that's the drink for me!"

But children inverted the ad's intended message explicitly—outrageously—by transforming it into a song about dangerous adults.
We might consider the themes of separation and abandonment
that populate children's lore (in fairy tales and lullabies, for example
[see Zipes 1997, 39–60; Hawes, 146–48]); this parody goes one step
further, staging what is perhaps the most primal existential anxiety
of children, the threat of filicide—expressed here as a mother who
would feed explosives to and poison her own little darling. In retali-
ation, the child, the intended victim, turns the tables and eliminates
the threat. On the most obvious level, this parody depicts a moment
of self defense against a menacing mother, but the scenario can also
be viewed more critically as a metaphor—a metaphor for the constant assault of toxic advertising that children face. So here we have a
reprisal against the opportunistic advertisers who would commodify
the normalized values of dominant adult culture and then force-feed
them to young consumers. It easy to see why children would appreciate this parody for its retribution, unconscious though it might be.

*Spoof Variety Pack: Antacid, Mattresses, Amusement Parks, Cigarettes,
and Bananas*

The last century has seen children increasingly enveloped by the
forces of consumerism; with the advent of television, they became

especially impressible by visual devices like animated commercials. For example, in the early days of television, Alka-Seltzer introduced its squeaky-voiced cartoon mascot Speedy, a sprightly lad composed of a pair of antacid wafers. The character was immediately appealing to a younger demographic, but interest waned during the social unrest of the 1960s, by which time Speedy had grown somewhat mawkish and stale—and Alka-Seltzer's share of the medicinal market ebbed proportionately. Fortunes reversed when the Tinker & Partners Ad Agency took on the Alka-Seltzer account and devised a strategy to increase the standard dosage from one to two tablets, which were then packaged in pairs in foil packets. Revenues soared as a result, and Speedy enjoyed a revival when in 1975 he first sang the effervescent earworm of a jingle that musically reinforced the double dose, indelibly etching it into the popular consciousness: "Plop, plop, / Fizz, fizz, / Oh, what a relief it is" (Wells 2002, 24–29). The hook of the jingle was its onomatopoetic appeal (Lindstrom 2008, 157–58), which embedded it in the minds of listeners but also left it open to parody. Children already knew well enough that Alka-Seltzer was associated with intestinal disturbance, among other symptoms. That, coupled with the sound-imitative lyrics and the notion of "relief," led them logically to connote the jingle as pertaining to bodily processes, a theme that always finds ample traction on the playground. Singing the tune, they would point to their backside with the word *plop*, and then to the genitals with *fizz*. And then they would sport an expression of relaxed contentment with the word *relief*. Notably, this parody operates differently from those above, which retool the verbal texts of original jingles to form new, comically subversive messages. Rather, the text of "Plop, plop, fizz, fizz" remains intact, unaltered—and the parody comes from the reconstituted scatological meaning made apparent by the accompanying gestures. Through kinesics and tone alone, the jingle is transformed into a sardonic celebration of the sounds and sensations of elimination.

All of the parodies we've examined here (and the Comet jingles in chapter 1) involve the ingestion of some well-branded product and address the implied dangers of voracious consumption. It seems fitting that these folk songs/chants, which are reactions to relentless advertising and branding, telegraph children's acute awareness of themselves as consumers. We might compare ads for Sleep Country Canada, a mattress retailer in Canada with more than 185 stores operating nationwide. Proliferating across airwaves, the company's brief, elaborately produced jingle—jaunty and memorable but overplayed—has been rated as one of Canada's catchiest advertising melodies: "Sleep Country Canada / Why buy a mattress anywhere else?"[5] The jingle certainly reverberates through the brains of children, who in summer camp sing: "Sleep Country Canada / Why buy a mattress, you've got a couch." What is written as a claim of brand superiority becomes for children a refreshingly anti-consumerist message: why buy a mattress at all when you can reasonably utilize the resources you already own? In the spirit of reduce, reuse, and recycle, this is an environmentally friendly parody. Another version is more frugal yet—even severely so: "Sleep Country Canada / Why buy a mattress, sleep on the floor."

A more localized bit of children's subvertisement in Canada has emerged around ads for Ontario's Marineland, a zoo and sea-themed amusement park close to Niagara Falls that opened in 1961. Despite a number of well-publicized legal and public relations entanglements stemming from unlawful animal capture, alleged ongoing animal abuse, and mismanagement (Diebel 2012; Diebel and Casey 2012b; Alam 2016; Casey 2016; Hudes 2017), the park has kept one rosy image of itself in the public eye through an enduring ad campaign featuring the buoyant jingle "Everyone Loves Marineland," heard widely throughout Ontario.

> There's a place I know in Ontario
> Where the sea lions kiss, so the story goes
> Its amazing shows and Friendship Cove
> Everyone loves Marineland!

Children have generated one playfully nonsensical parody:

> There's a place I know in Ontario
> Where the fish drink beer and eat Cheerios!
> It's a wonderful place to stare out into space
> Everyone hates Marineland.

Another variant includes the same surreal image of anthropomorphized fish drinking beer and eating breakfast cereal, but turns darker with an alternate third line:

> There's a place I know in Ontario
> Where the fish drink beer and eat Cheerios!
> It's a wonderful place *to get shot in the face*
> Everyone hates Marineland.

This is the prevailing rendition that circulates among children in southern Ontario, common enough to be considered something of a default version, although in recent years they occasionally substitute for the familiar second line a more trenchant lyric, "Where the fish all die and get burials." Now, children may not be fully aware of all the negative publicity that has bedeviled Marineland and its bellicose owner John Holer over the last decade, but they undoubtedly have absorbed some of the general gist by osmosis. All media outlets covered the controversies, and beginning in 2012, the *Toronto Star* mounted an investigative series called "Inside Marineland," which included extensive interviews with former employees/trainers who divulged troubling practices at the park. Organizations like PETA and Ocean Activists United publicly denounced Marineland as an "abusement park," and one woman, who became known as Marineland Mom, convinced her child's school to cancel a class trip to the park (Wells 2014). The exposés and negative publicity continued intermittently into 2020. So well known was the commercial jingle that it even became part of the story, with such headlines as "'People Don't Love Marineland Anymore': Ontario Law Leaves Orca Floating Alone in Niagara Falls" (Csanady 2015) and "Everyone Loves Marineland? Another Whale Dies at Ontario Water Park" (Mackinnon 2017).

Further, two gruesome incidents in particular gave rise to this "Everybody Loves Marineland" parody. It was alleged by a former supervisor and reported by the *Toronto Star* that John Holer once shot an injured fawn through the neck with a shotgun on park grounds and that he left the deer to choke on its own blood (Diebel and Casey 2012a). On another occasion, the supervisor claims, Holer shot two Labrador retrievers that had wandered from a neighbor's house onto Marineland property (Diebel and Casey 2013). These allegations, though not fully substantiated, received considerable exposure in the media and became the basis of children's humorously acerbic commentary on Marineland as "a wonderful place to get shot in the face." The original line about "Friendship Cove" is transformed antithetically into a graphic exposition on homicidal aggression. Violence perpetrated on innocent animals is a disturbing notion to children, and though they know that joking about such matters is frowned upon, humor about suffering and death can function as a device by which they neutralize and "domesticate" the uncomfortable cruelty of it all. This Marineland parody comments as well on the mediatization of violence and tragedy generally. As Elliott Oring has observed of other joke cycles on disaster, gallows humor like this can be regarded as "a rebellion against a world defined by media" and "part of a battle for the control of discourse about death and disaster" (1992, 38–39). Children are certainly not shielded from those media messages; at the same time that the satirical jingle derides Marineland and its ubiquitous advertising, it is a mechanism by which they grapple with distressing content.

Children's commercial parodies are abundant, the range of companies and products they target diverse—from gum, cola, and chocolate milk to antacid, mattresses, and amusement parks. Sometimes children's ludic interventions are blunt, just simple inversions of ad messaging in which the quality of a product is disparaged rather than lauded. The extremely successful slogan/jingle for Winston cigarettes from the 1950s, "Winston tastes good like a cigarette should," for example, was recast in children's parodies as "Winston tastes bad like the one I just had." Further ridicule was offered in these additions: "No flavor, no taste, just a 50 cent waste" and "No filter, no flavor, just plain old toilet paper." In other instances, the commercial material is repurposed to undermine the power of adults, as with parodies of "The Chiquita Banana song," first introduced as a radio jingle in 1944 and followed by an animated movie theater version that featured an anthropomorphized banana, Miss Chiquita, singing Carmen Miranda style. The catchy Latin tune and magnetic childhood appeal of a singing cartoon banana set the stage for this to be one of America's most popular and enduring commercial jingles. Children spoofed the original with a comical plot to eliminate the teacher, as one female informant remembered it:

> I'm Chiquita banana and I'm here to say
> If you want to get rid of your teacher today
> Just peel a banana and throw it on the floor
> And watch your teacher go flying out the door.

This archived version, collected in 1972, included the collector's contextual data: "She learned this song in second grade [c. 1960]. As she remembers, it was sung on bus rides, during recess, and at lunch, anytime the students got together and wanted to talk about the teacher."[6] Another informant recalled singing his version during the early 1970s:

> I'm Chiquita banana and I'm here to say
> If you want to kill your teacher there's a brand-new way
> Drop a banana peel on the floor
> And watch your teacher fly out the door.

The Chiquita brand of banana, well established as a market giant by then, is the slippery vehicle by which the students freed themselves of institutional authority.

Mocking McDonald's

No serious treatment of this topic could ignore the pervasive influence of McDonald's. In addition to being one of the first corporations to engage in lifestyle branding, McDonald's is well known for aggressively targeting children with a diverse arsenal of promotional strategies: child-friendly characters, Happy Meals, film and merchandising tie-ins, and so on. McDonald's is the world's largest distributors of toys, and the corporation operates more than 8,000 playgrounds in the United States alone (Koshuta 2007). It is no wonder, then, that the McDonald's brand is well stamped into children's awareness. The restaurant chain has kept its hired advertising agencies busy, with no fewer than thirty-seven separate ad campaigns since 1960. A few of the memorable ones:

Look for the Golden Arches! (1960–67)
McDonald's is your kind of place (1967–71)
You deserve a break today (1971–75)
We do it all for you (1975–79)
Nobody can do it like McDonald's can (1979–83)
You deserve a break today (1981–83)
That's my McDonald's (1981)
McDonald's and you (1983–84)
It's a good time for the great taste of McDonald's (1984–88)
It's Mac tonight (1985)
McDonald's is your place to be (1986)
The good time, great taste of McDonald's (1988–90)
You deserve a break today (1989–90)
Food, folks and fun (1990–91)
Do you believe in magic? (1992–97)
Have you had your break today? (1995–97)
Did somebody say McDonald's? (1997–2000)
We love to see you smile (2000–2003)
I'm lovin' it (2003–present)

"Your Kind of Place" in the late 1960s and into the 1970s is widely considered to be one of McDonald's' most successful campaigns.[7] Like "Pepsi Cola Hits the Spot" before it, this jingle is based on a familiar folk song, the Negro spiritual "Down by the Riverside," which circulated in the antebellum South and was recorded countless times in the twentieth century. McDonald's retooled the folk song, which by that time (1967–71) had surged back into popularity as an antiwar anthem during the Vietnam era. (A lyrical refrain from the song, "Study War No More," sometimes appears as its alternate title.) More critically, some would argue, McDonald's shamelessly capitalized on the song's currency, appropriating and commercializing it in a manner antithetical to its embedded ideology. In any case, here's how McDonald's rendered its first commercial adaptation for television in 1967, sung by children like earlier Bosco ads:

McDonalds is our kind of place [clap clap]
It's such a happy place [clap clap]
Hap- hap- hap- happy place [clap clap]

A clean and snappy place [clap clap]
McDonalds is our kind of place [clap clap]
It's such a happy place [clap clap]
McDonalds is our kind of place!
Your kind of place!

The soulful invocations of the old spiritual were effectively supplanted by peppy children's voices celebrating a disinfected consumerist paradise. The fixation on cleanliness is telling here; for
commercial purposes, the untidy associations of racial hardship
and social protest that "Down by the Riverside" carried with it
had to be sanitized. The overdubbed narration reinforces that
fixation: "Here's a plus—spill-proof lids on all beverages. Another plus—napkins as big as a bib. Quality, cleanliness, extra care
service. That's McDonald's." And the curious pitch to parents:
"McDonald's believes in getting food to your kids before they get
to each other," as if the food is some sort of opiate against childhood unruliness. But it's a catchy tune, to be sure, and children
were quick to invent new lyrics for it. While the original commercial obsesses over cleanliness and order, the children's parodies cel-
ebrate rowdiness and contamination:

McDonald's is your kind of place.
They serve you rattlesnakes,
French fries up your nose,
Pickles between your toes,
And don't forget those chocolate shakes,
They come from polluted lakes,
McDonald's is your kind of place.
The last time that I went there,
They stole my underwear,
I really didn't care,
It was my dirty pair,
The next time that you go there,
They'll serve my underwear,
McDonald's is your kind of place

Sometimes the parody would go on, like this one, for multiple verses, as if to tell us that just a single stanza could not contain the full

range of disgusting contaminations and putrefied substances that children wished to catalogue—the antipode of cleanliness. Choice snippets from other versions include these lines:

> Ronald is a mental case
> McDonald's ain't your kind of place

> Ketchup running down your back
> I want my money back
> before I have a heart attack!

> McDonald's was your kind of place
> Until we burned it down
> We burned it to the ground
> We even burned the clown
> McDonald's was your kind of place

"Your Kind of Place" parodies became a staple of North American children's lore, with remarkable longevity. We can only imagine how McDonald's executives may have winced at the thought of their most prized demographic—children—associating the brand with pollution, poor hygiene, vulgarity, heart disease, mental illness, arson, and murder. After all, studies have shown that advertisers, in establishing brand influence with children, are less interested in actual consumption or purchasing habits; they are more determined to forge early relationships (that may be exploited later) based on associative feelings and impressions (Cook 2010, 72; Lindstrom and Seybold 2004, 47).

Fortune 500 companies are vehement on that account and they summon considerable resources to make it happen. To wit, McDonald's became even more enterprising with a 1979 ad campaign featuring a group of African American girls jumping rope, double Dutch style, in front of a Harlem brownstone. Neighborhood spectators—peers only, no adults—cheer on the girls' gymnastic maneuvers. Launched perhaps as a corrective to earlier campaigns that had been ruthlessly mocked by children, this commercial was shrewd in its suggestion of "authenticity," targeted directly to urban youth culture as prepackaged folklore and mimicking a ludic vernacular that, traditionally, would be antithetical to all things adult or institutional. One way to fight subversion is to annex the media of disturbance. However, the accompanying jingle (sung by adults and pandering to kids) reminds us of the overriding corporate interests:

> McDonald's knows your double Dutch is really hard to beat
> 'Cause when you're jumping, you do something magic
>   with your feet.
> You're jumping up an appetite,
> and we'll give you a hand.
> You're the reason we do it,
>   If anyone can do it, McDonald's knows who can.

As a strategy of appropriation, it was not wholly successful from an advertising standpoint. But a year later, McDonald's recalibrated with a similar commercial that was more compelling to children and, in the end, more effective as an overall campaign. Instead of a purely urban setting like uptown New York, the new commercial was located more generically in the suburbs. As before, the focal point is a staged a double Dutch rope jumping session, but in this case the play occurs as part of a family get-together with three generations participating—gleeful parents and grandparents looking on approvingly. The most important distinction is that the adult-voiced (and thinly veiled corporatized) jingle from the earlier spot is replaced by an audio overdub that begins with kids themselves rhythmically chanting items from the McDonald's menu in cadence with the spinning ropes:

> Big mac, filet-o-fish, quarter pounder,
> French fries, icy Coke, thick shake,
> Sundaes, apple pies!

It is no less of a sales pitch, but because the children themselves are given a voice, it comes across as something like genuine playground folklore, albeit without any of the attendant defiance, irreverence, or creative mockery typical of children's peer-to-peer sport.

With this, McDonald's had devised a tactic to stem folkloric derision: the subversive potential of parody is neutralized when the expressive form is co-opted, then rendered civic, wholesome, and—most important—commercial. Here we see the quintessence of incorporation, which is control and containment—in this instance, control of the salable message and containment of disruptions to that message. By all estimates it was a successful strategy for McDonald's, as it continued over several years with a series of jump rope commercials that were then actively imitated rather than parodied on playgrounds—and eventually the content became a part of genuine folk culture with very little subversive manipulation by children. Children reciting a list of menu items from 1980s McDonald's commercials, which themselves had co-opted children's ludic folk forms, may be an early, pre-digital instance of what Christian Fuchs (2013) calls "surplus labor," manifesting when cultural participants propagate or repurpose media that promote commercial interests (220). The strategy was imitated later in an advertisement for the Kit Kat candy bar, which featured two young girls hand clapping to the infectious jingle "Gimme a break / Gimme a break / Break me off a piece of that Kit Kat bar" (Soileau 2016, 106). From there, the handclap replicated organically—and nearly verbatim—in children's folk culture, where it remains currently popular as evidenced by the numerous performed versions uploaded to YouTube.

In 1990–91, Ann Richman Beresin conducted a study of double Dutch jump rope play among third- through fifth-grade girls in an urban, working-class, racially integrated public schoolyard in Pennsylvania. The months-long investigation generated video footage covering twenty-seven days of recess and fifty-one days of live audio recording. Beresin observed that many of the more vintage traditional rhymes were "outshouted" by the newest one, called "Big Mac," which she labeled as a "corporate menu chant" and many of the girls identified as their favorite. In fact, "Big Mac" represented 40 percent of all the songs sung for double Dutch during the extensive study, far and away the most popular among the participants (Beresin 1999, 82–83). Since then, many variants have been documented, from virtual replications of the suburban double Dutch ad to elaborate hand-clapping versions with additional verses imported from children's lore and other McDonald's commercials. One striking example is a clapping exchange between a Peace Corps volunteer and a ten-year-old Senegalese girl named Aida Lo, recorded in Senegal and posted to YouTube in 2010:

Big mac, filet-o-fish, quarter pounder,
French fries, icy cold thick shake,
Sundae, apple pie.
You deserve a break today,
So get up in the morning and get away
To McDonald's, McDonald's
Where the dish ran away with the spoon! Oh yeah.

Amended to many North American versions as well, the "dish ran away with the spoon" coda is a curiosity. Certainly, it punctuates the gustatory theme, as dishes and spoons figure logically alongside the recitation of food items. But yoking the commercial chant together with a snippet of bona fide, and well-trod, children's folklore also provides a stamp of vernacular authenticity.

It's inconceivable that Aida Lo would have learned the rhyme among local peers in Senegal, since McDonald's does not operate or actively advertise there. Indeed, I discovered that she was taught the rhyme by one of the American Peace Corps volunteers who remembered it from her own youth, growing up in Pittsburgh in the 1990s. This exchange illustrates just how extensive and insidious the reach of advertising can be, in a slippery process that we might call folk marketing which, like marketing in general, has one primary imperative—exploiting and propagating brand equity—which can then be converted into capital value. However this folk form made its way into Aida Lo's ludic repertoire, we can be sure that the marketing department at McDonald's international would be pleased find it there. Just because McDonald's has no physical presence in Senegal currently doesn't mean that the country is not on the company's global conquest wish list. (It seems only a matter of time, as a new McDonald's restaurant opens up somewhere in the world about every seven hours.) On the playground, this jingle/rhyme morphed into the chant "Welcome to McDonald's," usually recited rapidly and accompanied by intricate hand-clapping movements:

Welcome to McDonald's, may I take your order?
Big Mac, small fries, Coca-Cola, apple pie.

This chant rhythmically simulates a transactional exchange in the service industry, and in their performance of it, with no hint of subversion, children are in effect portraying good consumerism; their enactment, lacking as it does suspicion or contempt for the corporate world, seems out of character with much of other children's ludic discourse around commercial culture. The children's folk right to undermine invasive corporate influence appears to have been waived in this instance.

Here we conclude on a cynical note, with the recognition that advertising can be cynical business. Decades ago, McDonald's lit upon a participatory marketing strategy that many advertisers now embrace fully—that is, specific groups of people are courted as "brand communities" that "form strong social bonds through common affinity for a brand, because, hopefully, these affective relations mean increased customer loyalty" (Jenkins, Ford, and Green 2013, 164). On the assumption that the best way to market to children is through other children, some companies have gone so far as to recruit kids to be brand ambassadors among their peers, including such insidious tactics as sponsored brand-themed sleepovers where children can test new products, while "secret agents" record the proceedings and report back to HQ for prizes (Nairn 2010, 109). Commercializing children's friendships this way is just one of a number of ethically questionable marketing tactics undertaken by companies in their persistent quest for more branding leverage.

* * *

For better or worse, children experience an immersive relationship with brands. They are potential lifetime customers and therefore primary targets for big businesses grooming them for profit (Mayo and Nairn 2009). Admirably, children employ folklore as a mechanism to defuse, interrupt, or undermine the advertising onslaught. But corporations take very seriously their mission to "trademark" the cognitive space of children's culture—to the point that even the folk process can be appropriated—incorporated, as we've seen, for commercial interests. And so the playground itself can be viewed as something of a branding battlefield.

6

"The Joke's on Us"

Deconstructing Metahumor

SELF-REFERENCE IS NOT NEW TO HUMAN EXPRESSION. *Hamlet* gives us a play within a play, one Escher hand draws another, Groucho Marx is unwilling to join a club that would have him as a member, *Seinfeld* characters promote a sitcom called *Jerry*—and so on. There are countless examples from popular culture. With the advent of social media, self-awareness has become exponentially more deliberate and calculated, and certainly well practiced (*selfie* was Oxford Dictionary's word of the year in 2013 [*twerk* also made the short list that year]). Additionally, with the emergence of reflexivity in the social sciences, scholars have become especially attuned to social performance and ethnography that "shows ourselves to ourselves" (Myerhoff 2007, 32). In this cultural and intellectual climate, metajokes have particular resonance. Like Escher's circuit of drawing hands, metajokes show us what jokes do—and in the process they repurpose and sometimes undermine themselves, tantamount to a form of auto-intervention. This chapter examines the generic boundaries and semantics of these offbeat jokes, which are metacultural affectations and adumbrations of folk forms already in circulation. Because some joking forms are so commonplace and immediately recognizable, they are immanently manipulable and perfectly suited for melding together the familiar and strange. In terms of production/reception, metajokes encapsulate perfectly

DOI: 10.7330/9781607329909.c006

the ambivalent—sometimes contradictory—nature of audience response: through parody and humorous gloss, they deconstruct the original forms that inspire them. Jokes find new (metacommunicative) life in folk culture as caricatures of themselves.

PUNCH LINES AND JOKE SCRIPTS

A rabbi walks into a bar with a frog on his shoulder.
The bartender says, "Hey, where did you get that?"
The frog says, "Brooklyn. They got hundreds of 'em."

In the world of jokes, where the fantastic and absurd are common, we can readily accept that a rabbi might indeed walk into a bar with a frog on his shoulder. The humor comes from the unexpected development of the frog talking. Here we see the effect of comic incongruity, which depends on unpredictability. The structural essence of incongruity in jokes is a tension between two oppositional scripts. The listener is (mis)guided into following the path of one of the two scripts but suddenly, in the punch line, another takes its place. As humor theorists Attardo and Raskin observed, a punch line "triggers the switch from the one script to the other by making the hearer backtrack and realize that a different interpretation was possible from the very beginning" (1991, 308). In the frog joke, there is an "appropriate incongruity" of interrelated domains, to use Oring's (1992, 1–15) terminology: the opening sentence depicts the rabbi as the active agent entering the bar, and we naturally assume that the bartender's "you" is addressing him. The punch line reveals otherwise, and it is the derailment of our assumptions and expectations that elicits the laugh. Our "getting" the joke presupposes a cognitive shift on our part when we "[recognize] the vector the narrative or sentence should have taken had it unfolded according to expectation, contrasting that against how it did unfold" (Brodie 2014, 26). In formal terms, the frog joke is quite conventional, characterized by a brief narrative opening in a familiar joke setting and a punch line that turns on the comic effect of thwarted expectations. It serves as a point of reference for another joke, comparable in its setting and cast of characters, that accomplishes something quite different in its punch line:

A priest, a rabbi, and a minister walk into a bar. The bartender
looks up and says, "Hey, what is this—some kind of joke?"

It is indeed some kind of joke, but we don't expect that observation to come from an imagined character within the text. As an
idiom in everyday parlance, the question "What is this—some kind
of joke?" is an expression of incredulity, and the referent has nothing to do with verbal jokes per se, but with actual lived situations.
It appears plausibly that way as part of the joke's fictive frame: we
might well imagine a real-life bartender saying something similar
were a real-life priest, rabbi, and minister to walk together into his
bar. But the idiom has a multivalent sense and that's why it works
well in the punch line here. As a comic device the meaning is only
denotative, and the bartender's *this* refers to the fiction where he
as a character exists. So he is literally—self-consciously—aware of
himself and the others as participants in the action. This textual
self-consciousness engenders a diversity of interpretations and
"stretches the imaginary world [of the joke] to breaking point,"
argues Alex Segal (2018, 7). The notable difference here is the fact
that the joke itself comprises the unexpected secondary script
upon which the humor hangs.

This kind of reflexivity in jokes is ponderable—certainly
compelling in analytical terms—and suggestive of a larger body
of metajokes: that is to say—simply, to begin with—jokes about
jokes/joking. Their self-awareness as a communicative form and
their circulation across folk and popular culture locates metajokes
in the realm of the folkloresque, "popular culture's own (emic) perception and performance of folklore" (Foster and Tolbert 2016,
5). Furthermore, since metajokes by definition are "treatments" of
other jokes, when promulgated through conduits of commercial
media they provide pop cultural commentary on folk ideas, notions
of genre, and audience expectation. The humor of a metajoke,
Attardo observes, derives from its "violation of the expectations
set by the activation of the genre 'joke'" (2014b, 417); metajokes
thus contain the seeds of their own deconstruction.

I am reminded of a few topical jokes about some tragic events
in recent history that all received extensive media coverage and

prompted much discussion. In the aftermath of the shocking mass suicide at the Jonestown compound in Guyana in 1978, I was earnestly asked by a friend why there were so few jokes about it. As I cogitated on the possible reasons, he answered dryly, "Because the punch lines were too long."[1] Later, in 1997, there was a frenzy of gallows humor following the automobile collision that caused Princess Diana's lamentable death in the Pont de l'Alma tunnel in Paris. Commenting on that fact, one colleague asked me rhetorically, "Don't all these Princess Diana jokes just drive you up the wall?" And when the Asian tsunami of 2004 was still a top story across news conduits, another colleague, aware of my interest in humor cycles, advised me to be on the lookout for tsunami jokes because surely they would be coming in waves.

In all of these instances, I recall that the tellers integrated the jokes into the surrounding (non-joking) conversation, catching me and other listeners off guard. As folk forms, these kinds of jokes operate similarly to anti-legends.[2] The benchmark is that one mode of discourse is disguised as another. What seemed at first to be discussions with friends *about* jokes were in fact jokes themselves, with discernible punch lines and the conventional joking device of puns related to particular details of the respective joke topics. Although they weren't initially perceived as such at the moment of their performance, these generically hybrid jokes have a "meta" quality in that they take on jokes as their subject.

Most of the metajokes that are the subject of this study work differently, however: from their beginnings they are framed as what we might consider typical narrative jokes, but then as they unfold they become notably atypical by their self-awareness. Incongruity is often an operative device in these jokes, but the violated expectation is not a function of some unanticipated twist in the narrative script (as in the frog joke); rather, the surprise comic moment occurs when the joke veers unpredictably to metanarrative by announcing its own status as joke, parsing its own characters, or pointing up the formulaic conventions of humor itself. Although metajoking is fashionable and appears frequently across contemporary popular media, it has been undertheorized by humor scholars, and I am hoping here to address that lack in some measure.

Comedian Bobcat Goldthwait's stand-up act included a bit in which he would proclaim loudly from the stage, "My wife is so fat," prompting the audience to respond, "How fat is she?" To this he would reply disdainfully, "She's just fat, okay, I can't make a joke about everything!" Of course, the entire exchange, which is clearly designed to elicit laughter, is a managed joke from the outset, but the audience is purposely misguided as the joke skews its anticipated paradigm, or template. In this case, the template had been firmly established by Johnny Carson on *The Tonight Show*. A tradition developed in the show's early years, when it was broadcast from the Rockefeller Center in New York (1962–72): Carson would comment during his monologue, "It was so [hot/cold/windy] . . ." and members of the audience would customarily call back in unison, "How [hot/cold/windy] was it?"—setting up Carson's riposte to complete the joke. As in, "It's so cold here in New York that the flashers are just describing themselves" (Kashner 2014). The recurring call-and-response bit became even more regular once the show moved to Burbank, California, in 1972. As a sort of tribute, the model was further reinforced, usually with bawdy undertones, by Gene Rayburn on *The Match Game* series. So, by the time Goldthwait took the stage as a stand-up comedian, this joke formula was well known in American popular culture, and the humor in his routine stemmed from the familiar made strange or unpredictable.

Through that lens, we might view other metajokes appearing in folk culture. Joke templates—that is, standard joke "types" with recurring characters, settings, and circumstances—are sometimes subverted for reflexive comic effect. Initially, we can consider one of the most tenacious joke templates, the chicken crossing the road. The form is so familiar that the riddling question "Why did the chicken cross the road?" began to elicit variable responses besides the original "To get to the other side" (e.g., "To get away from Colonel Sanders" or "To show the possum [or armadillo] that it could be done"). Notably, many of these alternate versions could stand alone and make comic sense to someone with no prior knowledge of the existing template. Other variations are more squarely metadiscursive because they trade on the audience's recognition of the form, like this one collected from an eleven-year-old boy in 2001: "Why did the dinosaur cross the road? Because chickens hadn't been invented yet." This joke registers only if the audience is familiar with the template, for the dinosaur anachronistically replacing the chicken—a sort of prehistoric ur-form—is the key to the humor. Or, similarly, this one, which puns on a double meaning: "Why did the turkey cross the road? Because he wasn't chicken." One variation has an essentialist appeal: "Why did the chicken cross the road? To have his motives questioned for years to come." In a single stroke, this metajoke abstracts the entire enterprise of the chicken-crossing-the-road template, at the same time that it structurally embodies the form it is ostensibly describing. Here, as with the dinosaur and turkey jokes, the comic value depends on an awareness of the prototype. These all might be considered joke parodies, intertextually resonating with a well-worn joking form. In a sense, every parody is metacommentary on another known text. That is not to say that all joke cycles—clusters of jokes around particular trending topics—operate necessarily as metajokes. However fashionable or tenacious they may be, popular joke cycles (or any jokes, for that matter) are metadiscursive only when they: (1) parody a known joking *form* (as with parodic joke templates), (2) take on jokes as their subject (metahumor), (3) are self-referential, (4) are shorthand allusions to jokes (that is, joke metonyms), or (5) undermine joking altogether in the form of anti-jokes (non-jokes posing as jokes).

TWISTED TEMPLATES

Some metajokes function on a two-part mechanism. The first is narrative orientation, which introduces the characters and the setting. At this point, the metajoke looks very much like other conventional narrative jokes. But then instead of proceeding into its next typical narrative stage—what Labov and Waletsky (1967) call the complicating action—the metajoke retreats essentially into typological summary. For instance: "Three blokes go into a pub. One of them is a little bit stupid, and the whole scene unfolds with a tedious inevitability" (Bailey 2004). This gibe comes from British comedian Bill Bailey, who has established himself as something of a specialist in metajoking. A recent interview in the *Guardian* introduced Bailey as one who "hates jokes—always has done. When somebody tells him one, he says, he feels as if he's being mugged—the buildup, the promise that he'll find this one funny, the forced reaction." His career effectively launched in 1994 when he received a call to fill in for another comedian who had canceled at the Joker Comedy Club in Essex. Recalling the fateful gig, Bailey says,

> The Joker is quite raucous: they like their comedy and they let you know one way or the other. Then some bloke said, "Oi, mate, tell us a joke!" I thought, "Oh my God, I can't think of any jokes at all." So I went, "OK, three blokes went into a pub," and straight away there was attention because this was something the audience could respond to . . . I'm thinking, "I'm so in the shit here." So I said, "I say three—it was probably more like four or five," and that got a couple of laughs. Then I said, "Well, I say five—it was 10. OK, 10 blokes go in a pub," and I say, "OK, there were quite a few more than that—20–30 blokes," and then it was 100, 200, a village, a small town, an area of Holland, northern Europe, and it went on and on, extrapolating this thing from three to most sentient blokes. "OK, the entire male population of the world goes into a pub and the first bloke goes up to the bar, and says, I'll get these." And I said, "What an idiot!" And it got a huge laugh, and I thought: that just came out of nowhere. (Hattenstone 2013)

Bailey stylized the joke (which voiced his long-held aversion to traditional one-liners) and made it a regular part of his act, later incorporating it into his 1995 comedy tour *Cosmic Jam*. An absurdly exaggerated extension of a conventional joke template, it opened the door for a particular brand of humor that would become his signature, what he regards as the "non-joke." As a comedian who travels on international tours, sells out stadium venues, and whose jokes appear all over the internet (often without attribution), Bailey has been instrumental in propagating and publicizing metajokes of this form. In the first episode of his stand-up/sketch comedy series *Is It Bill Bailey?* he told this condensed joke: "Three blokes go into a pub. Something happens. The outcome was hilarious!"[3]

Bailey's manipulation of these familiar joke templates is a co-optation of a folkloric form. Compare, for example, a similarly abridged joke from folk tradition that supplies an even more abbreviated summary: "A priest, a rabbi, and a minister get into a rowboat. Hilarity ensues."

Sometimes the generic summary creeps even into the joke's narrative orientation, like this: "Three people of different nationalities walk into a bar. Two of them say something smart, and the third one makes a mockery of his fellow countrymen by acting stupid."[4] Jokes of this sort lampoon the prescribed expectations of common joke templates—and if they strike us as funny, we are essentially laughing at our own joking conventions. One example is a classic riddle-joke template rendered almost clinically as a typological digest: "How many members of a certain demographic group does it take to screw in a light bulb? A finite number—one to screw in the light bulb and the remainder to act in a manner stereotypical of said group."[5] This is metadiscursive caricature, really—the joke template becomes the joke itself, contravening Oring's assertion that "the structure of a joke cannot be reduced to a logical or mathematical formula and still function as a joke" (2016, 188). Folklorists might regard this as an instance of type itself becoming variant.

These typological parodies make comic sense only when they are derived from well-trafficked forms. Not surprisingly, they appear often in the shtick of late-night television, which relies heavily on established comedic conventions and always chases the next cleverly winking reference for a knowing audience. Megan Kelly of *Fox News* invited a media firestorm in mid-December 2013 when she made the emphatic claim that Santa Claus is white, sparking vociferous commentary across cable media and the blogosphere, and dominating the news cycle for a full forty-eight hours. As a playful response, CNN's Don Lemon hosted a discussion panel of four different multicultural Santas (a white Santa, black Santa, Latino Santa, and Filipino Santa)—prompting Stephen Colbert to weigh in: "One white, one black, one Latino and one Filipino Santa? That reminds me of a great joke I can only tell to a white Santa" (*The Colbert Report*, 2013). Colbert's send-up manipulates the template of a familiar type of multiethnic slur; the humor relies solely on audience awareness of the type, but it is only an *allusion* to a (non-existent) joke that never actually gets told. Still, his jocular remark elicits the largest laugh of the segment.

Other commonly parodied types include the lightbulb joke, the bar joke—and the limerick. Gershon Legman's *The Limerick*, which remains the most comprehensive study of the subject, credits the genre as being "the only fixed poetic form original to the English language" and boldly claims that the limerick is "the *only* kind of newly-composed poetry in English, or song, which has the slightest chance whatever of survival" (1969, lxxii). Legman's (in)famous bluster notwithstanding, we can agree that the limerick, with its strict rules of rhyme and metrics, is perhaps the most formularized mode of folk poetry, and as such it lends itself to the same kind of metajoking typology we've already seen:

> There once was an X from place B,
> That satisfied predicate P,
> He or she did thing A,
> In an adjective way,
> Resulting in circumstance C.[6]

Showing and telling simultaneously, this limerick generically typifies the form it describes. Similarly, the topic of faulty scansion is expressed in a separate metrically "de-formed" limerick:

> There was a young man of Japan
> Whose limericks never would scan.
> When someone asked why,
> He replied with a sigh,
> "It's because I always try to get as many words into the
>   last line as I possibly can." (Attardo 2014a, 454)

In addition to reflexively toying with their own typological form like these limericks, metajokes may at the same time interrogate the boundaries of what is considered to be fair game topically, as Bailey demonstrates: "Three blind mice walk into a bar, but they are unaware of their surroundings, so to derive humor from them would be exploitive" (2004). Perhaps this satirizes hypersensitivity around handicapped jokes—or political correctness in general. In any case, structurally this is like Goldthwait's joke: it begins with a familiar trope that creates certain performative expectations, and the humor comes when those expectations are denied; what we get instead is the postured claim that, in the interest of propriety, the joke cannot be completed. The politics of humor is more aggressive in the following joke: "How many feminists does it take to screw in a light bulb? That's not funny!" The abrupt reply is a non sequitur—certainly not a viable answer to the posed question. It is, instead, the imported voice of censure. While on one level the joke impugns the very topic it raises, on another it is patently male chauvinistic, reinforcing a stereotype of militant feminists incapable of laughing at themselves or sexist jokes generally (Veatch 1998, 172; questioned by Oring 2016, 63).[7]

Sometimes the stereotype in the light bulb joke is a function of place. For instance, New Yorkers, fairly or not, are often typecast as impatient and belligerent—a perception institutionalized by the fact that *Travel + Leisure* magazine routinely ranks New York near the top of its annual "Rudest Cities in America" list. Of course, folklore has long reinforced that negative opinion: "How many New Yorkers does it take to screw in a light bulb? None of your fuckin' business!" (which seems to be a variation on the classic tourist's wisecrack to a New Yorker: "Can you tell me what time it is or should I just go fuck myself?"). Other light bulb jokes target groups because of their national identity, as with the common stereotype of Germans being authoritarian and militaristic, behavioral markers that read as equivalents of Nazism: "How many Germans does it take to change a light bulb? Ve are asking ze qvestions here!" (C. Davies 2011, 217).[8] Analysts, too, can find themselves in the dark, leaving us to ask, "How many Freudians does it take to change a light bulb?" The answer is "Two. One to hold the light bulb and one to hold the penis—I mean mother—I mean ladder." The verbal gaffes here seem at first disintegrative to the joke, but they fit thematically given the common caricature of doctrinaire Freudians, who are thought to link every morphemic misstep to some deeper phallic or maternal fixation. Like most light bulb jokes, these all tease out the stereotypes of selected target groups.

But they do so in nuanced ways. The highlighted stereotypes are not described or demonstrated in some action of the bulb changer (that would be typical); rather, the stereotypes infiltrate the verbal texture of the jokes themselves in the form of humorless censure or ungainly Freudian slips.

So hackneyed is the light bulb joke template that parodies of it need not even mention changing a light bulb, so long as the riddling construction "How many x does it take to y?" remains intact (where x stands for some targeted social group and y an identified task for members of that group to perform); that alone is sufficient to conjure up the conventional form. For example, "How many geeks does it take to ruin a joke? You mean nerd, not geek. And not joke, but riddle. Proceed." This joke, like the others, introduces an ancillary voice whose proscription against the posed question demonstrably answers the question. Thus, metajokes achieve a particular kind of comic traction by the ways in which they foster, and then promptly dislocate, our expectations about familiar, and somewhat predictable, joke structures. The violated expectation is largely a contrivance of destabilizing the anticipated generic "architecture" of the template.

SELF-REFERENTIAL JOKES

One form of self-reference occurs as jokes take jokes/joking as their subject. Jokes about the *fear* of joking, for instance, comprise a particular subtype of political metahumor that emerged in nondemocratic regimes during the Soviet era. These circulated during a time when telling, even listening and responding to, political jokes fell under article 58.10 of the Russian Soviet penal code, "Anti-Soviet and counter-revolutionary propaganda and agitation." In her recent study on the topic, Belarusian folklorist Anastasiya Astapova (2017) cites this brief joking exchange:

> "What is the hobby of Brezhnev?"
> "Collecting jokes."
> "So how many has he collected?"
> "Two camps [worth]."

As *collecting* is a term used by researchers who actively gather, archive, and classify compilations of jokes and other cultural material, it seems at first that Brezhnev may have some ethnographic interest as an armchair joke hobbyist; the trenchant punch line teaches us otherwise: that his interest lies not in the jokes themselves but rather in the unlawful tellers of them, who are then incarcerated—"collected"—in work camps for undermining the state. Astapova observes that variants of the joke have been told also about Stalin, Lavrentiy Beria (marshal of the Soviet Union and first deputy premier) and Alexandr Lukashenko (president of Belarus). The joke, she says, "mocks the fact that so many people are afraid, but does not dismiss the reasons for the fear." Beyond that, this sort of politically risky humor is a means by which "the regime, the leaders, the rhetoric, the incompetence, the hardships, the duplicity, the surveillance, and even the terror are domesticated and discounted" (Oring 2016, 126). No regime, regardless of how restrictive or ruthless, can completely control speech. Brave and defiant individuals (who might also be funny) give social resistance a voice, and naturally they gravitate toward expressive forms that have been prohibited by the state. Such is the case with a number of Soviet-era metajokes dealing with the spying on, arrest, and punishment of political joke tellers; these are jokes whose theme is the peril of joking in the face of totalitarianism. Christie Davies documented a few examples in Slovakia before the Berlin Wall came down.

> Prison conversation:
> "Why are you here?"
> "I told a joke."
> "And what brought you here?"
> "I listened to a joke."
> "And what about you?"
> "I am here because I was lazy! One evening I was at a party. Someone there told a joke. I went home wondering whether I should inform on them right away or wait until the next morning. 'Well,' I thought, 'tomorrow morning will do.' And they came for me during the night!"

Two judges are eating soup in the restaurant of the "pal-
ace." One with a spoon in his hand laughs.
"Why?"
"I heard a good joke today."
"Tell me."
"I can't tell you. I gave the man who told it five years."
"You call that a good joke? Good jokes get six years at
least." (2011, 227)

One raconteur described for Davies a version of "Modern Russian
roulette": "There are 12 of us telling political jokes. One of us is
an informer and we don't know who" (227). Another example is an
Iron Curtain classic about a joke competition, this variant among
the Romanian political jokes gathered by Robert Cochran: "Did
you hear about the political joke contest? Third prize is 100 lei
[Romanian currency], second prize is 1000 lei, first prize is fifteen
years" (1989, 270). Of course, as one might expect, earlier, when
the Nazis were in power, there are numerous instances of similar
joking, like this: "What is fratricide? If Hermann Goering slaugh-
ters a pig. What is suicide? If someone tells this joke in public"
(Lipman 1991, 52). Dangerous business, these jocular iterations are
maneuvers of reflexive subversion. Political jokes about joking become a natural, if perilous, idiom for defiant individuals inclined to
critique autocracies with strict proscriptions against political joking.
    Political humor notwithstanding, the reflexivity of jokes about
jokes is especially exaggerated when joke characters become self-
aware, recognizing themselves as types: "A priest, a rabbi, and a
minister are sitting together on a plane. The rabbi looks at the other
two and asks, 'Say, did you hear the one about us?'" Cognizant that
he inhabits "the one about us," the rabbi heralds another anticipated
joke performance, and we might guess where things could go from
there. If the rabbi were to relate *this* very joke, which itself frames
the beginning of another telling, it conceivably could stand as the
inaugural link in a perpetual chain of jokes within jokes, a comic
self-referential mise en abyme. Sometimes, the reflexivity extends
beyond characters' awareness of themselves as actors in the joke
script; they can self-recognize even at the level of text itself, as in

the meme that circulated widely in 2020 illustrating a rabbit, belly up to a bar and holding in its paws a pint of beer. The caption reads, "A priest, a rabbit, and a minister walk into a bar. The rabbit says, 'I might be a typo.'" Other examples carry us further yet into the metadiscursive, with characters who are not only self-aware or self-referential but also self-determining. Like Flann O'Brien's *At Swim, Two Birds*, in which the characters seize control of the novel, these jokes unfold by the prerogative of the characters.

> A newlywed couple, a blind man, a used car dealer, a proctologist, and a hooker, along with a nun, a man who just received a gorilla brain transplant, two Hassidic Jews, a stuttering hotel clerk, and a chicken are riding in a compact car. Suddenly, they hear a siren and a state trooper motions the vehicle to pull over. "License and registration," says the cop. "You've exceeded the legal character limit in this joke."

The notion that there exists some codified, enforceable set of joke regulations is playfully appropriate, for jokes *do* persistently violate what we might call statutes of expectation—and this one does so in a grandly overstated manner: the outrageous array of characters populating the joke could leave humor aficionados salivating at the boundless possibilities (besides just the comical image of them all stuffed into one small car).

Joke characters may behave unpredictably, and indeed punch lines often rely on that, but we still expect them to inhere within the fictive frame of the joke. When they do not, the anticipated path of the joke deviates into a particular genre of comic metadiscourse. For example, among the ubiquitous traveling salesmen in jokes, who find themselves fortuitously stranded at the houses of farmers with daughters, there are a few who step outside of, and rewrite, the conventional scripts of their own jokes: "A traveling salesman knocks on a farmer's door at night and says, 'Sorry to bother you, but my car has broken down. Can I stay the night?' The farmer replies, 'Sure, but you'll have to share a bed with my son.' The salesman says, 'Your son? Never mind. I must be in the wrong joke.'" Perhaps homophobic, or at least obstinately heteronormative, this salesman effectively ends the joke himself because the circumstances don't fit his own sexual proclivities. Alternately, a variant with the same standardized setup ends this way: "[The farmer says to the salesman,] 'Sure, I'll give you a bed for the night . . . But I gotta tell you that I have no daughter for you to sleep with like you always hear about in those jokes.' After thinking for a minute or two, the salesman says, 'How far to the next house?'" Meaning, effectively, how far to the next traveling salesman joke, where his sexual fantasy with a farmer's daughter might be realized. It's an intriguing thought—fictional characters drifting along in the universe of jokes searching for their most appropriate role and empowered to recast familiar texts along the way. It is an enactment of postmodernism: authorship itself is deposed.

JOKE METONYMS

As we have seen, some metajokes derive their humor from unexpected turns in narrative stance (from active narration to mediating summary), improbable shifts in voicing, and exaggerated reflexivity. There is another sort of metajoking, however—not jokes about jokes but rather joke metonyms, which are shorthand substitutions, typically just the decontextualized punch lines of larger narrative jokes. We might compare legend metonyms of the sort discussed in chapter 1, which "[recall] the whole story simultaneously present in the minds of the group's members, without interrupting the present topic of conversation to replay it" (Ellis 1989, 40). Or proverb metonyms for that matter, which operate similarly with abbreviated phrases like "gift horse," "spilled milk," or "silk purse," triggering unmistakable recollections of their fuller proverbial forms.

An important distinction, though, is that joke metonyms maintain a comic potential even when the "host" texts are unknown to the listener. That is to say, extracted punch lines can be inherently funny in their own right. There are websites dedicated to the "punch line only" format, and I remember playing this as a sort of party game when I was a teenager. Participants would recite just the punch lines from their favorite offensive jokes, invariably eliciting laughter from the other cohorts. Rarely are the punch lines obscene in and of themselves, but in a moment they conjure up flashes of elaborate *potential* plots with prurient details:

> "There's no way that kangaroo is left handed."
> "Dalai Lama, Dolly Parton—there's a difference?"
> "I got four weeks' vacation and five good leads."
> "Now wash your hands and make me a pastrami sandwich."
> "Hey, lady, how do you think I rang the doorbell?"
> "That's real nice music, mister, but I think your monkey's on fire."

William Safire's (1984) gloss on such joke leftovers as "dangling punch lines to forgotten stories, remaining in the language like the smile of the Cheshire cat" is an apt analogy if we remember Alice's astonishment at the disembodied grin: "Well! I've often seen a cat without a grin . . . but a grin without a cat! It's the most curious thing I ever saw in my life!" Oblique allusions to unknown texts, detached punch lines like these remain comically viable because they essentially invite listeners to create retroactively their own accompanying jokes.

The pop culture equivalent is a widely used television and film comedic device known as the "orphaned punch line." The action cuts to a new scene to show a character telling a joke in media res; the audience hears only the isolated joke punch line, detached from any narrative setup, and the reactions of other characters vary from "rip-roaring hilarity, monocle-popping disgust [to] a deathly quiet."[9] The orphaned punch lines are most often extracted from salacious jokes, allowing the filmmakers to insinuate a level of obscenity that would never be permitted overtly. For example, an allusion to a traveling salesman and farmer's daughter joke appears in a Laurel and Hardy film titled, appropriately enough, *Come Clean* (1931). Having asked his friend to distract their wives with a "funny story," Hardy returns to an apartment to find Laurel mid-sentence: ". . . then the farmer came in and he shot the traveling salesman," at which point Hardy's wife says, "How dare you?!" and attempts to slap Laurel across the face (missing, and slapping Hardy instead).[10]

In *Men in Black* a new scene begins with Tommy Lee Jones's character K telling a joke to Will Smith: "But, honey, this one's eating my popcorn!" It's the punch line to the old chestnut of a joke about the man who sneaks a chicken into a movie theater by stuffing the bird down his pants. The same orphaned punch line appears in *The Sting*, delivered in the background by an unnamed burlesque house comedian. Screenwriters sometimes invent the setups/punch lines outright, and when they do, they often introduce exceedingly peculiar narrative details just for fun, leaving the audience to ponder what joke could possibly accommodate such absurdity. That is probably the case with the orphaned punch line that appears in *Some Like It Hot*. Tony Curtis and Jack Lemmon, cross-dressed and traveling with a women's jazz band to hide from the mob, find themselves on a train with their band mates. Early in the trip, the trombonist begins an apparently off-color joke (about a girl tuba player stranded on a desert island with a one-legged jockey), but is stopped short by the band manager, who warns, "Now cut it out, girls, none of that rough talk." The action takes us away from that narration, until a full twenty minutes later in the film when we see the same character in a new scene delivering just the punch line "So the one-legged jockey says 'Don't worry about me, baby, I ride sidesaddle!'" (to uproarious laughter from the other characters). The sitcom *Night Court* had a running gag with an orphaned punch line plucked from a familiar joke about a lascivious nun: "Twenty dollars, same as in town!" There were occasional variations like "So Anna Karenina says, 'Twenty rubles, same as in St. Petersburg.'"

So popular were orphaned punch lines that they began to spring up in all types of mainstream entertainment, far afield from just film and TV sitcoms. David Letterman's recurring top ten list segment on *Late Night* once included the category "top ten punch lines to Scottish dirty jokes":

10. It took me a fortnight to get out of the thistles.
 9. I didn't know you could also get wool from them!
 8. It's not a bagpipe, but don't stop playing.
 7. What made you think I was talking about golf?

6. I've heard of comin' through the rye—but this is ridiculous!

5. Of course she's served millions—she's a McDonald.

4. Oh, so *you're* Wade Boggs.

3. Care to shake hands with the Loch Ness monster?

2. Who's burning argyles?

1. She's in the distillery making Johnnie Walker Red.

Likely, the entries on the list were all invented, written just for the show (I have been unable to identify from folk or popular sources the host jokes for any of these punch lines). However, in an interview with *Empire* magazine, comedian Leslie Neilsen admitted that he had forgotten the setup to his favorite joke, but well remembered the punch line (a variation of number 8 from Letterman's list): "It's not a bagpipe, lassie, but keep blowin'!"[11] Whether or not he truly had forgotten the joke's setup (or if the joke ever existed in the first place), Neilsen, a master of deadpan delivery, clearly played the punch line alone for all its *intrinsic* comedic value.

A 2010 television commercial for Miller Lite beer began with a young man at a bar telling a joke to his apparent girlfriend, delivering the (invented) orphaned punch line, "So I get to his house, and he has thirteen monkeys!" Her cued laughter is presumably an indication of their amicable relationship. Dave Barry's *Claw Your Way to the Top*, a send-up of job market and business success books, advises job candidates to begin letters of application this way: "So then the priest says to the rabbi, 'But how did you get the snake to wear lipstick?'" (Barry 1986, 18). The suggestion is that any employer receiving such a letter would be unable to resist calling the applicant in for an interview just to find out how the joke begins. One *Far Side* cartoon (July 1, 1994) by Gary Larson shows an anthropomorphized fork standing on a stage behind a microphone delivering stand-up comedy to an audience of other forks. The caption reads, ". . . And so the bartender says, 'Hey! That's not a soup spoon!' But seriously, forks . . ." In *Shrek Forever After*, the fourth and final installment of the *Shrek* tetralogy, Shrek can be heard telling the end of a joke to Rumpelstiltskin: "So, the centaur says, 'That's not the half I'm talking about.'" This is just a small sampling from among hundreds of instances of orphaned punch lines across popular media. These joke snippets all figure into the larger creative vision of their auteurs, but they also capture, in abridged fashion, mediated renditions of the folk processes of joke telling. Of course, television and film screenwriters, advertisers, humorists, and cartoonists have all witnessed authentic joke telling in natural contexts; these artistically manipulated detached punch lines metonymically reference those real-life folk performances—even as they metadiscursively play with the sense of authenticity and familiarity that such joke formats and types project. And like the adapted joke templates, these direct allusions/subversions to joking patterns make conscious use of the audience's indexical relationship to recognizable folk forms.

Metonyms of this sort invite another question: could a joke be reduced further yet, to a unit that is even more distilled than just its punch line? It might not surprise us that this question has been addressed in another metajoke:

> A new prisoner is at his first lunch. One of the other prisoners stands up and yells out, "73" and everyone laughs—they're banging trays on the table and laughing their heads off. Another prisoner stands up and yells, "139" and everyone laughs—even harder than before. So the new prisoner asks a guy next to him what's going on. "Oh, that? Well, we've been here so long that we just memorized a big book of jokes. We figure we save time by calling out the numbers of the jokes."
>
> So the new guy decides he'll give it a try. He stands up and calls out, "41." No one laughs—nothing. So he tries it again, louder: "41." Nothing. Then he asks the other prisoner, "What did I do wrong?" And the prisoner says, "Well, some people can tell jokes and some can't."[12]

In other versions, the new prisoner is told that no one laughs because his joke is in poor taste or that his timing is off. Whereas disembodied punch lines give the sense of narrative contexts, if only imagined ones, in this scenario, where the jokes (within the joke) are simplified to catalogue numbers, all performative elements are stripped away. This one may be a particular curiosity to contemporary humor theorists, who are inclined to pore over the social, situational, and textural complexities of joke performance. That a joke could be rendered funny, distasteful, or poorly timed under such circumstances is the implausibility that makes us laugh. Moreover, the joke may resonate especially with folklorists, who could hear it as a commentary on their discipline, or at least on a certain kind of folklorist. After all, folklore is the field that indexed and assigned type numbers to popular tales (e.g., ATU 510, ATU 300), and designated ballads by their numbered order in the Francis James Child compendium (e.g., Child 12, Child 84). Indeed, there was a moment in the history of folklore study when these index tags were bandied about as if they were narrative texts themselves.

ANTI-JOKES

The anti-joke, a locution bearing the formal features and linguistic markers of a conventional joke but delivered so as to offer no operative or even discernible punch line, presents another facet of metahumor. Whereas the switched scripts of more routine jokes elicit the sudden perception of appropriate incongruity (Oring 1992) from which the humor springs, anti-jokes effectively obliterate secondary scripts; that is, rather than deflecting expectations, anti-jokes effectively scrub them altogether.

Anti-jokes are intentionally not funny, and the irony is that some listeners with offbeat sensibilities find them funny for that reason alone. They often exploit familiar joke templates, as do other metajokes we've seen, but there is no punch line:

"What is a pirate's favorite letter of the alphabet?" "None. Historians have suggested that most pirates would have been illiterate."
[Traditional punch line: "R!" ("arrgh!")]

"What did one Frenchman say to the other Frenchman?" "I have no idea. I don't speak French."

"Why do undertakers wear ties?" "Because their profession is very serious, and it is important that their appearance has a degree of gravitas."

"Doctor, doctor. I feel like a pair of curtains."
    "That's the least of your worries. You're HIV positive."
    [Traditional punch line: "Pull yourself together, man!"]

A man says to his son, "If you keep masturbating, you'll go blind."
    The son replies, "That's never been scientifically proven."
    [Traditional punch line: "I'll stop when I need glasses."]

"Your mamma's so fat, we're all extremely concerned for her health."

"What's worse than biting into an apple and finding a worm?"
"The Holocaust."
    [Traditional punch line: "Finding half a worm."]

Like the long, drawn-out shaggy dog story with no point or punch line, the anti-joke builds expectation only to frustrate it. In social practice, however, the usually brief anti-joke aligns more closely with the simple misdirection-based prank. Tellers who knowingly catch their listeners off guard with anti-jokes presented as conventional jokes engage in "benign fabrication," a performative posture that Erving Goffman describes as "the intentional effort on the part of one or more individuals to manage activity so that a party of one or more others will be induced to have a false belief about what it is that is going on" (1974, 86). The key is the one-way ludic intention, as Moira Marsh has observed of practical jokes generally: "A practical joke is a scripted, unilateral play performance involving opposed parties—trickster and target—with the goal of incorporating the target into play without his or her knowledge, permission, or both" (2015, 12). The metajokes discussed earlier about the Jonestown massacre, death of Princess Diana, and the Asian tsunami were camouflaged in surrounding conversation, sprung on listeners unexpectedly from within what was assumed to be non-joking discourse. Conversely, anti-jokes, in their capacity as pranks, typically call attention to themselves as jokes and are performed accordingly; only with the execution of the deflated non–punch lines (or *flatlines*; see below) does the audience decode them as non-jokes.

The "punch" of a punch line is the snappy verbal hit at the end of a joke that elicits from the listener a reformulated perception of the joke setup, precipitating the emotional response of laughter. By that token, *punch line* is an inadequate term for the concluding tags of anti-jokes, since they supply no apparatus for the cognitive shift that normally resolves a joke, when the listener suddenly grasps a secondary script and comprehends the appropriate incongruity. Rather, the concluding line of an anti-joke is disinterested and abortive, punctuating the joke with a sober finality that works against the possibility of humor. A more apt term than punch line might be *flatline* since its function is purposely to make the joke fall flat, effectively killing the joke and thus "flatlining" it.

Sometimes anti-jokes are constructed in such a way that they neither replace nor recast a familiar punch line but rather amend the original with a dispiriting coda that derails the template altogether. Consider the classic joke:

> A horse walks into a bar, and the bartender says, "Why the long face?"

There is nothing unusual about a bartender asking a patron "Why the long face?" However, the relational frame of the horse, with its elongated equine facial features, is the conceptual mechanism by which the bartender's ordinary question transmutes into a laughter-inducing punch line (Stewart et al. 2002, 83). A number of anti-joking adaptations of this classic, however, tag on auxiliary flatlines that sabotage the humor. For example:

> A horse walks into a bar, and the bartender says, "Why the long face?" The horse says nothing because it is a horse and horses don't talk.

A similar variant adds a scatological detail:

> A horse walks into a bar, and the bartender says, "Why the long
> face?" The horse, incapable of understanding human language,
> promptly shits on the floor and leaves.

One version sustains the dramatic ethos of the original joke, reinforcing the magical idea that an anthropomorphized horse might
clomp its way into a bar and converse with a human, but the horse's
response to the bartender's query is anything but magical.

> A horse walks into a bar, and the bartender says, "Why the long
> face?" The horse responds, "Because I'm an alcoholic and it's tear-
> ing my family apart."

Not only does the horse behave as if human—drinking in a bar,
conversing as a patron—but he also suffers from (decidedly unfunny) human problems. And finally, in another variant, appearing
in an internet post titled "Kafka's Joke Book" (McNamee 2014),
the horse responds with bitter existential poignancy:

> A horse walks into a bar. The bartender asks, "Why the long
> face?"
>   "I was born into servitude, and when I die, my feet will be
> turned into glue," replied the horse.
>   The bartender realized he would not be getting a tip.

A Reddit thread called "It's the Anti-joke Chicken!" was created in 2011, featuring the picture of the disembodied head of a
rooster (not chicken) centered on a colorful starburst background,
a visual motif that became associated with a diverse body of visual/
verbal humor circulating on the internet as "animal advice memes"
(Dynel 2016). A chicken was chosen, presumably, to invoke the
well-trod "Why did the chicken cross the road?" joke cycle. Above
the rooster's head, users would generate text mimicking familiar
joke introductions, and underneath they would supply unexpected
anticlimactic responses. The forum proliferated hundreds of

anti-jokes like the ones discussed here, and derivatives of the anti-joke chicken appeared in other social media like the image board 4chan and meme generator Quickmeme. The idiosyncratic entries, often unfunny by design, weren't appreciated by all users. One commenter named Gabriot, for instance, used the common short riddle joke format to berate the meme: "What do you call an anti-joke chicken? A waste of bandwidth." The similar "Anti-joke Cat" Twitter account appeared about the same time and over the years has accumulated more than 200,000 followers who contribute their own examples.

There are multiple levels of enactment and subterfuge—and misguided expectation among the audience—as anti-joke aficionados perform versions of (what is perceived as) typical joke telling at the same time that they deliver essentially non-jokes. If there is any humor in these anti-jokes, it is a curious circumstance of the conventional humor having been expunged.

❋ ❋ ❋

Years ago, one of my brothers asked me, "What's wrong with lawyer jokes?" Before I could respond to what I thought was a foray into a theoretical discussion on humor, he shot back: "Lawyers don't think they're funny and no one else knows they're jokes." I laughed. And upon reflection, I think it was this exchange that sparked my initial interest in metajoking. What I didn't know at the time was that my brother's short riddle-form joke was an adaptation—distilled and made palatable for rapid transmission in oral folk culture—of a humorous anecdote told by former US Supreme Court chief justice William Rehnquist. Speaking to an audience of lawyers and nonlawyers at the dedication of a new building at the University of Virginia Law School in 1997, the chief justice explained: "In the past, when I've talked to audiences like this, I've often started off with a lawyer joke, a complete caricature of a lawyer who's been nasty, greedy and unethical. But I've stopped that practice. I gradually realized that the lawyers in the audience didn't think the jokes were funny and the non-lawyers didn't know they were jokes" (Galanter 2005, 3). Of course, Rehnquist's widely publicized commentary on the nature of lawyer jokes, since the 1980s one of the most active joke cycles in America (Galanter 2005; C. Davies

2011, 184–212), is itself a lawyer joke—a metajoke—and it points up precisely what we have seen in other examples: the dialogic relationship between one expressive form of folklore, mass culture, and popular media.

If we accept, as Greg Urban (2001, 4) posits, that metaculture necessarily engenders interpretation of and promotes the culture upon which it is based, then the study of metajokes will be seen as a useful exercise in interrogating the generic boundaries of jokes. Circulating robustly through contexts both folk and popular, metajokes certainly do propel joking culture. But since they are both jokes and non-jokes synchronously, subverting our expectations of how jokes operate in the first place, metajokes also undermine the whole enterprise of joking. E. B. White once quipped that "humor can be dissected, as a frog can, but the thing dies in the process and the innards are discouraging to any but the pure scientific mind" (White and White 1941, xvii). The hope with any analysis of jokes is that the metaphorical frog is not killed along the way; but metajokes, in a sense, dissect themselves, and they invite us to ponder, question, and refigure the joking devices that make us laugh. As expressive forms, metajokes by definition overtly or implicitly reference other antecedent jokes, and they do so in locutions distinctly postmodern, invoking "other discursive possibilities in a way that makes discourse itself a part of the topic of the art work" (Denith 2000, 184). Self-referential, self-aware, parodic, sometimes antithetical to common conventions of humor, metajokes work to disrupt the joking schema in which they operate.

Conclusion

Folklore, Media, and the Unruly Audience

FOR A SIGNIFICANT STRETCH OF ITS HISTORY, folklore as a field of study was predicated on a general antipathy toward mainstream media technologies, beginning with print. We can see this as early as 1888, when William Wells Newell, co-founder of the American Folklore Society and first general editor of the *Journal of American Folklore*, set about prescribing an operational framework of the field. The essential pillar of his conception was a narrowed preoccupation with oral tradition, the lore circulating strictly outside of print culture. Newell's mission statement in the inaugural issue of the journal celebrated the "freshness and quaintness which belongs only to the unwritten word" (1888b, 4). Folklore, he added in the following issue, "was invented to describe the unwritten popular traditions of civilized countries" (1888a, 163). Two years later, he proffered the now-classic definition of folklore as "oral tradition,—information and belief handed down from generation to generation without the use of writing" (1890, 134). Newell's formulations heralded the "American concept of folklore" (Dundes 1966), codified what Michael Bell considered the "initial institutional paradigm of emerging folklore research in America" (1973, 16), and established the identity of the discipline, in a sense, for nearly a century after (Kirshenblatt-Gimblett 1998b, 300–302). For a long while, the purity test of "genuine"

DOI: 10.7330/9781607329909.c007

folklore was its orality, while mediated communication, print and otherwise, remained suspect. Like early folklorists who decried printed broadsides as the death knell for authentic orally transmitted balladry, many twentieth-century folklorists projected their animus onto whatever emergent media technology might tarnish pure oral tradition.

But scholars grew to realize that folklore could not be strictly cordoned off from mass culture, and in the 1970s the theoretical winds began to shift accordingly. Richard Dorson, in his introduction to *Folklore and Folklife* (1972), hyperbolized the territorial apprehensions of some folklorists of the time: "Always the cry is that the flowers of tradition are being relentlessly crushed by the steamroller of industrial civilization. In a few more years, there will be no more folklore, and, *ergo*, no need for any folklorists" (41). Whether or not the old guard really were Luddites to such an extent, Dorson trumpeted the fact that folkloristic inquiry was beginning to veer into new territories of urban life and media. Not coincidentally, Dorson's recognition of the changing theoretical currents followed on the heels of the pacesetting "Toward New Perspectives in Folklore," a special issue of the *Journal of American Folklore* in 1971. It was there, among other significant contributions, that Dan Ben-Amos postulated his forward-looking definition of folklore as "artistic communication in small groups" (13)—an abstraction that Peter Narváez would later adapt in his analysis of the relationship between folkloristics, cultural studies, and popular culture. "The expressive use of communications media, mass produced goods, and mass mediated texts in small group contexts," Narváez argued, demonstrates a melding together of popular culture and folklore in performance (1992, 20), generating new portmanteau expressive forms he called "media lore" (1986).

About the same time that Narváez penned those observations, I was lucky enough to be studying with Linda Dégh in the last legend course that she taught at Indiana University. A seasoned folklore scholar whose classic monograph *Folktales and Society* was widely acclaimed as a model of small-community ethnography and whose program of field collection with *Indiana*

Folklore inspired and activated a generation of legend scholars, Professor Dégh in our class often lamented that the ground of traditional folklore study was shifting underneath our feet. Still, to her credit, Dégh just a few years later struck out into new territory with the publication of *American Folklore and the Mass Media* (1994). Her disciplinary purview opened up to consider "the diversity of mass media participation in the transmission of folklore" and reassess a wide array of electronic communications as "new vehicles" of dissemination (33). This was a notable shift, certainly for an old-school folklorist, but still it was a formulation in which media operated primarily as conduit or receptacle of folklore. Barbara Kirshenblatt-Gimblett contemporaneously identified an awakening "electronic vernacular" (1996), although it was to be a full decade yet before scholars moved substantively beyond the binary assumptions that had positioned pure folklore on one side and pure popular culture on the other (Bird 2006, 345), as in the folklore/popular culture continuum postulated earlier by Narváez and Laba (1986).

Mikel Koven's 2003 critical survey of folklore studies of film and television delineates what had been prevailing approaches up to that point: inquiries of (1) folklore *in* media, that is, the incorporation of folkloric material into media, which provided fuel for a generation of folklorists dedicated to "motif spotting"; (2) media *as* folklore, for example, cinematic adaptations of traditional narratives, like Disney film versions of Märchen; and (3) folklore as film, as in ethnographic documentaries (and related perspectives that regarded popular feature fiction film as something akin to "naïve ethnography" [180]). Further, Koven outlines (4) studies of a subgenre of narratives *about* media culture and technology, revisiting Sylvia Grider's "media narraforms" (1981) and Narváez's "media legends" (1986). Finally, Koven focuses on (5) fandom and audience studies, which examine subcultures of fans who become unorthodox, agentic users of the media texts that they saturate themselves in. He urges folklorists to embrace further audience-centered approaches like those modeled by Jenkins, who just three years later would remark that "convergence" culture "[throws] the media into flux" and "[expands] the opportunities for grassroots groups to speak back to the mass media" (2006, 259). Attention to this participatory impulse marked the next frontier of folklore and media studies.

By the 2010s, as the foothold of digital media was rapidly broadening, researchers began to plumb the deeper associative relationship between popular media and folklore as interwoven and dialogic. A diverse sampling of studies appeared, for example, on fairy tale and film (Greenhill and Matrix 2010; Zipes 2011a; Short 2014; Zipes, Greenhill, and Magnus-Johnston 2015), fairy-tale television (Greenhill and Rudy 2014), folklore and the internet (de Vos 2012; Foster 2012; Frank 2011), mediated legendry (Koven 2008; Kinsella 2011; Blank and McNeill 2018), and folkloristic approaches to all manner of digital culture (Miller 2008; Blank 2009, 2012; Blank and Howard 2013; Milner 2016). On top of that wave, in 2014 Utah State University's English department launched the Digital Folklore Project, a virtual research center co-founded and directed by folklorists Jeannie Banks Thomas and Lynne McNeill, which tracks popular strains of folklore across media, such as urban legends, internet memes, hashtags, and the like, and each year names a "digital trend of the year."

Unruly Audience is situated within this media/folkloristic landscape but also shares discourses with cultural, humor, consumer, and tourism studies. The connecting thread throughout is the transactional nature of folklore and popular media, each providing energy and action for the other. In that vein, the book is positioned as something of a companion volume to Foster and Tolbert's *The Folkloresque* (2016), which interrogates the "metadiscursive dimension of popular culture through which producers and consumers together engage in thoughtful evaluations of cultural forms that are the building blocks of new material" (25–26). It is an expressive process, Foster observes, emanating from the "symbiosis, and ultimately inseparability, of commercial production and folk creativity" (27). Among the manifestations of that creativity are the disruptive and participatory folk interventions in popular media like those analyzed in this volume.

SATIRE AND SUBVERSION

Colonel Bogey Parodies

By the eve of World War I, the English were skilled in the art of replacing familiar lyrics of popular tunes with new parodic lyrics, a practice stemming from the spirited verbal play within Victorian burlesque and musical theater. It was in that culture of parodic performance, amid the heightened anxiety of impending war, that Kenneth Alford penned his famous "Colonel Bogey March." The melody became popular almost instantly and the irreverent lyrics followed soon after. But this example is an unusual case, since the parodies did not really satirize existing lyrics—for there were none to satirize—and the original melodic "text" of the march remained unmolested. Rather, by their mismatch, the vulgar lyrics mocked the imperial, martial *spirit* of the tune. The process of folk intervention came into play as audiences repeatedly invented more and more irreverent lyrics, which were memorable and circulated widely, fracturing the melody's respectability and altering its cultural significance altogether. Even now, more than a century since its composition, the "Colonel Bogey March" has come to stand in Britain as "an unofficial national anthem to rudeness" (O'Grady 2010). The early Colonel Bogey parodies, which established a long tradition of jocular lyricizing around the march's melody, emerged naturally in anxious times of war and amid the comradery of soldiers who in the ranks enjoyed mild derision of martial dignity and sharper criticism of their common enemy.

Alternately, folk intervention can operate more subversively as a kind of guerilla communication critiquing corporate power and institutional authority—as with circulating jokes about Disney's *Snow White* and children's skewed imitations and mockery of the commercial world.

Snow White Jokes

A recent piece of street art features a stylized black silhouette of Disney's iconic Cinderella's castle. Close examination reveals the silhouette to be merely a tottering theatrical façade with visible braces and struts holding it upright. Clear enough as a symbol of (unstable) artifice, the propped-up castle is embellished with a caption: bold letters in distinctive Disney font that read simply, "Disillusioned." Obscene jokes about Disney's *Snow White* strike a similar chord, reframing our perceptions of Disney the company and its cultural productions. Widely recognized as "the one that started it all," *Snow White* in 1937 heralded themes that would become pillars of the Disney ethos: good triumphing over evil, romance, wish fulfillment, and "wholesome" values. The refrain of the dwarfs' "Washing Song" could stand as the company credo: "Ya gotta admit it's good, clean fun." Just as the character Snow White marshalled the collective labor of her animal friends to "tidy up the place," Walt Disney worked diligently to sanitize the classic fairy tale, reimagining the story and redacting its sexual undertones. Audience reception, however, remains untidy, regardless of the restraint or clarity of the purpose of production. The jokes about *Snow White* strip away the wholesome intent, including the adjunct cuteness, to unearth an antithetical universe that is profligate, cynical, even abusive.

Children's Commercial Parodies

It is well established that children use folklore to undermine and mock the most immediate institutions and adult authorities in their lives—parents, teachers, schools, principals, camp counselors, and so on. But since consumer culture captures children's attention and occupies their minds even more than these other targets and given that it provides resources by which children communicate and negotiate their identities (Buckingham 2011, 167–68), it is an even more formidable foil. Children are avid consumers at the same time that they are resourceful in appropriating and reworking messages from the commercial world. In 1984, Michael Jackson was severely burned while filming a Pepsi commercial: a premature stage explosion ignited his hair and he suffered second- and third-degree burns on his scalp. Extensive media coverage ensured that kids on the playground knew all about the incident, and even before the story faded from the headlines, there appeared new folk emendations to the popular clapping/skipping rhyme "Down by the Banks of the Hanky Panky." One excerpt went like this:

> Michael Jackson went downtown,
> Coca-Cola turned him down.
> Pepsi-Cola burned him up,
> So now he's drinking 7-Up.
> 7-Up's got no caffeine,
> So now he's drinking gasoline.
> Gasoline's not good for you,
> So now he's drinking Mountain Dew.
> Mountain Dew fell off the mountain,
> So now he's drinking from a fountain.
> Fountain broke, Michael choked,
> Now he's back to drinking Coke.

Driven by the topical news, this adaptation is built upon the operative line "Pepsi-Cola burned him up"; but the telling feature from a consumerist point of view is the itemized inventory of other popular soda brands that accumulated as the rhyme gained currency among children.[1] The rhyme demonstrates acute brand awareness, not surprising at a time when Coca-Cola and Pepsi were mounting combative ad campaigns in the so-called cola wars.

Often, from brand awareness comes brand derision, as with the familiar slogan/jingle "Everything's better with Blue Bonnet on it," which was refashioned by children as "Everything's better with blue vomit on it." Besides the appeal of the internal rhyme, regurgitation is a common subject in children's lore (see, e.g., the Comet rhymes above), and it is especially en-"grossing" to kids when they imagine vomit in the unnatural color of blue. No quantitative study has determined whether associating a given brand with a celebrity's sensational injury, for instance, or parodying an ad on the playground would inhibit the salability of a product. But such measurable results would be beside the point anyway. As the Knapps observe, children almost instinctively react against the "intrusive, we-know-best tone" (1976, 163) of commercials, and their mockery stems from the pleasures of seeing "the officious official [corporate] world turned upside down" (165). Parodies of commercials and refitted jingles appear on the playground precisely because the originals are catchy and memorable—and through their folklore children actively interact with and *perform* commercial culture even while they ridicule it.

PROACTIVE PARTICIPATION

A number of the case studies in this book demonstrate that intervention is not always expressed in terms of out-and-out resistance or subversion. Sometimes, rather, intervention is a function of grassroots *participation* at a generative level; that is, audiences actively assert their own tastes and sensibilities as they amend, adapt, or write over the cultural productions they consume. It is a disruption of sorts, but a participatory one as audiences "retrofit" mediated material to serve their own particular interests (Jenkins, Ford, and Green 2013, 27).

Touristic Performance at Rose Hall

The Rose Hall Plantation is a material site where tourists participate variously in performances of mediated history and culture. The divergent emphases of the daytime tours—historical and linear—compared to the nighttime tours—interactive and theatrical—are striking examples of what researchers have observed as discrete modes of tourism: *cultural tourism* and the more recently theorized *creative tourism* (see Thomas 2015, 72–73). The former entails a supply-side, unidirectional interpretation of culture delivered to tourists by trained docents, while the latter comprises the active involvement of tourists who, as more than mere spectators, interact with and "co-produce" the touristic experience (Richards and Wilson 2006; Tan et al. 2016, 981–2; Tan, Kung, and Luh 2013, 156). One model that we have seen for this patron involvement is the touristic legend trip, which occurs as active audiences conspire with existing narrative traditions to perform "enactment[s] of ambiguity" and consciously managed "experiential affirmation[s] of the weird or unexplainable" (McNeill and Tucker 2018, 16).

Artistic director Doug Prout's implementation of the interactive night tour at Rose Hall in 2011 coincided with a general "creative maelstrom" within the tourism industry at that time. Since then, creative content has been increasingly integrated into tourism products, and tourism itself has opened up as a creative arena wherein the experiences and reactions of participants constitute performances in their own right (Richards 2011, 1225–27). In keeping with notions of "experience economy" (Pine and Gilmore 1999), Prout enhanced the cultural value of the conventional touristic service at Rose Hall by reorchestrating the folklore as interactive experience. Though the night tours are scripted and have certain dramaturgical restrictions, as co-creations of producers and consumers, the (mutual) performances remain entirely emergent in the moment.

Through interactive participation, tourists bring a wide range of expectations, judgments, perceptions, moods, diverse points of view, and reactions that effectively reshape each night tour as an unduplicatable event, the antithesis of the "serial reproduction of culture" typical in many mass forms of cultural tourism (Richards 2011, 1225). The tours are attended by an eclectic mix of patrons: inquisitive tourists who have essentially stumbled onto the site; true believers, some genuinely afraid; pranksters who jump out and scare others; proponents who have brought their friends along; skeptics who doubt the supernatural; and so on. Collectively, in whatever configuration, the tourists form temporary creative networks with the hosts and together they generate wholly unique cultural performances—which are interventions against overdetermined supply-side tourism.

"That's What She Said" 2.0

When Michael Scott uttered his first "That's what she said" on *The Office* in 2005, there was no predicting how popular the joking form would become. TWSS and the British antecedents from which it derived had been in circulation for well over a century, but it was the television show and subsequent dissemination across digital culture that lifted the joke to the level of meme. Once mediatized, folklore is amplified; in the other direction, produced media diversifies as it spreads out into folk culture. As for the TWSS joke specifically, it emanated in various forms from media producers and audiences alike, but driven by different means and motivations. The process by which TWSS launched into viral circulation demonstrates perfectly a media dynamic delineated by Jenkins:

Some ideas spread top down, starting with commercial media and being adopted and appropriated by a range of different publics as they spread outward across the culture. Others emerge bottom up from various sites of participatory culture and getting pulled into the mainstream if the media industries see some way of profiting from it.

Participatory intervention of popular media draws its energy "not from destroying commercial culture but from writing over it, modding it, amending it, expanding it, adding greater diversity of perspective, and then recirculating it, feeding it back into the mainstream media" (Jenkins 2006, 268). From the standpoint of the audience, these participatory modifications refigure meaning as the digital universe provides a new framework of social power.

Like most memes, the TWSS meme enjoyed a meteoric rise to popularity and then tapered off. One can still stumble across the odd TWSS reference in popular culture, but they have for the most part evaporated. In some social contexts, the TWSS joking tagline has been reclaimed or reengineered in an effort to displace its ingrained sexism. For instance, more than one feminist group has appropriated the phrase as a rallying call to female empowerment, including the monthly gathering of women at the Social Study lounge in San Francisco and the Bristol Feminist Society, whose activist magazine is titled *That's What She Said*. In 2018, Denver-based artist and social activist Kimothy Joy produced a collection of watercolor portraits and inspirational quotes called *That's What She Said: Wise Words from Influential Women*. According to the publisher's descriptive blurb, the book "[reclaims] the derogatory cultural barb 'that's what she said,'" and "celebrates strong female leadership throughout history and empowers current and future generations to find their voices and inspire change in their communities." Indeed, encouraging women to find their voices runs counter to the schema of TWSS jokes, whose humor is based on the principle of silencing women and unilaterally reinscribing their discourse as sexual. A further suggestion that the chauvinistic joking phrase has been redefined and repurposed antithetically: Jodi Kantor and Megan Twohey's 2019 bestseller chronicling the rise of the Me Too movement is pointedly titled *She Said*.

"That's what she said" made its way into the Michael Scott's joking repertoire precisely because it was already hackneyed and inappropriate; as a dramatic device, his repeated use of it revealed something troubling about his character. The joke had something of a revival in folk culture following *The Office*, but it has unquestionably run its course. Further, considering the Me Too movement and the ethos of the post–Harvey Weinstein era, there is little place for it anymore. Meier and Medjesky (2018) argue that the TWSS joke cycle normalizes and perpetuates rape culture.[2] Their analysis of the joke's rhetoric of rape is attuned to the sensibilities of the moment, remarkably pertinent to the current conversations about sexual harassment and sexual violence:

> Even though "she" is the subject of the joke's phrase, "she" is always an object to be used by the joke and its teller. In this way, just as "she" lacks individual identity, "she" also lacks the capacity to speak for herself because we are always told what "she said." We cannot know what "she said" because "she" is forbidden from actually speaking. Instead, we are *always* told what "she" said and that "she" spoke at all. More to the point, we are *never* told that "she" said anything indicating her consent. If "she" cannot say "yes," then she also cannot say "no," thus rendering the sexual encounter imagined by the joke teller and audience entirely non-consensual. (9)

There has been some Hollywood chatter about a possible reboot of *The Office*, with hints that some principal cast members might return. The speculation remains unconfirmed, but if there were to be a new generation of *The Office*, the TWSS joke would not likely be a recurring comedic device as it was before. It is so flatly out of step with the current zeitgeist that there would simply be no taste for it on a network program.

Metajokes as "Self-Intervention"

Quantitative studies of humor have well demonstrated the difficulties of operationalizing jokes in computational terms (Hempelmann 2008; Taylor 2017). They have also shown—predictably—that empirical inquiries of humor are confounded when the data set becomes more abstruse, as with metadiscursive and anti-jokes, for example (Sjöbergh and Araki 2007). That is to say, computers can recognize and to some degree emulate predictable joke templates, but jokes that purposely violate their own generic expectations are for computers indecipherable enigmas. Synthetically programmed joking aside, the humor that emanates from face-to-face human interaction is exponentially more complex, especially in the realm of metajokes, which disrupt, undermine, question, and refashion the very joking conventions that they ostensibly employ. As we have seen, this arena of metadiscursivity takes various forms: parodies of joking forms, that is, templates ("Why did the turkey cross the road? It was the chicken's day off"); metahumor, jokes about jokes ("What's the difference between a good joke and a bad joke timing" [spoken with no pause] . . . "dang it!"); self-referentiality (a long traveling salesman joke that ends with the punch line, "Pardon me, I must be in the wrong joke"); truncated joke metonyms (the stand-alone punch line "Do you think I wished for a twelve-inch pianist?"); and anti-jokes ("What's the difference between a blonde and a bowling ball? A blonde is a living person with a specific hair color, and a bowling ball is an inanimate object used in the sport of bowling"). The self-aware, the self-referential, the metonymic, the antithetical—these are all crosscurrents of postmodernism. Metahumor presents us with a noteworthy case in social practice as certain jokes can be both this and that simultaneously, just as they can effectively reconstitute the very enterprise of joking.

❊ ❊ ❊

Audiences are not just unquestioning and inert spectators of the mediated cultural forms they consume. Even in the face of structural constraints, they find cracks where they might assert personal agency: they rearrange, parody, subvert, augment, and participate in the production of those forms such that the meaning is transformed and the material becomes more relevant to their own circumstances. By various means, audience interventions challenge institutional media with active (often public) social engagement emanating from what Leah A. Lievrouw calls "commons knowledge," which mobilizes "deliberative and participatory democratic practices against the prerogatives of technocratic elites" (2011, 182; see also Benkler 2007). Folklore is instrumental in these grassroots transfigurations of mediated culture, where we see, for example, cheeky soldiers singing derisive wartime ditties, legend-tripping tourists, internet users creating and spreading transient viral memes, children parodying commercial ads on the playground, and a wide array of irreverent joke tellers. These are the sorts of participants who comprise the unruly audience.

Notes

INTRODUCTION

1. The conventional view of a sender, a message, and a receiver is articulated in the well-known and often-cited model of communication posited by Shannon and Weaver 1963.

2. For example, *Big Brother* has perhaps the highest shoot ratio in television history. See Jones 2003, 409.

CHAPTER 2. "THERE'S DIRTY WORK AFOOT"

1. The wide array of critical studies on Disney's use and manipulation of fairy-tale sources includes Stone 1975; Trites 1991; Hastings 1993; Zipes 1995; Wood 1996; O'Brien 1996; Hoerrner 1996; Zipes 1997; Dundes and Dundes 2000; Craven 2002; Do Rozario 2004; Hurley 2005; Bruce 2007; Lester 2010; England, Descartes, and Collier-Meek 2011.

2. http://samuraifrog.blogspot.ca/2006/01/disneys-folly-notes-on-snow-white.html.

3. According to Jonathan Rosenbaum (2018), this image of the opening book to begin the story may have been influenced by a shot from Leni Riefenstahl's *The Blue Light* (1932). But Disney's repeated use of the device in animated features (*Pinocchio*, 1940; *Cinderella*, 1950; *Sleeping Beauty*, 1959; *Sword in the Stone*, 1963; *Jungle Book*, 1967; *Robin Hood*, 1973; several *Winnie the Pooh* films; and others) developed it into something of a convention. The opening shots of these other films, like that of *Snow White and the Seven Dwarfs* before them, make a visual claim for the provenance and textual/cultural authority of their respective tales. Regarding this trope in Disney's *Sleeping Beauty*, see Schacker (2019, 179).

4. Excerpts from this production meeting are also housed at the British Film Institute (BFI) in London: "*Snow White and the Seven Dwarfs* Collection, Item I—Extracts from Story Conference Notes, 26 July 1934—8 June 1937. Copied by David R. Williams in August 1987 with some notes and comments throughout made by him." I am indebted

to the institute for access to these documents; subsequent extracts are referenced as: BFI, "Extracts from Story Conference Notes," with story conference date.

5. The phallic suggestions were highlighted by Anne Sexton (1971), whose feminist poem "Snow White and the Seven Dwarfs" describes the dwarfs as "those little hot dogs." And the dwarfs are not the first Disney characters to be viewed thus. In 1940, the psychoanalyst Fritz Moellenhoff interpreted the figure of Mickey Mouse as "a phallus but a desexualized one" (31).

6. A larger role was originally contemplated and sketched for the prince but it never developed. It involved his imprisonment by the queen, and—common in romances—a rescue and escape sequence. In the end, the episode was deemed unnecessary to the overall story as the romantic theme was already well established in the opening; this is just one among countless examples of Disney's relentless editing in the interest of dramatic economy.

7. Grumpy's prominence is suggested even in the color of his clothing: his magenta-hued jerkin stands out among the other dwarfs, who are toned more muted russet, gray, and tan (Frome 2013, 463–64).

8. Jones (1985) analyzes this version of the joke:

> Well, Snow White was staying with the seven dwarfs, and she had to go into her room to change for dinner. The seven dwarfs decided that they wanted to see what was going on, so they went outside to see if they could peek in her window, but the window was too high, so they got up on one another's shoulders until they were all seven stacked up together, and the top one could peek in the window. Well, she starts to undress, and the top dwarf looks in and whispers back down to the one under him, "She's taking off her blouse," who whispers to the one below him, "She's taking off her blouse," and he whispers, "She's taking off her blouse" to the one below him and so on down to the bottom. Well, the top dwarf looks in again and he sees that she's taking off her skirt, so he whispers, "She's taking off her skirt," and the dwarf below him whispers to the dwarf below him, "She's taking off her skirt," who whispers to the next dwarf, "She's taking off her skirt" and so on. Then the top dwarf looks in and sees that she's taking off her bra, so he whispers, "she's taking off her bra," and it gets passed on down the line, "She's taking off her bra," "She's taking off her bra." Then the top dwarf peeks in and sees that she's taking off her panties so he whispers back down, "She's taking off her panties," and the rest of the dwarfs pass it on down the line, "She's taking off her panties," "She's taking off her panties." Then the top dwarf looks in and hears somebody knocking on the door and Snow White goes to the door and starts to open it, so he whispers down, "Somebody's coming, somebody's coming" and

the next dwarf goes, "Me too," and the one after him goes, "Me too," and the rest go, "Me too, Me too!" (103–4)

He mentions another variant in which one dwarf peeps through the keyhole and the other six queued in the hallway sequentially pass his reports down the line.

9. This comment, proffered by Disney shortly after the film's opening, has been frequently misquoted in both popular and academic sources, for example, in Bell, Haas, and Sells 1995. There, the quote is an epigraph for the introduction, appearing as "We just make the pictures, and let the professors tell us what they mean," attributed to Walt Disney but with no citation.

10. As with the shape and properties of character figures themselves, the symbolism of their appendages has been analyzed as well. The rounded "trinity of wafers," as Ub Iwerks described the circles that comprise Mickey Mouse's face, have been associated with pudgy babies, women's bottoms, and women's breasts (see Eisen 1975, 35); and the long elastic ears of Mickey's precursor Oswald the Rabbit, according to Donald Crafton (1982, 294), are noticeably phallic.

11. BFI, "Extracts from Story Conference Notes," January 7, 1937.

12. BFI, "Extracts from Story Conference Notes," November 11, 1936. See also Gould 1979. The dwarfs and animals were drawn and animated with exaggerated cuteness in mind, while the characters of the queen, huntsman, prince, and Snow White were extended studies of hyperrealism, leading to what would become the "aesthetic blueprint for much of the Disney-Formalist period" (Pallant 2010, 345), which reached its zenith with *Bambi* in 1942.

13. See, for example, the comments of sequence director Perce Pearce, BFI, "Extracts from Story Conference Notes," November 3, 1936: "Walt feels very strongly the point that we have got to keep these little fellows *cute*—mustn't get grotesque. In some cases you want to see how far it has developed in the early stages from the first reel. The head size has a definite bearing on it. We are playing with figures with bulgy noses and features. Walt points out that the animators must always try to feel the *cuteness* in the personal treatment of all these characters. This is a hard thing to catch . . . Dopey could become very grotesque, unless he is kept in a *cute* little manner. He must be funny, but if he isn't kept funny in a *cute* little way, he ceases to be funny and becomes imbecilic . . . He is not goofy, a freak, but a *cute* little elfish guy, child-like in his reactions and actions to things" (emphasis added). Cuteness was a device employed by Disney's to make the dwarfs "likeable and familiar, rather than strange and uncanny" (Davis 2013, 94).

14. The merchandising was extensive, as Ernest Larsen notes: "No fewer than seventy corporate licenses were granted for dozens of items carrying the Snow White stamp" (1998, 32). See also Wasko 2001, 14.

15. See the introduction to the English translation of Kühne-Harkort's play in Jarvis and Blackwell 2001, 299.

16. See, for example, "General Characteristics and Personalities of All Dwarfs," BFI, "Extracts from Story Conference Notes," December 15, 1936.

17. Since the company banner bears the founder's full name—Walt Disney—many presume the corporate logo to be just a stylized version of Walt's own signature, but that has been largely debunked. See *Big Cartoon News* n.d.

18. There were, however, some technical problems with animation in the final scene. Culhane points to the noticeable trembling and shaking of the prince, which apparently was the result of an unnamed artist's careless tracing of the live action. "It must have been a heartbreaking decision for Walt" to leave the animation of the prince uncorrected, Culhane writes, but it was "an indication of the dangerous financial condition of the studio at that time, and the breakneck speed of production as the release date grew nearer and nearer" (1986, 180).

CHAPTER 3. HAUNTING VISITORS

1. Drawn in part from one typical composite version of the legend of Annie Palmer, pitched to tourists, at http://www.jamaicatravelandculture.com/destinations/st_james/rose-hall/white-witch.htm.

2. https://rosehall.com/rose-hall/.

3. In 1920, for instance, a Swiss travel agency marketed excursions to Verdun, guaranteeing "an unbelievably impressive picture of horror and frightfulness" (Kraus 1970, 70).

4. What percentage of that amount goes directly to the guide is not known. (Incidentally, the working wage in Jamaica is currently about US $11 a day).

5. See, for comparison, St. George 1995.

6. Compare Aarne-Thompson-Uther Tale Type 326, "The Youth Who Wanted to Learn What Fear Is," in which a young man goes out into the world to "discover" fear and endures a series of frightening episodes in that effort. This appears in the Grimms' 1857 edition of *Kinder und Hausmärchen* as "A Tale about the Boy Who Went Forth to Learn What Fear Was" (see Zipes 2003) and in Andrew Lang's *Blue Fairy Book* (1889) as "The Tale of a Youth Who Set Out to Learn What Fear Was."

7. https://www.islandroutes.com/caribbean-tours/jamaica/1/montego-bay/1672/rose-hall-great-house-night-experience/.

8. Roy Wilder (1998, 31) claims that the pathway between the kitchen and dining room on southern plantations was referred to as a "whistle walk" because slaves serving food were required to whistle to show that they were not eating the food along the way. But there appears to be no historical support for this apocryphal notion.

CHAPTER 4. "THAT'S WHAT SHE SAID"

1. The art mistress and the gardener were popularized by the British actress Beryl Reid in the 1950s BBC radio series *Educating Archie* (Mieder 1977, 192). The Windmill Theatre remained opened all during the war, offering performances even during the Blitz. The theater's famous motto, "We never closed," was on occasion playfully recast as "We never clothed." My friend David Page, a British expat and investment portfolio manager who now lives in Toronto, reflected on the routine use of the jocular phrase "as the vicar said to the tart" during his childhood in Essex. The vicar form of the joke was preferable to the bishop, Page said, because as a quintessential local character type, the vicar was more relatable to English villagers. In an interview, he remembered that the quip would appear "fluidly and frequently" at family gatherings around holidays or other family celebrations like weddings or christenings:

> We'd have these huge, what we call knees-ups. And the big part of
> those things would be music and laughter. And so the music would
> come from, you know, somebody getting drunk and playing the
> piano. Not by any means unique to England at all, but then around
> that there'd be a few drunk uncles. And they would kind of riff off
> one another. There'd be a lot of this kind of back-and-forth humor.
> So it was those kinds of environments where these types of jokes
> would be heard. And also, as opposed to, say, today, people would say
> things that were cheekier—bawdy humor, as we call it in England.
> And there'd be minimal, if any, concern about the kids being nearby
> and hearing it. Whereas today, you would put hands over their ears or
> wouldn't even have them in the room, because political correctness
> has divorced us of some of this humor. So I can remember, certainly,
> uncles and whatever, saying these things when I was a kid, and
> everyone bursting into laughter. And probably laughing at it myself,
> not knowing at all what the innuendo meant, but just realizing it was
> funny and it got that reaction from people.

2. https://www.youtube.com/watch?v=ETFwAjNsyiU.
3. For example, "[Subject x] stuck [object y] in" and "[Subject x] could eat [object x] all day."
4. The URL for Unruh's blog is https://isleyunruh.com/.

CHAPTER 5. "YOUR KIND OF PLACE"

1. The doubled amount for a nickel was an important part of the campaign, as Pepsi's main competitor, Coca-Cola, sold only six ounces for the same price in their famous tiny wasp-waisted bottles. Accompanying slogans on Pepsi ad illustrations included: "Bigger, better," "Bigger bottle, bet-

ter flavor," "America's biggest nickel's worth," "Twice the fun with Pepsi," "Certified quality, and more of it," and "A nickel drink worth a dime."

2. The lyrics were penned by John Woodcock Graves, whose friend and compatriot John Peel was known locally as an avid huntsman. On occasion, Peel's mother sang "Bonnie Annie" to her grandson, which, overheard by Graves, provided the tune for his lyrics "Do ye ken John Peel?" (Campbell 1972). In part:

> Do ye ken John Peel with his coat so grey?
> Do ye ken John Peel at the break of day?
> Do ye ken John Peel when he's far, far away
> With his hounds and his horn in the morning.
> Twas the sound of his horn brought me from my bed
> And the cry of his hounds has me oftimes led
> For Peel's view holloa would wake the dead
> Or a fox from his lair in the morning.

"John Peel" became widely known "not only in hunting circles but at social, festive, and dance gatherings all over the world where the English tongue is spoken" (Gilchrist 1941, 82). It was included in Charles Villiers Stanford's 1906 *National Songbook*, sung in countless London pubs and dance halls in the following decades.

3. "I Love Bosco" was written by Joan Edwards and Lyn Duddy for the Wallerstein Company in 1955.

4. Another version:

> I love Bosco, it's the drink for me.
> Mommy put it in my milk and almost poisoned me.
> While she wasn't looking, I put it in her tea.
> Dun dun dun da [from the theme song of the police drama *Dragnet*]
> The cops are after me!

5. https://www.huffingtonpost.ca/2012/11/12/canadian-jingles-25 -catchy-songs_n_2118837.html.

6. Collected by Sheila Ann Marin from a twenty-year-old white female. Text and collector's report from Fife Folklore Archives, Utah State University, 1972. See Bronner 1988, 110, 155.

7. Second only to "You Deserve a Break Today," named by *Advertising Age* as the best ad campaign of the twentieth century.

CHAPTER 6. "THE JOKE'S ON US"

1. More than 900 adherents of the cult leader Jim Jones died on November 18, 1978, by drinking grape Flavor Aid laced with cyanide. In reference to that event, the phrase "drink the Kool Aid" has come to denote blind obedience to any religious or political cause.

2. The term *anti-legend* was coined by John Vlach (1971) to designate presumed horror stories, usually narrated by children, that reveal themselves in the end to be jokes.

3. Episode 1 (1998), 1:36.

4. Eriksgata2, "anti-joke chicken," n.d., http://www.quickmeme.com /meme/2p4s/ (accessed December 15, 2014).

5. Mr.Tea, *The Escapist,* April 18, 2010, http://www.escapistmagazine .com/forums/read/18.189302-Anti-Joke-time?page=1.

6. "The Limerick," Snowclones Database, March 17, 2008, http:// snowclones.org/2008/03/17/the-limerick/.

7. Gendered sensitivities to that stereotype were recently challenged by Australian comedian Hannah Gadsby, whose 2018 Netflix special *Nanette* is widely acclaimed as a radical interrogation of conventional stand-up comedy and jokes generally. Openly gay and known for frank discussion of sexuality in her performances, Gadsby was chided from some quarters for "[having] not enough lesbian content." In the act itself, she reflects on that critique:

> I should quit. I'm a disgrace. What sort of comedian [*gestures to self*] can't even make the lesbians laugh? Every comedian ever. [*audience laughter*] Oh, that's a good joke, isn't it? Classic. It's bulletproof, too. Very clever, because it's funny . . . because it's true. [*audience laughter*] The only people who don't think it's funny are us lezzes. But we've got to laugh, because if we don't—proves the point. [*audience laughter*] Check mate!

8. For his full discussion of jokes directed at the stereotype of German militarism, see Christie Davies 1990, 202-19.

9. http://tvtropes.org/pmwiki/pmwiki.php/Main/OrphanedPunch line.

10. The Motion Picture Productions Code of 1930 included "traveling salesmen and farmer's daughter jokes" on its list of "profanity." This scene from *Come Clean* remained uncut, however, as the code was merely advisory and not much heeded until it became enforced censorship law in 1934. See David Hayes, "Laurel & Hardy vs. the Censors," n.d., http://laurelhardy .dhwritings.com/Censorship.html (accessed December 15, 2014).

11. "Leslie Neilsen," *The Empire*, n.d., http://www.empireonline.com /interviews/interview.asp?IID=1127 (accessed December 15, 2014).

12. Other variants of the joke, with their own subtexts, have monks telling jokes at a monastery, old folks at a convalescent home, or locals at an Irish pub while a curious outsider is visiting for the first time (thanks to Charles Doyle and Tim Tangherlini, respectively, for pointing out these last two).

CONCLUSION

1. Pepsico owns all of these sodas except Coke, but children at the time were not likely to have known that.

2. Though published in 2018, Meier and Medjesky's very timely article "*The Office* Was Asking for It: 'That's What She Said' as a Joke Cycle That Perpetuates Rape Culture" was submitted to *Communication and Critical/Cultural Studies* well before the sexual harassment and rape allegations against Harvey Weinstein were made public in October 2017.

References

Adams, Erik. 2013. "Last Call for 'That's What She Said' Jokes: *The Office* Is Closing." *A.V. Club*, May 16. http://www.avclub.com/article/last-call-for -thats-what-she-said-jokesi-the-offic-97815.

Adler, Judith. 1989. "Travel as Performed Art." *American Journal of Sociology* 94 (6): 1366–91.

Ainsztein, R. 1969. Review of *The Death of Adolf Hitler: Unknown Documents from Soviet Archives*, by Lev Bezymenski. *International Affairs* 45 (2): 294–95. http://dx.doi.org/10.2307/2613016.

Alam, Hina. 2016. "Marineland Charged with Animal Cruelty." *Toronto Star*, November 25.

Allan, Robin. 1999. *Walt Disney and Europe*. Bloomington: Indiana University Press.

Andresen, Lee. 2003. *Battle Notes: Music of the Vietnam War*. Superior, WI: Savage.

Astapova, Anastasiya. 2017. "Joking about the Fear (of Joking)." Paper presented at the Annual Meeting of the American Folklore Society, Minneapolis, October 21.

Attardo, Salvatore, ed. 2014a. "Limericks." In *Encyclopedia of Humor Studies*, 450–45. London: Sage.

Attardo, Salvatore, ed. 2014b. "Meta-joke." In *Encyclopedia of Humor Studies*, 417–18. London: Sage.

Attardo, Salvatore, and Victor Raskin. 1991. "Script Theory Revis(it)ed: Joke Similarity and Joke Representation Model." *Humor: International Journal of Humor Research* 4 (3–4): 293–347.

Ayres, Brenda. 2003. "The Poisonous Apple in *Snow White*: Disney's Kingdom of Gender." In *The Emperor's Old Groove: Decolonizing Disney's Magic Kingdom*, edited by Brenda Ayres, 39–50. New York: Peter Lang.

Baer, Florence E. 1983. "Wellerisms in *Pickwick Papers*." *Folklore* 94 (2): 173–83.

Bailey, Adrian. 1982. *Walt Disney's World of Fantasy*. New York: Everest House.

Bailey, Bill. 2004. *Bill Bailey Live—Part Troll*. Universal Pictures. DVD.

Bans, Lauren. 2010. "That's What She Said? Yeah, Give It a Rest." *GQ*, August 3.

Barrier, Michael. 1999. *Hollywood Cartoons: American Animation in Its Golden Age*. Oxford: Oxford University Press.

Barry, Dave. 1986. *Claw Your Way to the Top: How to Become the Head of a Major Corporation in Roughly a Week*. Emmaus, PA: Rodale.

DOI: 10.7330/9781607329909.c008

Bart, Peter. 1996. "Disney's Ovitz Problem Raises Issues for Showbiz Giants." *Daily Variety*, December 16.

Bastard, Alexander, Comte de. 1850. *Bulletin des Comités Historiques*, II: 172.

Bedi, Joyce, and Joseph N. Tatarewicz. 2016. "Hollywood Geek Fest—The Oscars Side Party: Two Proudly Geeky Historians Offer an Appreciation of the Winners of the Academy's Scientific and Technical Awards." Lemelson Center for the Study of Invention and Innovation, February 29. https://invention.si.edu/hollywood-geek-fest-oscars-side-party.

Behlmer, Rudy. 1982. *America's Favorite Movies: Behind the Scenes*. New York: Ungar.

Bell, Elizabeth, Lynda Haas, and Laura Sells, eds. 1995. *From Mouse to Mermaid: The Politics of Film, Gender, and Cultures*. Bloomington: Indiana University Press.

Bell, Michael J. 1973. "William Wells Newell and the Foundation of American Folklore Scholarship." *Journal of Folklore Research* 10(1/2): 7–27.

Ben-Amos, Dan. 1971. "Toward a Definition of Folklore in Context." In "Toward New Perspectives in Folklore," special issue, *Journal of American Folklore* 84 (331): 3–15.

Bendix, Regina. 1997. *In Search of Authenticity: The Formation of Folklore Studies*. Madison: University of Wisconsin Press.

Bendix, Regina F. 2018. *Culture and Value: Tourism, Heritage, and Property*. Bloomington: Indiana University Press.

Benkler, Yochai. 2007. *The Wealth of Networks: How Social Production Transforms Markets and Freedom*. New Haven, CT: Yale University Press.

Beresin, Ann Richman. 1999. "Double Dutch and Double Cameras: Studying the Transmission of Culture in an Urban Schoolyard." In *Children's Folklore: A Sourcebook*, edited by Brian Sutton-Smith, Jay Mechling, Thomas W. Johnson, and Felicia R. McMahan, 75–91. Logan: Utah State University Press.

Bettelheim, Bruno. 1989. *The Uses of Enchantment: The Meaning and Importance of Fairy Tales*. New York: Vintage.

Bezymenski, Lev. 1968. *The Death of Adolph Hitler: Unknown Documents from Soviet Archives*. New York: Harcourt, Brace & World.

Big Cartoon News. n.d. "The Secret History of Walt Disney's Signature." http://blog.bcdb.com/lies-disney-told/walt-disneys-signature/.

Biggs, Sarah J. 2013. "Knight v Snail." *British Library Medieval Manuscripts Blog*, September 26, 2013. http://britishlibrary.typepad.co.uk/digitised manuscripts/2013/09/knight-v-snail.html.

Bird, Harry Lewis. 1947. *This Fascinating Advertising Business*. Indianapolis: Bobbs-Merrill.

Bird, S. Elizabeth. 2006. "Cultural Studies as Confluence: The Convergence of Folklore and Media Studies." In *Popular Culture Theory and Methodology*, edited by Harold E. Hines Jr., Marilyn F. Motz, and Angela M. S. Nelson, 344–55. Madison: University of Wisconsin Press.

Birthisel, Jessica, and Jason A. Martin. 2013. "'That's What She Said': Gender, Satire, and the American Workplace on the Sitcom *The Office*." *Journal of Communication Inquiry* 37 (1): 64–80.

Blank, Trevor J., ed. 2009. *Folklore and the Internet: Vernacular Expression in a Digital World*. Logan: Utah State University Press.

Blank, Trevor J., ed. 2012. *Folk Culture in the Digital Age: The Emergent Dynamics of Human Interaction*. Logan: Utah State University Press.

Blank, Trevor. 2013. *The Last Laugh: Folk Humor, Celebrity Culture, and Mass-Mediated Disasters in the Digital Age*. Madison: University of Wisconsin Press.

Blank, Trevor J., and Robert Glenn Howard, eds. 2013. *Tradition in the Twenty-First Century: Locating the Role of the Past in the Present*. Logan: Utah State University Press.

Blank, Trevor J., and Lynne S. McNeill, eds. 2018. *Slender Man Is Coming: Creepypasta and Contemporary Legends on the Internet*. Logan: Utah State University Press.

Bolland, Brian. 2006. *The Art of Brian Bolland*. Portland, OR: Image Comics.

Bolter, David, and Richard Grusin. 1999. *Remediation: Understanding New Media*. Cambridge, MA: MIT Press.

Brodie, Ian. 2014. *A Vulgar Art: A New Approach to Stand-Up Comedy*. Jackson: University Press of Mississippi.

Bronner, Simon. 1988. *American Children's Folklore*. Littlerock, AR: August House.

Brophy, John, and Eric Partridge. 1965. *The Long Trail: What the British Soldier Sang and Said in the Great War of 1914–18*. London: Andre Deutsch.

Brownlow, Kevin. 1996. *David Lean: A Biography*. New York: St. Martin's.

Bruce, Alexander M. 2007. "The Role of the 'Princess' in Walt Disney's Animated Films: Reactions of College Students." *Studies in Popular Culture* 30 (1): 1–25.

Brunette, Peter. 1980. "Snow White and the Seven Dwarfs." In *The American Animated Cartoon*, edited by Danny and Gerald Peary, 66–75. New York: E. P. Dutton.

Bruns, Axel. 2008. *Blogs, Wikipedia, Second Life, and Beyond: From Production to Produsage*. New York: Peter Lang.

Buckingham, David. 2011. *The Material Child: Growing Up in Consumer Culture*. Cambridge: Polity.

Burn, Andrew. 2016. "Children's Playground Games in the New Media Age." In *Children's Games in the New Media Age: Childlore, Media and the Playground*, edited by Andrew Burn and Chris Richards, 1–30. London: Routledge.

Busby, Roy. 1976. *British Music Hall: An Illustrated Who's Who from 1850 to the Present Day*. London: Paul Elek.

Byrne, Eleanor, and Martin McQuillan. 1999. *Deconstructing Disney*. London: Pluto.

Byrnes, Holly. 2009. "Beer Ad Shows Drunk Snow White in Bed with Dwarves." *Sydney Daily Telegraph*, October 15.

Camille, Michael. 1992. *Image on the Edge: The Margins of Medieval Art*. London: Reaktion Books.

Campbell, A. W. 1972. "Graves, John Woodcock (1795–1886)." In *Australian Dictionary of Biography*. Melbourne: Melbourne University.

Canady, John. 1973. "The Art So to Speak of Walt Disney." *New York Times*, October 28.

Carnegie, James. 1973. *Some Aspects of Jamaica's Politics: 1918–1937*. Kingston: Institute of Jamaica.

Casey, Liam. 2016. "Marineland Charged for Five Counts of Animal Cruelty in Ongoing Investigation." *Toronto Star*, December 4.

Cash, Johnny. 1973. *Any Old Wind the Blows*. Columbia Records.

Castello, James. 1868. *Legend of Rose Hall Estate in the Parish of St. James, Jamaica*. Falmouth, Jamaica: *Falmouth Post*.

Chesterton, G. K. 1911. *Appreciations and Criticisms of the Work of Charles Dickens*. New York: E. P. Dutton.

Chronis, Athinodoros. 2005. "Co-constructing Heritage at the Gettysburg Storyscape." *Annals of Tourism Research* 32 (2): 386–406.

Clarke, Roger. 2012. *Ghosts: A Natural History: 500 Years of Searching for Proof*. New York: St. Martin's.

Clements, William M. 1980. "The Chain on the Tombstone." In *Indiana Folklore: A Reader*, edited by Linda Dégh, 259–64. Bloomington: Indiana University Press.

Cleveland, Les. 1994a. *Dark Laughter: War and Song in Popular Culture*. Westport, CT: Praeger.

Cleveland, Les. 1994b. "Singing Warriors: Popular Songs in Wartime." *Journal of Popular Culture* 28 (3): 155–75. http://dx.doi.org/10.1111/j.0022-3840.1994.2803_155.x.

Cochran, Robert. 1989. "'What Courage!' Romanian 'Our Leader' Jokes." *Journal of American Folklore* 102 (405): 259–74.

The Colbert Report. 2013. Episode 1283. December 12.

"Complete Vocabulary of Spoken English." 1973. *Punch*, October 10, 511.

Cook, Daniel Thomas. 2008. "The Missing Child in Consumption Theory." *Journal of Consumer Culture* 8 (2): 219–43.

Cook, Daniel Thomas. 2010. "Commercial Enculturation: Moving beyond Consumer Socialization." In *Childhood and Consumer Culture*, edited by David Buckingham and Vebjørg Tingstad, 63–79. New York: Palgrave Macmillan.

Corbett, Christopher. 1993. "So, Just Who Is a Khaki Kind of Guy?" *Los Angeles Times*, September 5. http://articles.latimes.com/1993-09-05/opinion/op-32104_1_khakis.

Corner, John. 1983. "Textuality, Communication and Power." In *Language, Image, Media*, edited by Howard Davis and Paul Walton, 266–81. Oxford: Blackwell.

Coven. 1969. *Witchcraft Destroys Minds and Reaps Souls*. Mercury Records.

Crafton, Donald. 1982. *Before Mickey: The Animated Film, 1898–1928*. Cambridge, MA: MIT Press.

Craven, Allison. 2002. "Beauty and the Belles: Discourses of Feminism and Femininity in Disneyland." *European Journal of Women's Studies* 9 (2): 123–42.

Croce, Paul Jerome. 1991. "A Clean and Separate Space: Walt Disney in Person and Production." *Journal of Popular Culture* 25 (3): 91–103.

Croxton, Katie. 2014. "Snow White, the Grimm Brothers and the Studio the Dwarfs Built." In *Walt Disney, from Reader to Storyteller: Essays on the Literary*

Inspirations, edited by Kathy Merlock Jackson and Mark I. West, 21–30. Jefferson, NC: McFarland.

Csanady, Ashley. 2015. "'People Don't Love Marineland Anymore': Ontario Law Leaves Orca Floating Alone in Niagara Falls." *National Post*, May 29.

Culhane, Shamus. 1986. *Talking Animals and Other People*. New York: St. Martin's.

Curley, Robert. 2018. "The Caribbean's Best Golf Courses and Golf Resorts." https://www.tripsavvy.com/caribbean-golf-courses-and-golf-resorts -1488134.

Davies, Christie. 1990. *Ethnic Humor around the World*. Bloomington: Indiana University Press.

Davies, Christie. 2001. "Humour Is Not a Strategy in War." *Journal of European Studies* 31: 395–412.

Davies, Christie. 2011. *Jokes and Targets*. Bloomington: Indiana University Press.

Davies, Owen. 2007. *The Haunted: A Social History of Ghosts*. New York: Palgrave.

Davis, Amy M. 2013. *Handsome Heroes and Vile Villains: Men in Disney's Feature Animation*. New Barnet, Herts, UK: John Libbey.

De Caro, Frank. 2015. "The LaLaurie Haunted House, Ghosts, and Slavery." In *Putting the Supernatural in Its Place*, edited by Jeannie Banks Thomas, 24–48. Salt Lake City: University of Utah Press.

Dégh, Linda. 1994. *America Folklore and the Mass Media*. Bloomington: Indiana University Press.

Dégh, Linda, and Andrew Vázsonyi. 1976 (1971). "Legend and Belief." In *Folklore Genres*, edited by Dan Ben-Amos, 93–123. Austin: University of Texas Press.

Delaure, Marilyn. 2017. "The Yes Men: An Interview." In *Culture Jamming: Activism and the Art of Cultural Resistance*, edited by Marilyn Delaure and Moritz Fink, 418–22. New York: New York University Press.

De la Ville, Valérie-Inés, and Valerie Tartas. 2010. "Developing as Consumers." In *Understanding Children as Consumers*, edited by David Marshall, 23–40. London: Sage.

Denith, Simon. 2000. *Parody*. London: Routledge.

De Lisser, Herbert G. 2007 (1929). *The White Witch of Rose Hall*. London: Macmillan Caribbean.

De Souza, M. C. 1891. *Tourist's Guide to the Parishes of Jamaica. Together with an Account Descriptive of the Jamaica Exhibition*. Kingston: publisher unknown.

De Vos, Gail. 2012. *What Happens Next? Contemporary Urban Legends and Popular Culture*. Santa Barbara, CA: Libraries Unlimited.

Dickens, Charles. 1868 (1837). *The Pickwick Papers*, 4 vols. New York: Hurd and Houghton.

Diebel, Linda. 2012. "Marineland Animals Suffering, Former Staffers Say." *Toronto Star*, August 15.

Diebel, Linda, and Liam Casey. 2012a. "Marineland: Allegations of Poor Treatment of Deer, Bears." *Toronto Star*, September 8.

Diebel, Linda, and Liam Casey. 2012b. "Marineland: Environment Ministry Launches Probe into Mass Animal Graves." *Toronto Star*, December 20.

Diebel, Linda, and Liam Casey. 2013. "Marineland Owner John Holer Shot Dead Neighbours' Dogs, According to Witnesses." *Toronto Star*, March 5.

Disney, Walt. 1937. "Why I Chose *Snow White.*" *Photoplay Studies* 10 (3): 7–8.

Donahue, Jennifer. 2014. "The Ghost of Annie Palmer: Giving Voice to Jamaica's 'White Witch of Rose Hall.'" *Journal of Commonwealth Literature* 49 (2): 243–56.

Dorfman, Ariel, and Armand Mattelart. 1984. *How to Read Donald Duck: Imperialist Ideology in the Disney Comic.* New York: International General.

Do Rozario, Rebecca-Anne C. 2004. "The Princess and the Magic Kingdom: Beyond Nostalgia, the Function of the Disney Princess." *Women's Studies in Communication* 27 (1): 34–59.

Dorsey, Paul. 1937. "Mouse and Man." *Time*, December 27: 19–21.

Dorson, Richard M. 1972. *Folkore and Folklife.* Bloomington: Indiana University Press.

Dorson, Richard M. 1973. "Is Folklore a Discipline?" *Folklore* 84 (3): 177–205.

Dorson, Richard M. 1976. *Folklore and Fakelore: Essays toward a Discipline of Folk Studies.* Cambridge, MA: Harvard University Press.

Dorson, Richard M. 1977. *American Folklore.* Chicago: University of Chicago Press.

Douglas, Mary. 2002 (1966). *Purity and Danger: An Analysis of the Concepts of Pollution and Taboo.* London: Routledge.

Douny, Laurence. 2017. "The Commodification of Authenticity: Performing and Displaying Dogon Material Identity." In *Indigenous Tourism Movements*, edited by Alexis C. Bunten and Nelson H. H. Graburn, 140–62. Toronto: University of Toronto Press.

Doyle, Charles Clay. 1981. "Folk Epigraphy by Subtraction." *Midwestern Journal of Language and Folklore* 7 (1): 49–50.

Du Gay, Paul, Stuart Hall, Linda James, Hugh Mackay, and Keith Negus. 1997. *Doing Cultural Studies: The Story of the Sony Walkman.* London: Sage.

Dundes, Alan. 1966. "The American Concept of Folklore." *Journal of the Folklore Institute* 3 (3): 226–49.

Dundes, Lauren, and Alan Dundes. 2000. "The Trident and the Fork: Disney's *The Little Mermaid* as a Male Construction of an Electral Fantasy." *Psychoanalytic Studies* 2 (2): 117–30.

Dynel, Marta. 2016. "'I Has Seen Image Macros!' Advice Animal Memes as Visual-Verbal Jokes." *International Journal of Communication* 10: 660–88.

Edensor, T. 2000. "Staging Tourism: Tourists as Performers." *Annals of Tourism Research* 27: 322–44.

Edwards, Jim. 2009. "Disney Frowns at 'Ho White and the 7 Dwarves' Beer Ad." CBS News Moneywatch, October 19. https://www.cbsnews.com/news/disney-frowns-at-ho-white-and-the-7-dwarves-beer-ad/.

Eisen, Armand. 1975. "Two Disney Artists." *Crimmer's: The Harvard Journal of Pictorial Fiction* (Winter): 35–44.

Eisenstein, Elizabeth. 1983. *The Printing Revolution in Early Modern Europe.* Cambridge: Cambridge University Press.

Ellis, Bill. 1989. "When Is a Legend? An Essay in Legend Morphology." In *The Questing Beast: Perspectives in Contemporary Legend IV*, edited by Gillian Bennett and Paul Smith, 31–53. Sheffield, UK: Sheffield Academic Press.

Ellis, Bill. 2003. *Aliens, Ghosts, and Cults: Legends We Live.* Jackson: University Press of Mississippi.

England, Dawn E., Lara Descartes, and Melissa A. Collier-Meek. 2011. "Gender Role Portrayal and the Disney Princesses." *Sex Roles* 64 (7–8): 555–67.

Era. 1895. "A Chat with Lottie Collins." August 10.

Fagan, Robert. n.d. "White Witch Golf Course Casts a Magical Jamaican Golf Spell." Course review for *The A Position.* http://theaposition.com/robert fagan/golf/courses-and-travel/14627/white-witch-golf-course-casts-a -magical-jamaican-golf-spell.

Feifer, M. 1985. *Going Places: The Ways of the Tourist from Imperial Rome to the Present Day.* London: Macmillan.

Fine, Gary Alan. 1979. "Small Groups and Culture Creation: The Idioculture of Little League Baseball Teams." *American Sociological Review* 44 (5): 733–45.

Fine, Gary Alan. 1985. "The Goliath Effect: Corporate Dominance and Mercantile Legends." *Journal of American Folklore* 98 (397): 63–84.

Fine, Gary Alan. 2012. *Tiny Publics: A Theory of Group Action and Culture.* New York: Russell Sage.

Fiske, John. 1989. *Reading the Popular.* Boston: Unwin Hyman.

Fiske, John. 2011. *Television Culture.* 2nd ed. New York: Routledge.

Forgacs, David. 1992. "Disney Animation and the Business of Childhood." *Screen* 33 (4): 361–74.

Foster, Michael Dylan. 2012. "Photoshop Folklore and the 'Tourist Guy': Thoughts on the Diamond Format and the Possibilities of Mixed-Media Presentations." *New Directions in Folklore* 10 (1): 85–91.

Foster, Michael Dylan, and Jeffrey A. Tolbert. 2016. *The Folkloresque: Reframing Folklore in a Popular Culture World.* Logan: Utah State University Press.

Francis, W. Nelson, and Henry Kučerna. 1979. *The Standard Corpus of Present-Day Edited American English, for Use with Digital Computers.* Providence, RI: Department of Linguistics, Brown University.

Frank, Russell. 2011. *Newslore: Contemporary Folklore on the Internet.* Jackson: University Press of Mississippi.

Frayling, C., B. Godfrey, Z. Schwartz, and P. Wells. 1997. "Disney Discourse: On Caricature, Conscience Figures and Mickey Too." In *Art and Animation,* edited by P. Wells, 4–9. London: Academy Editions.

Freitag, Tilman G. 1994. "Enclave Tourism Development: For Whom the Benefits Roll?" *Annals of Tourism Research* 21 (3): 538–54.

Frome, Jonathan. 2013. "*Snow White:* Critics and Criteria for the Animated Feature Film." *Quarterly Review of Film and Video* 30 (5): 462–73.

Fuchs, Christian. 2013. "Class Exploitation on the Internet." In *Digital Labor: The Internet as Playground and Factory,* edited by Trebor Scholz, 211–24. New York: Routledge.

Gabler, Neal. 2006. *Walt Disney: The Triumph of the American Imagination.* New York: Random House.

Gadsby, Hannah. 2018. *Nanette.* Directed by Jon Olb and Madeleine Parry, performance by Hannah Gadsby. Guesswork Television. Netflix.

Gainesville Sun. 1982. "Seven-Up Officials Waging Campaign against Caffeine," March 5, 6B.

Galanter, Marc. 2005. *Lowering the Bar: Lawyer Jokes and Legal Culture.* Madison: University of Wisconsin Press.

Garfield, Bob. 1999. "Ad Age Advertising Century: The Top 100 Campaigns." *Advertising Age*, March 29, 82.

Gelder, Ken. 2007. *Subcultures: Cultural Histories and Social Practice.* New York: Routledge.

Gervais, Ricky. 2007. *Ricky Gervais Live 3—Fame.* Universal Pictures. DVD.

Gilchrist, Anne G. 1941. "The Evolution of a Tune: 'Red House' and 'John Peel.'" *English Folk Dance and Song Society* 4 (2): 80–84.

Giroux, Henry A. 1999. *The Mouse That Roared: Disney and the End of Innocence.* New York: Rowman & Littlefield.

Gjoni, Edlira. 2017. "From Passive Viewers to Content Generators: Audience Role on TV Programs and Online Media." *Journalism and Mass Communication* 7 (2): 63–67.

Gmelch, George. 2003. *Behind the Smile: The Working Lives of Caribbean Tourism.* Bloomington: Indiana University Press.

Goffman, Erving. 1974. *Frame Analysis: An Essay on the Organization of Experience.* New York: Harper & Row.

Goldstein, Diane E., Sylvia Ann Grider, and Jeannie Banks Thomas. 2007. *Haunting Experiences: Ghosts in Contemporary Folklore.* Logan: Utah State University Press.

Gottzén, L. 2012. "Money Talks: Children's Consumption and Becoming in the Family." In *Children, Childhood and Everyday Life: Children's Perspectives*, edited by Mariane Hedegaard, Karin Aronsson, Charlotte Højholt, and Oddbjørg Skjær Ulvik, 91–108. Charlotte, NC: Information Age.

Gould, Stephan Jay. 1979. "Mickey Mouse Meets Konrad Lorenz." *Natural History* 88 (May): 30–36.

Graham, Al. 1944. "Jingle—or Jangle." *New York Times Magazine*, October 29, 26.

Grant, John. 2001. *Masters of Animation.* London: Watson-Guptill.

Graves, Richard. 1999. "The Real Colonel Bogey." *Music and Vision*, April 7.

Gray, Jonathan, Jeffrey P. Jones, and Ethan Thompson. 2009. "'The State of Satire, the Satire of State." In *Satire TV: Politics and Comedy in the Post-Network Era*, edited by Jonathan Gray, Jeffrey P. Jones, and Ethan Thompson, 3–36. New York: New York University Press.

Greenhill, Pauline, and Sidney Eve Matrix, eds. 2010. *Fairy Tale Films: Visions of Ambiguity.* Logan: Utah State University Press.

Greenhill, Pauline, and Jill Terry Rudy, eds. 2014. *Channeling Wonder: Fairy Tales on Television.* Detroit: Wayne State University Press.

Grider, Sylvia. 1981. "The Media Narraform: Symbiosis of Media and Oral Tradition." *Arv* 37: 125–31.

Griffin, Martyn, Nancy Harding, and Mark Learmonth. 2017. "Whistle While You Work? Disney Animation, Organizational Readiness and Gendered Subjugation." *Organization Studies* 38 (7): 869–94.

Grover, Ron. 1991. *The Disney Touch: How a Daring Management Team Revived an Entertainment Empire.* Homewood, IL: Business One Irwin.

Haig, David. 2020. *From Darwin to Derrida: Selfish Genes, Social Selves, and the Meanings of Life.* Cambridge, MA: MIT Press.

Hakewill, James. 1825. *A Picturesque Tour of the Island of Jamaica, from Drawings Made in the Years 1820–1821*. London: Hurst, Robinson.

Hall, Gary. 1973. "The Big Tunnel." *Indiana Folklore* 6: 139–73.

Hall, Stuart. 2000 (1973). "Encoding/Decoding." In *Media Studies: A Reader*, 2nd ed., edited by Paul Marris and Sue Thornham, 51–61. New York: New York University Press.

Hanks, Michele. 2015. *Haunted Heritage: The Cultural Politics of Ghost Tourism, Populism, and the Past*. Walnut Creek, CA: Left Coast.

Harmes-Liedtke, Ulrich. 2012. "Complexities of Tourism Development—Viewpoints of Development Practitioner." *Journal of Public Policies and Territories* 3: 45–56.

Harold, Christine. 2004. "Pranking Rhetoric: 'Culture Jamming' as Media Activism." *Critical Studies in Media Communication* 21 (3): 189–211.

Hassall, John, illus. 1921. *Blackie's Popular Nursery Stories*. London: Blackie & Son.

Hastings, A. Waller. 1993. "Moral Simplification in Disney's *The Little Mermaid*." *The Lion and the Unicorn* 17: 83–92.

Hattenstone, Simon. 2013. "Bill Bailey: Bill's Excellent Adventure." *Guardian*, April 19. http://www.theguardian.com/culture/2013/apr/19/bill-bailey -interview-qualmpeddler.

Hawes, Bess Lomax. 1974. "Folksongs and Function: Some Thoughts on the American Lullaby." *Journal of American Folklore* 87 (3): 140–48.

Heath, Chip, Chris Bell, and Emily Sternberg. 2001. "Emotional Selection in Memes: The Case of Urban Legends." *Journal of Personality and Social Psychology* 81: 1028–41.

Hellekson, Karen, and Kristina Busse, eds. 2006. *Fan Fiction and Fan Communities in the Age of the Internet: New Essays*. Jefferson, NC: McFarland.

Hempelmann, C. F. 2008. "Computational Humor: Beyond the Pun?" In *The Primer of Humor Research*, edited by V. Raskin, 333–60. Berlin: Mouton De Gruyter.

Hoerrner, Keisha L. 1996. "Gender Roles in Disney Films: Analyzing Behaviors from *Snow White* to *Simba*." *Women's Studies in Communication* 19 (2): 213–28.

Holliss, Richard, and Brian Sibley. 1987. *Snow White and the Seven Dwarfs and the Making of the Classic Film*. New York: Simon & Schuster.

Hollon, John. 2007. "Office Training." *Workforce Management* 86 (5): 34.

Holly, Donald H., Jr., and Casey E. Cordy. 2007. "What's in a Coin? Reading the Material Culture of Legend Tripping and Other Activities." *Journal of American Folklore* 120 (477): 335–54.

Holstein, William J. 2004. "Jamaican Witchcraft: At the Ritz-Carlton, Rose Hall, Golf and Legend Meet." *Chief Executive*, March, 60–61.

Holzer, Hans. 2004. *Ghosts: True Encounters with the World Beyond*. New York: Black Dog & Leventhal.

Hudes, Sammy. 2017. "Marineland Charged with Six New Counts of Animal Cruelty." *Toronto Star*, January 9.

Inge, M. Thomas. 2004. "Art, Adaptation, and Ideology: Walt Disney's *Snow White and the Seven Dwarfs*." *(Retrospectives) Journal of Popular Film and Television* 32 (3): 132–42.

Ironside, Rachael. 2018. "The Allure of Dark Tourism: Legend Tripping and Ghost Seeking in Dark Places." In *The Supernatural in Society, Culture, and History*, edited by Dennis Waskul and Marc Eaton, 95–115. Philadelphia: Temple University Press.

Jarvis, Shawn C., and Jeannine Blackwell, eds. and trans. 2001. *The Queen's Mirror: Fairy Tales by German Women, 1780–1900*. Lincoln: University of Nebraska Press.

Jenkins, Henry. 2006. *Convergence Culture: Where Old and New Media Collide*. New York: New York University Press.

Jenkins, Henry. 2013. *Textual Poachers: Television Fans and Participatory Culture*. New York: Routledge.

Jenkins, Henry, Sam Ford, and Joshua Green. 2013. *Spreadable Media: Creating Value and Meaning in a Networked Culture*. New York: New York University Press.

Jin, Huimin. 2012. *Active Audience*. Bielefeld, Germany: Transcript Verlag.

Johnston, Lauren. 2009. "Disney Sees Red over Beer Ad Showing 'Ho White' Smoking in Bed with Seven Dwarves: Report." *New York Daily News*, October 16.

Jones, Janet Megan. 2003. "'Show Your Real Face': A Fan Study of the UK *Big Brother* Transmissions (2000, 2001, 2002); Investigating the Boundaries between Notions of Consumers and Producers of Factual Television." *New Media and Society* 5 (3): 400–421.

Jones, Steven Swann. 1985. "Joking Transformations of Popular Fairy Tales: A Comparative Analysis of Five Jokes and Their Fairy Tale Sources." *Western Folklore* 44 (2): 97–114.

Joy, Kimothy. 2018. *That's What She Said: Wise Words from Influential Women*. New York: Harper Collins.

Kantor, Jodi, and Megan Twohey. 2019. *She Said: Breaking the Sexual Harassment Story That Helped Ignite a Movement*. New York: Penguin.

Kashner, Sam. 2014. "*Theeeeere's* Johnny!" *Vanity Fair*, January 27. http://www .vanityfair.com/hollywood/2014/02/johnny-carson-the-tonight-show.

Kaufman, J. B. 2012. *The Fairest of Them All: The Making of Walt Disney's "Snow White and the Seven Dwarfs."* San Francisco: Walt Disney Family Foundation.

Kelley, Greg. 2012. "Colonel Bogey's March through Folk and Popular Culture." In *Warrior Ways: Explorations in Modern Military Folklore*, edited by Tad Tuleja and Eric Elaison, 205–221. Logan: Utah State University Press.

Kelley, Greg. 2015. "'The Joke's on Us': An Analysis of Meta-Humor." In *The Folkloresque: Reframing Folklore in a Popular Culture World*, edited by Michael Dylan Foster and Jeffrey A. Tolbert, 205–220. Logan: Utah State University Press.

Kiddon, Chloé, and Yuriy Brun. 2011. "That's What She Said: Double Entendre Identification." *Proceedings of the 49th Annual Meeting of the Association for Computational Linguistics: Short Papers—Volume 2*, 89–94. Portland, OR: Association for Computational Linguistics.

Kinsella, Michael. 2011. *Legend Tripping Online: Supernatural Folklore and the Search for Ong's Hat*. Jackson: University Press of Mississippi.

Kinsey, Alfred C., Wardell B. Pomeroy, Clyde E. Martin, and Paul H. Gebhard. 1998. *Sexual Behavior in the Human Female*. Bloomington: Indiana University Press.

Kirshenblatt-Gimblett, Barbara. 1996. "The Electronic Vernacular." In *Connected: Engagements with Media*, edited by George E. Marcus, 21–66. Chicago: University of Chicago Press.

Kirsenblatt-Gimblett, Barbara. 1997. "Afterlives." *Performance Research* 2 (2): 1–9.

Kirshenblatt-Gimblett, Barbara. 1998a. *Destination Culture: Tourism, Museums, and Heritage*. Berkeley: University of California Press.

Kirshenblatt-Gimblett, Barbara. 1998b. "Folklore's Crisis." *Journal of American Folklore* 111 (441): 281–327.

Klein, Naomi. 2000. *No Logo*. Toronto: Vintage Canada.

Klugman, Karen. 1995. "Under the Influence." In *Inside the Mouse: Work and Play at Disney World*, edited by the Project on Disney, 98–109. Durham, NC: Duke University Press.

Knapp, Mary, and Herbert Knapp. 1976. *One Potato, Two Potato: The Folklore of American Children*. New York: Norton.

Koshuta, John. 2007. "McDonald's Marketing Focused on Children, New Report States." *Natural News*, December 7. https://www.naturalnews.com/022334 _McDonalds_fast_food_marketing.html#ixzz2UnxZl9M7.

Koven, Mikel. 2003. "Folklore Studies and Popular Film and Television: A Necessary Critical Survey." *Journal of American Folklore* 116 (460): 176–95.

Koven, Mikel J. 2008. *Film, Folklore and Urban Legends*. Lanham, MD: Scarecrow.

Krassner, Paul. 2012. *Confessions of a Raving, Unconfined Nut: Misadventures in the Counterculture*. Berkeley, CA: Soft Skull.

Kraus, Karl. 1970 (1920). "Tourist Trips to Hell." In *No Compromise: Selected Writings of Karl Kraus*, edited by Frederick Ungar, 69–75. New York: Ungar.

Kuenz, Jane. 1995. "Working at the Rat." In *Inside the Mouse: Work and Play at Disney World*, edited by the Project on Disney, 110–62. Durham, NC: Duke University Press.

Kupfer, David. 2009. "In the Jester's Court: Paul Krassner on the Virtues of Irreverence, Indecency, and Illegal Drugs." *The Sun Magazine*, February.

Labov, William, and Joshua Waletsky. 1967. "Narrative Analysis: Oral Versions of Personal Experience." In *Essays on the Visual and Verbal Arts*, edited by June Helm, 12–44. Seattle: University of Washington Press.

Lang, Andrew. 1889. *The Blue Fairy Book*. London: Longmans, Green and Co.

Larsen, Ernest. 1998. "Compulsory Play." *Nation*, March 16.

Lawrence, Elizabeth. A. 1986. "In the Mick of Time: Reflections on Disney's Ageless Mouse." *Journal of Popular Culture* 20 (2): 65–72.

Legman, Gershon. 1968. *No Laughing Matter*. Vol. 1. Bloomington: Indiana University Press.

Legman, Gershon. 1969 (1964). *The Limerick*. New York: Bell.

Lennon, J., and M. Foley. 2000. *Dark Tourism: The Attraction of Death and Disaster*. London: Continuum.

Lester, Neal A. 2010. "Disney's *The Princess and the Frog*: The Pride, the Pressure, and the Politics of Being a First." *Journal of American Culture* 33 (4): 294–308.

Lievrouw, Leah A. 2011. *Alternative and Activist New Media.* Cambridge: Polity.

Lindahl, Carl. 2005. "Ostensive Healing: Pilgrimage to the San Antonio Ghost Tracks." *Journal of American Folklore* 118 (468): 164–85.

Lindstrom, Martin. 2008. *Buy•ology: Truth and Lies about What we Buy.* New York: Crown.

Lindstrom, Martin. 2011. *Brandwashed: Tricks Companies Use to Manipulate Our Minds and Persuade Us to Buy.* New York: Crown.

Lindstrom, Martin, and Patricia Seybold. 2004. *Brandchild: Remarkable Insights into the Minds of Today's Global Kids and Their Relationships with Brands.* Rev. ed. London: Kogan Page.

Lipman, Steve. 1991. *Laughter in Hell: The Use of Humor during the Holocaust.* Northvale, NJ: Jason Aronson.

Lippard, L. R. 1999. *On the Beaten Track: Tourism, Art, and Place.* New York: New Press.

Lomas, L. 1994. "Mystifying Mystery: Inscriptions of the Oral in the Legend of Rose Hall." *Journal of West Indian Literature* 6 (2): 70–89.

Louis, J. C., and Harvey Z. Yazijian. 1980. *The Cola Wars.* New York: Everest House.

Lyall, Sarah. 2010. "In BP's Record, a History of Boldness and Costly Blunders." *New York Times,* July 12.

Macalister, Terry, and Eleanor Cross. 2000. "BP Rebrands on a Global Scale." *Guardian,* July 25. http://www.theguardian.com/business/2000/jul/25/bp.

MacCannell, Dean. 1989. *The Tourist: A New Theory of the Leisure Class.* 2nd ed. Berkeley: University of California Press.

Macdonald, Lyn. 1993. *Somme.* Harmondsworth, UK: Penguin.

Mack, Walter, and Peter Buckley. 1982. *No Time Lost.* New York: Atheneum.

Mackie, Erin. 2006. "Jamaican Ladies and Tropical Charms." *Ariel: A Review of English Literature* 37 (2): 189–220.

Mackinnon, Ancelene. 2017. "Everyone Loves Marineland? Another Whale Dies at Ontario Water Park." *Cantech Letter,* August 15.

Magelssen, Scott. 2011. "Tourist Performance in the Twenty-First Century." In *Enacting History,* edited by Scott Magelssen and Rhona Justice-Malloy, 174–202. Tuscaloosa: University of Alabama Press.

Mahoney, Rosemary. 1994. "Scenes from Central Park." *Johns Hopkins Magazine,* September. http://www.jhu.edu/jhumag/994web/global1.html.

Maoz, D. 2006. "The Mutual Gaze." *Annals of Tourism Research* 33: 221–39.

Margolick, David. 2005. *Beyond Glory: Joe Louis vs. Max Schmeling, and a World on the Brink.* New York: Knopf.

Marsh, Jackie, and Julia C. Bishop. 2014. *Changing Play: Play, Media and Commercial Culture from the 1950s to the Present Day.* New York: Open University Press.

Marsh, Moira. 2015. *Practically Joking.* Logan: Utah State University Press.

Martyris, Nina. 2015. "The Sam Weller Bump: Dickens as Authorpreneur." *Paris Review,* April 14.

Mayo, Ed, and Agnes Nairn. 2009. *Consumer Kids.* London: Constable & Robinson.

McGowan, David. 2016. "'And They Lived Happily Ever After???!': Disney's Animated Adaptation of *Snow White and the Seven Dwarfs* (1937) and Fleischers' *Gulliver's Travels* (1939)." In *It's the Disney Version! Popular Cinema and Literary Classics*, edited by Douglas Brode and Shea T. Brode, 1–12. New York: Rowman & Littlefield.

McLeod, Kembrew. 2017. "The Day I Killed Freedom of Expression." In *Culture Jamming: Activism and the Art of Cultural Resistance*, edited by Marilyn Delaure and Moritz Fink, 393–401. New York: New York University Press.

McNamee, John. 2014. "Kafka's Joke Book." *McSweeney's Internet Tendency*, March 19.

McNeill, Lynne S., and Elizabeth Tucker. 2018. *Legend Tripping: A Contemporary Casebook*. Logan: Utah State University Press.

Mechling, Jay. 1986. "Children's Folklore." In *Folk Groups and Folk Genres*, edited by Elliott Oring, 91–120. Logan: Utah State University Press.

Meier, Matthew R., and Christopher A. Medjesky. 2018. "*The Office* Was Asking for It: 'That's What She Said' as a Joke Cycle That Perpetuates Rape Culture." *Communication and Critical/Cultural Studies*, 15 (1): 2–17.

Meley, Patricia M. 1990. "Adolescent Legend Trips as Teenage Cultural Response: A Study of Lore in Context." *Mid-American Folklore* 18 (1): 1–26.

Merritt, Karen. 1988. "The Little Girl/Little Mother Transformation: The American Evolution of 'Snow White and the Seven Dwarfs.'" In *Storytelling in Animation: The Art of the Animated Image*, vol. 2, edited by John Canemaker, 105–21. Los Angeles: American Film Institute.

Mieder, Wolfgang. 1997. "Welleristic Addenda to the *Dictionary of Wellerisms*." *Proverbium* 14 (2): 187–217.

Mieder, Wolfgang, and Stewart A. Kingsbury. 1994. *A Dictionary of Wellerisms*. Oxford: Oxford University Press.

Miller, Kiri. 2008. "Grove Street Grimm: 'Grand Theft Auto' and Digital Folklore." *Journal of American Folklore* 121 (481): 255–85.

Milner, Ryan M. 2013. "Hacking the Social: Internet Memes, Identity Antagonism, and the Logic of Lulz." *The Fibreculture Journal* 22 (Dec. 1).

Milner, Ryan M. 2016. *The World Made Meme: Public Conversations and Participatory Media*. Cambridge, MA: MIT Press.

Moellenhoff, Fritz. 1940. "Remarks on the Popularity of Mickey Mouse." *American Imago* 1 (3): 19–32.

Morris, Margaret. 1985. *Tour Jamaica*. Kingston, Jamaica: Gleaner.

Moses, Louis J., and Dare A. Baldwin. 2005. "What Can the Study of Cognitive Development Reveal about Children's Ability to Appreciate and Cope with Advertising?" *Journal of Public Policy and Marketing* 24 (2): 186–201.

Mosley, Leonard. 1992. *Disney's World: A Biography*. Lanham, MD: Scarborough House.

Mould, Tom. 2018. "A Doubt-Centered Approach to Contemporary Legend and Fake News." *Journal of American Folklore* 131 (522): 413–20.

Myerhoff, Barbara G. 2007. *Stories as Equipment for Living*. Ann Arbor: University of Michigan Press.

Nairn, Anges. 2010. "Children and Brands." In *Understanding Children as Consumers*, edited by David Marshall, 96–114. London: Sage.

Narváez, Peter. 1986. "'The Folklore of Old Foolishness': Newfoundland Media Legends." *Canadian Literature* 108: 125–43.

Narváez, Peter. 1992. "Folkloristics, Cultural Studies, and Popular Culture." *Canadian Folklore* 14: 15–30.

Narváez, Peter, and Martin Laba, eds. 1986. *Media Sense: The Folklore-Popular Culture Continuum*. Bowling Green, OH: Bowling Green State University Popular Press.

Nash, Dennison. 1989. "Tourism as a Form of Imperialism." In *Hosts and Guests: The Anthropology of Tourism*, 2nd ed., edited by Valene Smith, 37–52. Philadelphia: University of Pennsylvania Press.

Newell, William Wells. 1888a. "Folk-lore and Mythology." *Journal of American Folklore* 1 (2): 163.

Newell, William Wells. 1888b. "On the Field and Work of a Journal of American Folk-lore." *Journal of American Folklore* 1 (1): 3–7.

Newell, William Wells. 1890. "The Study of Folk-lore." *Transactions of the New York Academy of Sciences* 9: 134–36.

Nissenbaum, Asaf, and Limor Shifman. 2017. "Internet Memes as Contested Cultural Capital: The Case of 4chan's /b/ Board." *New Media and Society* 19 (4): 483-501.

Nugent, Frank S. 1938. "One Touch of Disney: And New York Surrenders to the Genial Warmth of His *Snow White* Fantasy." *New York Times*, January 23.

O'Brien, Donough. 2000. *Fringe Benefits*. London: Bene Factum.

O'Brien, Pamela Colby. 1996. "The Happiest Films on Earth: A Textual and Contextual Analysis of Walt Disney's *Cinderella* and *The Little Mermaid*." *Women's Studies in Communication* 19 (2): 155–83.

Official Comedy. 2012 (June 28). "That's What She Said: Jokes through the Ages" Video file. https://www.youtube.com/watch?v=3xNq8Ve_wOw.

O'Grady, Sean. 2010. Minor British Institutions: Colonel Bogey. *Independent Online*, September 18.

Oldman, D. 1992. "Adult-Child Relations as Class Relations." In *Childhood Matters*, edited by Jens Qvortrup, Marjatta Bardy, Giovannia Sgritta, and Helmut Wintersberger, 43–58. Aldershot, UK: Avebury.

Olesker, Michael. 1993. "From Hitler to Hemingway, Joke Is on Gap." *Baltimore Sun*, September 23. http://articles.baltimoresun.com/1993-09-23/news/1993266063_1_wore-khakis-gap-corbett-wrote.

Opie, Iona, and Peter Opie. 1959. *The Lore and Language of Schoolchildren*. Oxford: Oxford University Press.

Opie, Iona, and Peter Opie. 1984. *Children's Games in Street and Playground*. Oxford: Oxford University Press.

Opie, Iona, and Peter Opie. 1997. *Children's Games with Things*. Oxford: Oxford University Press.

Oring, Elliott. 1992. *Jokes and Their Relations*. Lexington: University of Kentucky Press.

Oring, Elliott. 2014a. "Memetics and Folklore: The Applications." *Western Folklore* 73 (4): 455–92.

Oring, Elliott. 2014b. "Memetics and Folklore: The Theory." *Western Folklore* 73 (4): 432–54.

Oring, Elliott. 2016. *Joking Asides: The Theory, Analysis, and Aesthetics of Humor.* Logan: Utah State University Press.

Oring, Elliott. 2019. "Oppositions, Overlaps, and Ontologies: The General Theory of Verbal Humor Revisited." *Humor* 32 (2): 151–70.

Pallant, Chris. 2010. "Disney Formalism: Rethinking 'Classic Disney.'" *Animation* 5 (3): 341–52.

Pallant, Chris. 2011. *Demystifying Disney: A History of Disney Feature Animation.* London: Bloomsbury.

Paravisini-Gebert, Lizabeth. 1990. "The White Witch of Rosehall and the Legitimacy of Female Power in the Caribbean Plantation." *Journal of West Indian Literature* 4 (2): 25–45.

Partridge, Eric. 1977. *A Dictionary of Catch Phrases: British and American, from the Sixteenth Century to the Present Day,* edited by Paul Beale. London: Routledge.

Pattullo, Polly. 2005. *Last Resorts: The Cost of Tourism in the Caribbean.* London: Latin America Bureau.

Pellegrini, Anthony D., ed. 1995. *The Future of Play Theory: A Multidisciplinary Inquiry into the Contributions of Brian Sutton-Smith.* Albany: State University Press of New York.

Pettitt, Tom. 2005. "Body and Environment in the Contemporary Legend: Articulation vs. Containment." *Contemporary Legend,* n.s., 8: 47–66.

Phillips, Gene D. 2006. *Beyond the Epic: The Life and Films of David Lean.* Lexington: University Press of Kentucky.

Pimple, Kenneth D. 1996. "The Meme-ing of Folklore." *Journal of Folklore Research* 33 (3): 236–40.

Pine, Joseph, and James Gilmore. 1999. *The Experience Economy.* Cambridge, MA: Harvard Business School Press.

Pollack-Pelzner, Daniel. 2011. "Dickens and Shakespeare's Household Words." *ELH* 78 (3): 533–56.

Pullen, Kirsten. 2005. *Actresses and Whores: On Stage and in Society.* Cambridge: Cambridge University Press.

Quarterly Review. 1837. Review of *Pickwick Papers,* by Charles Dickens. 59: 484–518.

Radford, Ben. 2010. *Scientific Paranormal Investigation.* Corrales, NM: Rhombus.

Randall, Lilian M. 1962. "The Snail in Gothic Marginal Warfare." *Speculum* 37 (3): 358–67.

Rattle, Alison, and Allison Vale. 2005. *Hell House: And Other True Hauntings from around the World.* New York: Sterling.

Redlich, Fritz. 1999. *Hitler: Diagnosis of a Destructive Prophet.* New York: Oxford University Press.

Richards, Greg. 2011. "Creativity and Tourism: The State of the Art." *Annals of Tourism Research* 38 (4): 1225–53.

Richards, Greg, and Julie Wilson. 2006. "Developing Creativity in Tourist Experiences: A Solution to the Serial Production of Culture?" *Tourism Management* 27 (6): 1209–23.

Richards, Jeffrey. 2001. *Imperialism and Music: Britain 1876–1958*. Manchester: Manchester University Press.

Ritzer, George, and Allan Liska. 1997. "'Mcdisneyization' and 'Post-Tourism': Complementary Perspectives on Contemporary Tourism." In *Touring Cultures: Transformations of Travel and Theory*, edited by Chris Rojek and John Urry, 96–109. New York: Routledge.

Roberts, Andrew. 2008. "Did Hitler Really Only Have ONE Testicle? A Historian Sorts the Extraordinary Truth from the Far-Flung Myths about the Führer." *Mail Online* (London), November 20. http://www.dailymail .co.uk/news/article-1087380/Did-Hitler-really-ONE-testicle-A-historian -sorts-extraordinary-truth-far-flung-myths-Fuhrer.html.

Robertson, Glory. 1968. "The Legend of Rose Hall." *Jamaica Journal* 2 (4): 6–12.

Roby, John. 1849. *The History of the Parish of St. James, in Jamaica*. Kingston: R. J. De Cordova.

Rojek, Chris. 1993. *Ways of Escape: Modern Transformations in Leisure and Travel*. London: Macmillan.

Rose Hall, Jamaica: The Story of a People, a Legend, a Legacy. 2004. Montego Bay, Jamaica: Rose Hall Limited.

Rosenbaum, Jonathan. 2018. "Dream Masters I: Walt Disney (Part One)." January 4. https://www.jonathanrosenbaum.net/2018/01/walt-disney/.

Rosenbaum, Ron. 1998. *Explaining Hitler: The Search for the Origins of His Evil*. New York: Harper Collins.

Rosenbaum, Ron. 2008. "Everything You Need to Know about Hitler's 'Missing' Testicle: And Why We're So Obsessed with the Führer's Sex Life." *Slate. com*, November 28. http://www.slate.com/articles/life/the_spectator /2008/11/everything_you_need_to_know_about_hitlers_missing_testicle .html.

Rosenberg, Leah Reade. 2007. *Nationalism and the Formation of Caribbean Literature*. New York: Palgrave.

Russ, Joanna. 1985. *Magic Mommas, Trembling Sisters, Puritans and Perverts: Essays on Sex and Pornography*. Trumansberg, NY: Crossing.

Safire, William. 1984. "Punch-line English." *New York Times*, March 11, A28.

Sale, Roger. 1978. *Fairy Tales and After: From Snow White to E. B. White*. Cambridge, MA: Harvard University Press.

Schacker, Jennifer. 2019. "Long Ago and Far Away: Historicizing Fairy-Tale Discourse." In *Teaching Fairy Tales*, edited by Nancy L. Canepa, 174–80. Detroit: Wayne State University Press.

Schickel, Richard. 1997. *The Disney Version: The Life, Times, Art, and Commerce of Walt Disney*. 3rd ed. Chicago: Ivan R. Dee.

Seaton, A. V. 1996. "Guided by the Dark: from Thanatopsis to Thanatourism." *International Journal of Heritage Studies* 2: 234–44.

Seeger, Pete. 1959. *Folk Songs for Young People Sung by Pete Seeger*. Folkways Records.

Segal, Alex. 2018. "Jokes, Aporia and Undecidability." *European Journal of Humour Research* 6 (1): 1–11.

Sexton, Anne. 1971. "Snow White and the Seven Dwarfs." In *Transformations*, 3-10. Boston: Houghton Mifflin.

Shannon, Claude E., and Warren Weaver. 1963. *The Mathematical Theory of Communication*. Champaign: University of Illinois Press.

Sherman, Josepha, and T. K. F. Weisskopf. 1995. *Greasy Grimy Gopher Guts: The Subversive Folklore of Childhood*. Little Rock, AR: August House.

Shifman, Limor. 2014. *Memes in Digital Culture*. Cambridge, MA: MIT Press.

Shore, Joseph, comp. 1970 (1911). "The True Tale of Rose Hall." In *In Old St. James, Jamaica: A Book of Parrish Chronicles*, edited by John Stewart. London: Bodley Head.

Short, Sue. 2014. *Fairy Tale and Film: Old Tales with a New Spin*. London: Palgrave.

Shortsleeve, Kevin. 2004. "The Wonderful World of the Depression: Disney, Despotism and the 1930s; or, Why Disney Scares Us." *Lion and the Unicorn* 28 (1): 1–30.

Sjöbergh, J., and K. Araki. 2007. "Recognizing Humor without Recognizing Meaning." In *Proceedings from 7th International Workshop on Fuzzy Logic and Applications: Applications of Fuzzy Sets Theory*, edited by Francesco Masulli, Sushmita Mitra, and Gabriella Pasi, 469–76. Berlin: Springer.

Sklar, Robert. 1980. "The Making of Cultural Myths—Walt Disney." In *The American Animated Cartoon*, edited by Danny and Gerald Peary, 58–65. New York: E. P. Dutton.

Smith, Neville. 2001. *Dear Dr. Goebbels*. BBC, November 30.

Soileau, Jeanne Pitre. 2016. *Yo' Mama, Mary Mack, and Boudreaux and Thibodeaux: Louisiana Children's Folklore and Play*. Jackson: University Press of Mississippi.

Solis, Santiago. 2007. "Snow White and the Seven 'Dwarfs'—Queercripped." *Hypatia* 22 (1): 114–31.

Solomon, Charles. 1998. "Fairy Tale Ending to a Real Disney Story. Film: Studio Restores Walt's First Animated Work—Long Lost, but Rediscovered by Chance." *Los Angeles Times*, July 17.

Sparrman, Anna, Bengt Sandin, and Johanna Sjöberg, eds. 2012. *Situating Child Consumption: Rethinking Values and Notions of Children, Childhood and Consumption*. Lund, Sweden: Nordic Academic Press.

Stewart, I., D. Barnes-Holmes, S. C. Hayes, and R. Lipkens. 2002. "Relations among Relations: Analogies, Metaphors, and Stories." In *Relational Frame Theory*, edited by S. C. Hayes, D. Barnes-Holmes, and B. Roche, 73–86. Boston: Springer.

St. George, Robert Blair. 1995. "Ritual House Assaults in Early New England." In *Fields of Folklore: Essays in Honor of Kenneth S. Goldstein*, edited by Roger D. Abrahams, 253–72. Bloomington, IN: Trickster Press.

Stone, Kay. 1975. "Things Walt Disney Never Told Us." *Journal of American Folklore* 88 (347): 42–50.

Sturken, Marita, and Lisa Cartwright. 2018. *Practices of Looking: An Introduction to Visual Culture*, 3rd ed. New York: Oxford University Press.

Surlin, Stuart H., and Eugene D. Tate. 1976. "*All in the Family*: Is Archie Funny?" *Journal of Communication* 26 (4): 61–68.

Tan, Siow-Kian, Shiann-Far Kung, and Ding-Bang Luh. 2013. "A Model of 'Creative Experience' in Creative Tourism." *Annals of Tourism Research* 41: 153–74.

Tan, Siow-Kian, Siow-Hooi Tan, Ding-Bang Luh, and Shiann-Far Kung. 2016. "Understanding Tourist Perspectives in Creative Tourism." *Current Issues in Tourism* 19 (10): 981–87.

Taylor, John P. 2001. "Authenticity and Sincerity in Tourism." *Annals of Tourism Research* 28 (1): 7–26.

Taylor, Julia M. 2017. "Computational Treatments of Humor." In *The Routledge Handbook of Language and Humor*, edited by Salvatore Attardo, 456–71. New York: Routledge.

Tedder, Michael. 2013. "*The Office* Finale Recap: That's All She Said." *The Vulture: Devouring Culture*, May 17. http://www.vulture.com/2013/05/office-finale-recap-thats-all-she-said.html.

Telotte, J. P. 2008. *The Mouse Machine: Disney and Technology*. Urbana: University of Illinois Press.

Thigpen, Kenneth A., Jr. 1971. "Adolescent Legends in Brown County: A Survey." *Indiana Folklore* 4 (2): 141–215.

Thomas, Bob. 1958. *Walt Disney, the Art of Animation: The Story of the Disney Studio Contribution to New Art*. New York: Simon & Schuster.

Thomas, Jeannie Banks. 2003. *Naked Bodies, Warrior Joes, and Other Forms of Visible Gender*. Urbana: University of Illinois Press.

Thomas, Jeannie Banks. 2015. "Which Witch Is Which? Salem, Massachusetts." In *Putting the Supernatural in Its Place: Folklore, the Hypermodern, and the Ethereal*, edited by Jeannie Banks Thomas, 49–89. Salt Lake City: University of Utah Press.

Thompson, Ethan. 2009. "'I Am Not Down with That': *King of the Hill* and Sitcom Satire." *Journal of Film and Video* 61 (2): 38–51.

Tincknell, Estella, and Parvati Raghuram. 2002. "Big Brother: Reconfiguring the 'Active' Audience of Cultural Studies?" *European Journal of Cultural Studies* 5 (2): 199–215.

Torben, Rick. 2015. "Social Media and the Oil Spill Disaster." June 24. https://www.torbenrick.eu/blog/social-media/social-media-and-the-oil-spill-disaster/.

Trendell, John. 1991. *Colonel Bogey to the Fore: A Biography of Kenneth J. Alford*. Dover: Blue Band Magazine; printed by A. R. Adams & Sons.

Trites, Roberta. 1991. "Disney's Sub/Version of Andersen's 'The Little Mermaid.'" *Journal of Popular Film and Television* 18 (4): 145–52.

Tropic Lightning News. 1968. "SSG Jones Sets High in Re-up Bonus." August 12, 1.

Tucker, Elizabeth. 2008. *Children's Folklore: A Handbook*. Westport, CT: Greenwood.

Urban, Greg. 2001. *Metaculture: How Culture Moves through the World*. Minneapolis: University of Minnesota Press.

Urry, John, and Jonas Larsen. 2011. *The Tourist Gaze 3.0*. London: Sage.

Veatch, Thomas C. 1998. "A Theory of Humor." *Humor: International Journal of Humor Research* 11 (2): 161–215.

Vidmar, Neil, and Milton Rokeach. 1974. "Archie Bunker's Bigotry: A Study in Selective Perception and Exposure." *Journal of Communication* 24 (1): 36–47.

Vlach, John. 1971. "One Black Eye and Other Horrors: A Case for the Humorous Anti-legend." *Indiana Folklore* 4: 95–140.

Waddell, Rev. Hope Masterson. 1863. *Twenty-Nine Years in the West Indies and Central Africa: A Review of Missionary Work and Adventure, 1829–1858.* London: T. Nelson & Sons.

Waite, Robert G. L. 1977. *The Psychopathic God: Adolph Hitler.* New York: Basic Books.

Waldman, Katy. 2011. "[Subject] Could Eat [Object] All Day. That's What She Said." *Slate*, May 3.

Wasko, Janet. 2001. *Understanding Disney: The Manufacture of Fantasy.* Oxford: Polity.

Waskul, Dennis. 2018. "Ghosts and Hauntings: Genres, Forms, and Types." In *The Supernatural in Society, Culture, and History*, edited by Dennis Waskul and Marc Eaton, 54–75. Philadelphia: Temple University Press.

Watts, Steven. 1997. *The Magic Kingdom: Walt Disney and the American Way of Life.* Columbia: University of Missouri Press.

Wearing, Stephen, and Simon Darcy. 2011. "Inclusion of the 'Othered' in Tourism." *Cosmopolitan Civil Societies Journal* 3 (2): 18–34.

Weems, Scott. 2014. *Ha! The Science of When We Laugh and Why.* New York: Basic Books.

Wells, Jon. 2014. "Mother Convinces School to Cancel Class Trip to Marineland." *Toronto Star*, March 15.

Wells, Mary Lawrence. 2002. *A Big Life in Advertising.* New York: Touchstone.

White, E. B., and Katharine S. White, eds. 1941. *A Sub-treasury of American Humor.* New York: Coward-McCann.

Wilder, Roy. 1998. *You All Spoken Here.* Athens: University of Georgia Press.

Willett, Rebekah. 2016. "Remixing Children's Cultures: Media-Referenced Play on the Playground." In *Children's Games in the New Media Age: Childlore, Media and the Playground*, edited by Andrew Burn and Chris Richards, 133–51. London: Routledge.

Williams, Tammy Ronique. 2012. "Tourism as a Neo-colonial Phenomenon: Examining the Works of Pattullo and Mullings." *Caribbean Quilt* 2: 191–200.

Wood, Naomi. 1996. "Domesticating Dreams in Walt Disney's *Cinderella*." *Lion and the Unicorn* 20 (2): 25–49.

Yates, Geoffrey. 1965a. "The Rose Hall Legend: Was It Really Annie?" *Kingston Gleaner*, December 5, 7.

Yates, Geoffrey. 1965b. "The True Tale of the 'White Witch of Rose Hall': Death of a Legend." *Kingston Gleaner*, November 21, 7.

Young, Brian. 2010. "Children and Advertising." In *Understanding Children as Consumers*, edited by David Marshall, 115–31. London: Sage.

Zipes, Jack. 1995. "Breaking the Disney Spell." In *From Mouse to Mermaid: The Politics of Film, Gender, and Culture*, edited by Elizabeth Bell, Lynda Haas, Laura Sells, 21–42. Bloomington: Indiana University Press.

Zipes, Jack. 1997. "Once upon a Time beyond Disney: Contemporary Fairy-Tale Films for Children." In *Happily Ever After: Fairy Tales, Children, and the Culture Industry*, 89–110. New York: Routledge.

Zipes, Jack, trans. 2003. *The Complete Tales of the Brothers Grimm*. Toronto: Bantam.

Zipes, Jack. 2006. *Fairy Tales and the Art of Subversion: The Classical Genre for Children and the Process of Civilization*. 2nd ed. London: Routledge.

Zipes, Jack. 2008. "What Makes the Repulsive Frog So Appealing: Memetics and the Fairy Tale." *Journal of Folklore Research* 45 (2): 109–43.

Zipes, Jack. 2011a. *The Enchanted Screen: The Unknown History of Fairy-Tale Films*. New York: Routledge.

Zipes, Jack. 2011b. "The Meaning of the Fairy Tale with the Evolution of Culture." *Marvels & Tales: Journal of Fairy-Tale Studies* 25 (2): 221–43.

Zipes, Jack, Pauline Greenhill, and Kendra Magnus-Johnston, eds. 2015. *Fairy Tale Films beyond Disney: International Perspectives*. New York: Routledge.

Index